MURDER AT THE FARM

MURDER AT THE FARM

Who Killed Carl Bridgewater?

Paul Foot

SIDGWICK & JACKSON
LONDON

501931

First published in Great Britain in 1986
by Sidgwick and Jackson Limited
1 Tavistock Chambers, Bloomsbury Way
London WC1A 2SG

ISBN 0-283-99165-8

Typeset by Rapidset and Design Limited

Printed and bound in Great Britain by
Butler & Tanner, Frome, Somerset

CONTENTS

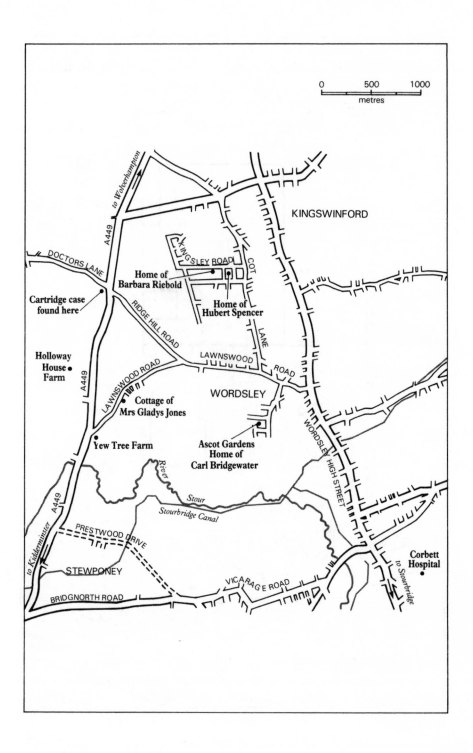

0   500   1000
metres

KINGSWINFORD

to Wolverhampton

A449

DOCTORS LANE

Cartridge case
found here

KINGSLEY ROAD

Home of
Barbara Riebold

Home of
Hubert Spencer

COT

RIDGE HILL ROAD

LANE

Holloway
House
Farm

A449

LAWNSWOOD ROAD

LAWNSWOOD

ROAD

WORDSLEY

Cottage of
Mrs Gladys Jones

Yew Tree Farm

Ascot Gardens
Home of
Carl Bridgewater

WORDSLEY HIGH STREET

River

Stour

Stourbridge Canal

A449

PRESTWOOD DRIVE

to Kidderminster

STEWPONEY

VICARAGE ROAD

Corbett
Hospital

to Stourbridge

BRIDGNORTH ROAD

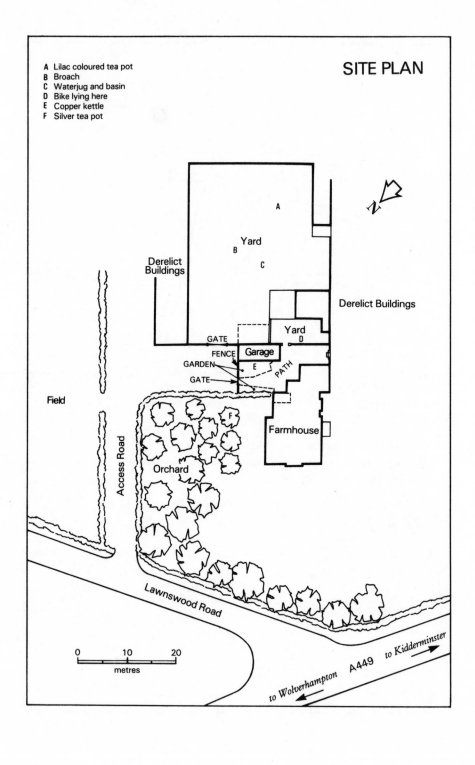

A Lilac coloured tea pot
B Broach
C Waterjug and basin
D Bike lying here
E Copper kettle
F Silver tea pot

SITE PLAN

Yard

Derelict
Buildings

Derelict Buildings

Yard

GATE

FENCE

Garage

GARDEN

GATE

PATH

Field

Access Road

Farmhouse

Orchard

Lawnswood Road

0   10   20
metres

to Wolverhampton   A449   to Kidderminster

INTRODUCTION

This book was inspired by a remarkable and courageous woman. In February 1980, I received this letter at the *Daily Mirror*, where I had just started to write a weekly column:

Dear Mr Foot,
My son, along with three other men, has been found guilty of murder – a very horrible murder of a newspaper boy named Carl Bridgewater from Staffordshire. My son is the youngest of the accused, Michael Hickey. He is innocent beyond doubt. Indeed, so are the other three accused with him. They were found guilty on circumstantial evidence. Not one piece of factual evidence was produced in court.
Hopefully, this is where I think you may be able to help me. Since this trial ended I have been doing a lot of investigations myself. I won't stop fighting until I've proved my son's innocence, but I must find someone who will at least listen to me, and look at the evidence I have in my possession. Hopefully, that someone will be your good self.

The letter was signed Ann Whelan, and the address was a council estate in Hollywood, a Midlands village just south of the Birmingham border.

I was cautious. The Carl Bridgewater case had finished three months earlier in much publicity. The jury verdict had been unanimous. There had been an unchallenged confession from one of the accused.

I responded politely, but guardedly. I did not meet Ann and her husband Fred until October that year (1980). In that month I wrote the first of many articles on the case in my column.

I met the Whelans again in December 1981 after their son and his fellow defendants were refused leave to appeal. Ann asked me to write a book on the case. I put her off. I was involved in another book at the time, and had discovered when writing about James Hanratty, who was hanged in 1962 for the A6 murder, just how much work is involved in

ix

challenging a jury verdict in a celebrated case. She persisted doggedly through 1982 and 1983. At one stage she sought others who might do the job, but without success. In these years, my doubts about the case slowly evaporated, but I was reluctant to commit myself.

It was Michael Hickey who tipped the balance. In the winter of 1983/4 he went on the roof of Gartree prison, near Leicester, in protest against his conviction for the murder of Carl Bridgewater. He stayed there for an astonishing eighty-nine days in conditions which defy belief. It suddenly was obvious that if Michael could spend a whole winter on a prison roof, I could write a book.

I have been lucky with documents. All the statements produced at the trial, which amount to nearly 1,500 pages, were immediately handed over to me by Ann Whelan. The transcript of the trial – nineteen volumes, and another 1,500 pages – was obtained for me by the *Daily Mirror*. This was by no means the only measure of the support I have had for this story from the two editors of the *Daily Mirror* over the past six years – Michael Molloy and Richard Stott. Though my obsession with the case became a standing joke in the *Mirror* offices, no one there ever discouraged me from it. Hugh Corrie, the *Mirror*'s top lawyer, went through the text with me to shield it, where possible, from libel. There is no surer hand at this in all the country.

I have had unstinting help from two solicitors. Tony Fryer was solicitor at the trial to one of the accused men, Jimmy Robinson. He has gone to the most extravagant and generous lengths to help me. For instance, he typed from his notes the four closing speeches of the barristers at the trial, and sent them to me.

In 1985, Jim Nichol, Michael Hickey's solicitor, started work on a petition to the Home Secretary to refer the case to the Court of Appeal. He got permission from the Director of Public Prosecutions to see the statements which were not produced at the trial, but which were available to the defence before it. There were some 7,000 of these, and almost all of them had not been looked up by the defence lawyers at the time of the trial. The DPP also gave Jim Nichol permission to see the statements which he had specifically withdrawn from the defence at the time.

Jim Nichol spent two weeks in Newcastle-under-Lyme, Staffordshire, under police supervision reading and recording from these statements. He concentrated on statements made about car sightings.

Through his mother, Michael Hickey has made all the statements which Jim Nichol recorded available to me. I can, as a result, give a much clearer picture of the car sightings than the one which emerged at the trial.

Jim Nichol was also approached by the family of Pat Molloy, another of the convicted men, who died in prison. He agreed to act on their behalf, and he collected from Molloy's former solicitors in Tamworth all the dead man's legal papers. All these are quite new to the case. They too have been made available to me by the Molloy family, to whom I am very grateful. They are invaluable to this account.

Without the help of these two solicitors, who have worked for their clients far beyond the call of duty, I would not have been able to proceed.

I was not able to interview the convicted men. Prison regulations bar authors or journalists from talking to prisoners about anything which might appear in print. I have been flung out of too many prisons to try again with such well-known inmates. So I wrote to the Home Office asking for permission for one interview with each of the three men. Permission was refused. Michael Molloy, then editor of the *Daily Mirror*, wrote on 25 October 1984 to the Home Secretary of the time, Leon Brittan, asking if the rules could be waived in view of my long interest to the case.

Mike Molloy offered to stand by any undertaking which did not inhibit my freedom to report what I discovered.

The answer came on 26 November, in a letter signed by Christine Heald, a Home Office official:

> We do permit, in fact we encourage representatives from the media to visit establishments and on occasions to speak to individual prisoners. However, these visits have always aimed at improving the public's knowledge of prison conditions and prisoners' reactions to them, and our practice has been to refuse requests from the media to interview named prisoners about their individual cases. Your request has been very carefully considered, but I am afraid that we do not feel we can make an exception in this case.

Though I could not see the three men, I could read their letters. Carol Bradbury, who was living with Jimmy Robinson at the time of his arrest, welcomed me into her home on two occasions and spoke with great vigour and conviction about Robinson's innocence of the murder. She let me have six exercise books in which were faithfully pasted all the letters written to her by Jimmy Robinson in 1979 (during most of which he was on remand), 1980 and 1981. The letters make intriguing reading at many different levels. Like Michael Hickey's letters, all of which Ann handed over in an enormous parcel, they shed a lot of light on the case. I have quoted from them freely.

Vincent Hickey was much less co-operative. His mother, Ann Hickey, worked hard to persuade him to help me. Her influence produced two huge letters from Vincent in 1985, which gave me specific answers about the alibi. Finally, in January 1986, Ann Hickey handed me a long report which Vincent wrote with the help of a Home Office psychiatrist in 1983. The report, protesting his innocence throughout, goes a long way to explaining Vincent's extraordinary behaviour in 1978.

In trying to interview key witnesses in the case, I have come across more hostility than in any other case I can remember.

Again and again I have been turned away, often with force or the threat of force.

In February 1984 I was interrupted during a polite conversation in his home with Don Spencer, brother of the murderer of Hubert Wilkes, by his wife Valerie. When she found out who I was, Mrs Spencer unleashed a magnificent tirade against me and all I stood for, at the climax of which she grabbed hold of me and pushed me out of her house. Philip Wilkes, son of the murdered farmer, would not let me into his house to talk to him. Neither would his sister Jean, a witness to her father's murder. Mrs Janet Spencer, another witness to that murder, visited me at the *Daily Mirror* in 1980, and begged me not to proceed with any more articles which linked her husband to the Carl Bridgewater murder. I could not give her any such promise, but I have not pestered her since. I made special trips from London to see two of Spencer's former fellow-workers at Corbett Hospital, Mrs Barbara Riebold (in 1984) and Mrs Celia Johnson (in 1986). Both would not let me past the door. Linda Galvin, a former girlfriend of Vincent Hickey, and a crucial alibi witness, also refused to talk about the case.

I owe special thanks, then, to the people who did help me, at no advantage to themselves. These included Farmer Michael Howard of Droitwich; Dr Angus Macdonald, who first discovered the body of the murdered boy; Richard Rogerson, administrator of Corbett Hospital; Barry Chambers of Ambulance Control, Dudley, and several other ambulance officers in the area who want to be anonymous; Fred Jones (who has since died); Andrew Zannetos, garage proprietor; William Mee; Paul and Gayle Wyton; and Yvonne Hall-Annieson. Janet Cotter has helped me a lot with the Spencer mystery. Friends and relatives of the convicted men who have helped me include John Smith, David Kane, Sean Tierney, Susan Bennett, Albert Chatterly, Joe Hickey, Reg Hickey, Les and Nancy Godridge, Dave Waller and Dennis Nott. Ann Whelan's two neighbours, Jean Hunter and Jenny Powell, who were quickly swept into her campaign, have helped in all sorts of ways.

My thanks also to reporter Bill Jacobs, to the staffs of the *Birmingham Evening Mail, Daily Express,* and *The Star*.

I was lucky, for the second time in my life, to have the book edited by Jane Heller. She told me one evening at 9 p.m. that there were a 'few points' which needed clearing up. I left at 6.10 a.m. Most of the 'points' (mistakes) had been dealt with.

The book was typed out at great speed by Diana Miller and Yola Pegasiou. My thanks to them.

As the book was being completed, I wrote to Mr Robert Stewart, who had been in charge of police inquiries following the murder of Carl Bridgewater and of Hubert Wilkes. In 1985, Mr Stewart, then a detective chief superintendent, left the police force and took up a new post as chief security officer at GCHQ, the government's intelligence headquarters at Cheltenham.

Dear Mr Stewart,
    I heard that you had been appointed head of security at GCHQ, and the Foreign Office News Department kindly agreed to pass this on.
    I have, as you may know, been very interested for many years in the Carl Bridgewater murder, and its aftermath. I am writing a book about this, and have come across several matters which I would like to discuss with you. I wonder if you would give me an hour or so of your time for this. I appreciate that you are a busy man, but it would be wrong for me not to approach you, since you were in charge of the case.
    You will, of course, know that I take the view that the wrong men were convicted of the murder, but I still have an open mind on the matter.
    I would of course be happy to come to Cheltenham if you agree to an interview.

The reply was dated 7 May 1986. It was brief:

Dear Mr Foot,
    I received your letter on returning to the office yesterday, 6th May, 1986.
    I have noted what you say but there are no matters which I would wish to discuss with you, and, in the circumstances, cannot agree to your request.

There was another, much grimmer responsibility I could not duck. In 1985 I wrote to Brian and Janet Bridgewater, the parents of the murdered boy, at their home in Wordsley. I explained that I was greatly interested in the case, and believed that the wrong men had been convicted of their son's murder. I said there were a number of questions which I wanted to ask, but would not press them in any way.

There was, understandably, no reply. Rather than leave it there, I called one summer evening in June 1985 at their home. They invited me in. I tried to explain the reason for what I was doing. They both heard me out politely, and, without much enthusiasm, tried to answer my questions. I realised at once that they were not in the least bit interested in my inquiries. Nor was there any reason why they should be. Each time the case got any publicity, they said, the suffering of that awful September came back to haunt them. Whoever did the murder was to them of small significance compared to the fact that their son was gone.

I mumbled a promise not to print pictures of Carl any more in my *Mirror* column and left. The visit reminded me that whatever the merits of investigative journalism, it has its dark side too.

For what after all *is* the point of devoting so much time and effort to absolving known criminals of a particular offence? Were not all four men convicted of killing Carl Bridgewater lags and thugs from the Birmingham underworld? Indeed, were they not convicted – at the same time as the Bridgewater trial – of outrageous armed robberies?

The first, rather obvious answer is that any system of prosecution and justice which accepts conviction for one offence because the accused have been guilty of other ones is immediately suspect. The second, even more obvious, is that if the real criminals escape conviction, they are free to strike again.

The bulk of this book was written in a hectic and almost sleepless month (January 1986) in the Whelans' flat. Most of the time, the entire flat was covered with documents. Ann Whelan was like a walking and talking encyclopaedia on the case. She turned herself into a thorough and patient investigator. 'You talk too much; you don't *listen*,' she once rebuked me – perhaps the best journalistic advice I have ever had. If ever she went off the rails into the fantasies which are so alluring in such cases, she was brought up sharp by Fred's common sense and cheerfulness, both of which were inexhaustible.

There has been about Ann Whelan's campaign not a trace of pride or side or selfishness. The whole of her intelligence and energy has been crammed up to the single purpose of freeing her son. The odds against her have been enormous. She has been obstructed, smeared, even accused of threatening people twice her size. She has no wealth, no connections, nothing but her fighting spirit which seems to grow in ferocity as her son sinks deeper into despair.

If this book goes even a little way to achieving her only ambition, it will have achieved its purpose.

CHAPTER ONE
Murder

Carl Bridgewater was late for his last paper round because he had to go to the dentist. In his school break he called in at Davies's newsagents to warn Mr Davies about this. Carl was keen to keep the round, since he had only recently been taken on as a regular. Mr Davies thanked him for his trouble.

Carl rode to the dentist on his bike, straight from school. He was seen early, and was away by a quarter to four. In a few minutes he was at the paper shop, and off on his round before four o'clock.

The round took him out of the small West Midlands town of Wordsley, where he lived, down Lawnswood Road into the country. Most of his calls were in two leafy suburban cul-de-sacs off Lawnswood Road, Hunters Ride and Lawnswood Drive. At a quarter past four he rode up to the gate of Weather Oaks, Lawnswood Drive, where Mrs Osborne was talking to a man. 'I'll take that, love,' she called out, and Carl handed her the paper. A couple of houses later he was finished with Lawnswood Drive and was on to the big house, White Friars, where they took two newspapers. He left his bike in the road, ran in with the papers, and came back. As he was getting on his bike again, a car passed. There were four workers in it from the Severn Trent Authority works up the road. A teenager in the back, Richard Parkes, hailed him: 'Hello, there, how's it going?' Carl nodded, smiled, mounted his bike, and followed the car over the brow of the hill.

This was the best part of the run, especially on a fine autumn day like this one, Tuesday, 19 September 1978. Carl was thirteen. He loved his bicycle and was one of the best cyclists in his class. It was an easy sweep down the hill of Lawnswood Road, past Mr and Mrs Jones's cottage on the left, to the farm at the bottom of the hill. Only three papers to go. The first had to be taken to Yew Tree Farm. Then he had to pop across the main road at the end to one house on the other side, then back again to Yew Tree Cottage, then home. His yellow bike sailed down the hill towards the farm.

An hour later, Dr Angus Macdonald was making his way home down the same road. A Scottish chest physician, Dr Macdonald had settled in this comfortable neck of the West Midlands some thirty years previously. He was based at Wordsley Hospital and known throughout the neighbourhood as someone who not only treated his patients but cared about them as well.

Much of his work was with old people. He liked to keep in regular touch with his patients even if they didn't immediately need his help. He often interrupted his journey home to Prestwood, in the country just outside Wordsley, by calling at Yew Tree Farm. It was occupied by Fred Jones, a retired farmer, and his cousin, Mary Poole. Miss Poole had been in hospital recently, and was very frail.

On an impulse, Dr Macdonald swung his car off Lawnswood Road into the track which led to the back of Yew Tree Farm. All traffic to the farm went this way. Although there was a front gate leading out into the A449, and a drive up to the farm from there, no one had used either for years. The doctor drove down the track, turned right into the farmyard, stopped his car, and walked through the open wicket gate to the back door.

'I don't know if you go for this sort of thing,' he said to me some years later, 'but I felt as I walked up there that something was very strange about the place. It was something to do with the wind, I don't know.'

As he got to the door, he could see that something was very strange. The paintwork of the door around the Yale lock was battered and the wood around the lock had been chipped away. The door was ajar.

'I could see they'd been done,' he says. 'Fred and Mary were always talking about burglars, and now they'd come.' For a moment he hesitated. Was it dangerous to go in? Then, remembering how old and arthritic both his patients were, he took courage and strode into the house, into the living room.

'The place was in chaos,' he said. That was what he first noticed. Crockery had been swept off the surfaces, and the cupboards ransacked. But he had little time for inspection. Something far more horrible than burglary had happened. On the settee in the middle of the room lay the body of the newspaper boy. His feet were on the ground and his head was resting on a bolster at the end of the settee. It was swimming in blood. The newspaper bag, with only two papers in it, was slung over his back. Another newspaper for that day lay in a box attached to the back door. Dr Macdonald walked to the phone, and then stopped. 'Something in my army training told me not to touch anything,' he said. He rushed from the room. Minutes later he was in his own front room, dialling the police station at Kinver.

The doctor chose Kinver because it was, by a short head, the nearest police station. It was also, by a short head, staffed by the appropriate police force. In his short bicycle ride that afternoon, Carl Bridgewater had crossed the boundary between the West Midlands, which is policed

2

by the second biggest force in England, into Staffordshire, whose police force is one of the smallest.

Staffordshire sits on top of the West Midlands industrial complex, which runs from Coventry in the east through Birmingham to Wolverhampton in the north-west and Stourbridge in the south-west. A slim peninsula of Staffordshire probes down to the west of the West Midlands, covering its western flank. Wordsley is on the western edge of the West Midlands. Just outside it runs the county boundary, which Carl crossed. When he was killed, he was in Staffordshire.

PC Michael Fallon took Dr Macdonald's call at almost exactly 5.30 p.m. In seven minutes his police car was parked outside Yew Tree Farm.

PC Fallon followed Dr Macdonald's route through the open back door of the farm and into the living room where the boy lay. He heard a noise behind him and spun round to find the doctor, who had come straight back again. Dr Macdonald felt the boy's pulse and pronounced him dead.

The constable noticed that a ground-floor window at the front of the farmhouse was open, and that the floor in front of it was covered with broken glass. He went upstairs and made a quick search of the bedrooms to satisfy himself that the house was empty. Then he phoned his police station and called for help. Within minutes two other constables arrived from Kinver, and the three men searched the house again. They discovered that the entire house had been left in disorder. They secured the back door and crept out through the open window, waiting for senior officers, who had now been told of a murder, to come from Wombourne and from police headquarters thirty miles away at Stafford.

At 7.30 p.m. the occupants of Yew Tree Farm returned from their day out in the country. Fred Jones and Mary Poole had been taken for a drive by their friend and fellow Methodist, Mrs Kit Parrot. The trio had driven out to Wenlock Edge, Shropshire. It was a fine day, and they had taken their time coming home. They were surprised on their arrival to find the back drive choked with police cars. One of the policemen told them what had happened. After a hurried conference, Dr Macdonald offered the two old people a bed at his house, and they left.

By this time the head of Staffordshire CID, Detective Chief Superintendent Robert Stewart, had arrived at the farm to take charge. The grim faces of his men were enough to tell him that this was no ordinary inquiry. It was plain at once that the newspaper boy had been murdered for no better reason than that he had interrupted an armed robbery.

With the night closing in, there was little Chief Superintendent Stewart or his force could do on site. Soon after nine o'clock a Home Office pathologist from Birmingham University, Dr Benjamin Davis, arrived at the farm and took samples from the body and from the scene of the crime. He was followed by Sergeant Vincent Potts, for ten years a scene-of-crime officer at Stafford police headquarters. Sergeant Potts made a cursory search of the farm, and ordered photographs to be taken. His main work had to wait until morning. At 10 p.m. undertakers from Wordsley came to collect the boy's body and take it to the mortuary at Wordsley Hospital. There it was identified by Carl's grieving father, Brian Bridgewater, a Wordsley pipe-fitter, and inspected again by Dr Davis. The doctor's conclusion was simple: Carl had been shot through the left side of the head by a single bullet from a shotgun. The gun had been held close to his head when it went off; no more than four feet away.

The farm, meanwhile, had been sealed off, and two police left to guard it. There was, however, at least one job which could be done that night. Fred Jones and Mary Poole, diverted from their home to Dr Macdonald's, might be able to shed some light on the awful crime which had taken place in their farmhouse. Detectives went to Dr Macdonald's house and interviewed Mr Jones. Their conversations went on well into the night.

Fred Jones said he was seventy-two and had been a farmer all his life – at Claverley, Shropshire. His wife died in 1968, when he handed over his farms to his sons. In 1973 he decided to join his cousins, Jack and Mary Poole, at Yew Tree Farm. They too had retired. Jack Poole had sold the farm to a big landowner, Jack Foulkes, of Stourton Hall, on condition that he and Mary could live in the farmhouse for the rest of their lives. Foulkes had let the land at Yew Tree to the farmer next door, Hubert Wilkes, of Holloway House Farm. Most of the work at Yew Tree was supervised by Hubert Wilkes' elder son Anthony, who was a frequent visitor to the farmhouse.

Jack Poole had died the previous December (1977). Since then Fred and Mary had lived on their own in the farmhouse. They both suffered from arthritis. Occasionally, Fred would go for a drink with Dr Macdonald, or with one of his sons, but for the most part the couple were housebound. They had few visitors. Milk was delivered early in the morning on Tuesdays and Thursdays, bread on Mondays, Wednesdays and Fridays. The Wolverhampton-based evening paper, the *Express and Star*, was delivered every day by Carl Bridgewater, who seldom came into the house but always left his bike in the yard to walk up to the door and put the paper into the box on the other side of it.

Some months ago the son of a friend, who was an auctioneer, had called to look round the furniture and household goods, and had remarked that many of them were valuable antiques. The farm occasionally hosted the meet of the Albrighton hunt. On these occasions several hunters used the toilets. Try as he could, however, Fred Jones could

4

think of very few occasions when strangers had been anywhere near his house.

The expedition that afternoon had been entirely unplanned, he said. Mrs Parrot had offered to take him and Mary for a drive. She had arrived at about eleven in the morning, after the cleaner had left, and taken Mary into Wordsley to get her pension. While the two women were gone, Fred had put his dog, Skip, in the kitchen, and secured the locks.

At Much Wenlock they had a meal, and visited a friend.

In all this, there was very little to help the police. The isolation of the couple tended to suggest that any robbery of the farm was a chance effort, and a lucky one for the robbers, since the old people so rarely left the house together.

Then, as he racked his memory, Fred Jones started to tell other stories about the farmhouse which painted a rather different picture. He said:

> Just prior to Jack Poole's death in December last year we suddenly started getting telephone calls at the house. When we answered, all that we heard was the receiver being replaced. This sort of thing started in the middle of November and for a period of about three weeks we had about a dozen such calls, mainly around 9.30 to 10 p.m. After Jack's death these calls continued for another two weeks but less frequently. There were occasions when I was in bed that the telephone rang and I didn't answer it. Once one morning we had two such calls at about 6.30 a.m. At no time did any friends or members of the family tell me that they had telephoned and received no answer. Since about the middle of December we didn't receive any more calls.
>
> But then suddenly, two or three weeks before the murder, the calls started again. They were more sporadic, and there were much less than previously. They went on for a week or so, and then stopped again.

Other weird things had happened. In 1974, Anthony Wilkes, who organised work on the farm, had been annoyed by dogs who were attacking his sheep. He put a notice in the paper warning that if he found any dogs straying on his land he would shoot them. He got an unexplained, anonymous phone call warning that if the caller's dogs were shot, the farm's buildings would be burnt down. Not long afterwards, Wilkes shot a couple of dogs. A few nights later the outbuildings to the farm, not a hundred yards from the farmhouse, were badly damaged by fire.

Then there was the curious story of the disappearing money. The previous April, said Fred Jones, he'd got £70 in cash in rent for stabling horses on his old farm at Claverley. He'd put the money at the bottom of the top righthand drawer of his chest of drawers in his bedroom. On 19 August, exactly a month before the murder, he'd got the envelope out to put another fiver in it. The £70 had gone.

The missing money worried him a lot, and set him thinking. He remembered an occasion a few weeks previously, about the beginning of August, when he and his cousin had gone to visit relations in Birmingham. He had left a key under a slate on the coalhouse window ledge for his neighbour, Mrs Gladys Jones, to let the dog out. When he came home that night, he'd gone to get the key and found it lying 'at a completely different angle from which I'd left it, and it was obvious that it had been moved from its original position'. He had asked Gladys Jones if she had let the dog out but she told him she had not.

Since losing the money, he had deliberately left small amounts of money about the house where the cleaner or any other visitor could find it. But none of that money had gone missing. He had not mentioned the incident because he had not wanted to impugn the honesty of the cleaner whom he trusted. Ever since, he had worried about the moving key and the missing money. So he had fitted another Yale lock on the door to the sitting room.

Other things mysteriously vanished from the farm in August and September. A wood-chopper went from the scullery and a scythe from the garden. Fred Jones asked Anthony Wilkes whether he'd taken them. Wilkes vigorously and convincingly denied it. These strange events persuaded Fred Jones to take the family silver out of the cupboards and put it in his safe.

At the end of his interview that Tuesday night, Fred Jones promised to go to the farm the next morning to check all his property and see what was missing. He was questioned closely about his dog. He insisted he had left the dog in the kitchen. Yet Sergeant Potts on his cursory examination of the farmhouse had come across the dog in the scullery, a room just inside the back door.

The story told by Fred Jones that September evening suggested that the farmhouse had, for some months, been the object of mysterious and macabre scrutiny by someone who knew it. It helped form the police view that the crime they were investigating had been the work of someone local who had been spying on the farm for some time, and who may have struck before, on the only other occasion in the previous two months when Fred Jones and Mary Poole had both left the house.

This notion had already suggested itself to Chief Superintendent Stewart and his colleagues in answer to a vital question: what was the motive for this murder? Carl Bridgewater could hardly have stood in the way of an adult robber, and could have been restrained if he had.

The chief superintendent and all his officers were struck by the position of the dead boy on the settee. At first sight, it looked as though he was asleep. His head rested on a bolster, and his feet were dangling down. There was no sign that he had been involved in a fight with his killer. It looked as though he had sat down on the settee of his own free will. Somehow, the absence of a struggle made the crime even more disgusting.

The next day's *Express* and *Star* (20 September) quoted DCS Stewart as saying: 'I am satisfied that Carl disturbed or came across intruders forcing entry to the house. Why they felt obliged to shoot a lad who could do them no physical harm is beyond me.'

After Stewart's first press conference, which was held only twenty-four hours after the murder, the *Express and Star* of 21 September reported: 'Mr Stewart said there was a strong possibility that Carl recognised his attackers. "I tend to go for the view that the motive was that he could have recognised his assailant," he said.'

This was reported in headlines all over the country. The *Birmingham Evening Mail* of 21 September had: 'THE VICTIM OF A LOCAL GANG. Chief Supt. Bob Stewart said: "I have got to consider that the lad recognised one of them."'

The *County Express* of 22 September, which circulated weekly in Stourbridge and Wordsley, carried as its front page headline the question: 'DID CARL KNOW HIS KILLERS? Carl Bridgewater may have lost his life because he recognised the raiders he disturbed in the lonely farmhouse. This theory was put forward by police chiefs. They believe the brutal killing may have been the work of local men.'

All these hunches in those very early days assumed that Carl was murdered by 'a gang', or by killers. This seems to have been Stewart's view from the very first day, and it was supported by the thorough search of the house and grounds which was led, from first light on the morning after the murder, by Sergeant Potts and a team of fifty police.

Every room in the house had been 'gone over'. In some bedrooms the drawers had been completely removed, in others left open. Plants had been knocked over, and the contents of boxes and even a sewing basket scattered on the floor. All this was routine for a random burglary. One precious find was a button on the sill of the downstairs window that had been broken.

Outside in the grounds, however, detectives found various antiques. In the yard, overgrown with scrub, at the side of the house, there was a basin, a water jug, a brooch, and in the far corner a lilac-coloured teapot. In the untended and overgrown orchard on the other side of the house was a silver-coloured teapot, under an apple tree. A large copper kettle was also found by the garage, near the wicket gate which opened on to the path to the back door.

Fred Jones confirmed that all this property had come from the house.

Finally, Carl's bicycle was not down on the ground in the yard where he normally left it, but over a wall in a pigsty, immediately to the right of the farmhouse back door.

After close consultation with Fred Jones, Sergeant Potts and his men drew up a list of several items which undoubtedly had gone missing from the house. The list, which was distributed to the press by the end of the week in the hope that some of it might already have found its way into the hands of fences or into an antique shop, read like this: from the sitting room, a copper warming pan, which Fred Jones valued at £100; two brass meat jacks and a large copper kettle (not the one found outside). From the hall, a large green canvas shopping bag (£5) and two brass candlesticks (£10). From the billiard room, a set of fire irons, a meat carving set, a pink glass biscuit barrel, an oak tantalus with three cut-glass decanters. From the bedrooms, two sweet dishes, a ladies' key-wind pocket watch, a heavy double silver watch chain, two pairs of gold and silver cuff links.

Fred Jones rather generously put the total value of the haul at £508, and this was the sum eventually agreed with his insurance company. The police put it lower. Newspapers blazed abroad the fact that Carl's killers had got away with no more than £100 worth of goods.

The inventory of the stolen property was the easiest part of Sergeant Potts' job that morning. More difficult was the search for forensic clues, especially for fingerprints, footprints and tyre prints. This continued for more than a day. Every possible item which could have been touched by an intruder was microscopically examined. So was the ground outside the house. On the Thursday morning (21 September) Chief Superintendent Stewart told the *Express and Star* that the forensic search had been 'fruitful'. The *Birmingham Evening Mail* that day was much more explicit: 'PRINTS COULD TRAP CARL'S KILLER', it declared in a headline, and reported: 'The net was closing around the killers of 13-year-old Midland newsboy Carl Bridgewater this evening as vital clues were found to his murder.' The prints, the report went on, were on the 'stolen goods which had been dumped in the farmhouse yard'.

The fingerprints, moreover, did not match those of the people who lived in the house, or of the cleaner. On Friday, 22 September, the police took the entire windowframe which had been broken into and some of the carpet near the settee where the boy was murdered and subjected them to detailed tests for prints of fingers and of feet. Once again, prints appeared on both items which did not match those of Fred Jones or Mary Poole or the cleaner.

All this was 'fruitful' but it did not get the detectives much closer to the identity of the murderer. For this, the police needed help from the public and especially from the motoring public.

What kind of car visited Yew Tree Farm that fatal afternoon? This question dominated the first few days of the inquiry and the whole history of the case.

At once, the police, whose inquiry team had risen to 200, found a lead. Mrs Gladys Jones, the close friend of the old people who lived at the farm, who was trusted with the whereabouts of the back door key on their previous outing that summer, lived in a cottage at the top of a slight rise which overlooks the farm. From her garden, she could look directly down on the farm and its back driveway.

Within an hour of the discovery of the body, PC John Crowe was at Mrs Jones' cottage to take a statement from her. In that statement, Mrs Jones was specific: 'At about 4 p.m. on the afternoon of Tuesday 19th September, 1978, I was in the garden of my home, and on looking towards Yew Tree Farm, I saw a light blue Ford Cortina estate car parked in the gateway of Yew Tree Farm. The vehicle had its boot lifted and was close to the farm's back door.'

She had then gone inside, she said, but at about 4.30 p.m., when she came out again, the car was gone.

This vital information was immediately transmitted by the police to other forces in the area, and to the newspapers.

The first edition of the *Birmingham Evening Mail* the following day had this: 'Detectives today circulated a description of a car. . . The car they are seeking is light blue and is described as a Ford Cortina type of vehicle.'

The later edition of the *Mail* had: 'A blue car, *possibly an estate car*, was seen in the driveway at about 4.30 p.m. yesterday, but no people were seen by the witness.'

In the *Express and Star*, this version had changed very slightly: 'More than 50 police are taking part in the murder hunt, and they want to trace a blue car, *probably* an estate which was seen in the farm driveway. . .'

The *County Express* (which came out on the Friday but went to press on the Wednesday) had: 'The police's main lead is the sighting of a blue car in the farm drive at 4.30 p.m. *It could have been* an estate car.' (Author's emphasis throughout.)

The qualifications were soon dropped from the police statements. Before long all the papers and television bulletins were referring definitely to an estate car. On Sunday, 24 September, Mrs Jones made a full statement to the police:

At about 4.00 p.m. that afternoon I was in the rear garden of my home. I looked in the direction of Yew Tree Farm, and in the drive immediately in front of the front door I saw a vehicle parked. I could clearly see that it was a blue estate vehicle. It was facing towards my home, and I could see that the tailgate was raised. I could not see anyone with the vehicle. I thought at first that the vehicle belonged to Mrs Julie Jones, daughter-in-law of Mr Fred Jones, because she has a blue estate. . .

On looking more carefully at the vehicle I could see that it was not Julie's vehicle as it was the wrong colour blue. I decided to get an even better view to see just who it was. I walked from the garden into the field where I had a completely uninterrupted view of the farm and the vehicle. I then saw that it was a lighter blue than Julie Jones's vehicle. I would not commit myself completely to the make, but I am more or less sure that it was a Ford Cortina. It was most certainly a vehicle of the Cortina size. I stood in the field for a good five minutes waiting to see who came to the vehicle, but no one did.

After about five minutes I collected my washing from the line and went into the house, where I remained until about 4.30 p.m. I then went out into the rear garden again and saw that the estate vehicle had gone.

Mrs Jones' description of the car on 24 September differed slightly in two respects from what she had said on the evening of the murder. The 'boot' of the car in her statement on the 19th had become a 'tailgate', and in her second statement she 'could not commit herself completely to the make' of the car, as she had done on the murder evening. But the most interesting part of the statement gave a reason for her original certainty about the make. *She had seen a blue Ford Cortina estate at the farm before.* This could have influenced her not just as to the make but also as to whether or not the car was an estate. In May 1983, I went with Ann Whelan to Yew Tree Farm. We parked a blue Vauxhall Viva saloon with its back to the farm, and its boot up. We walked to Mrs Jones' cottage and looked down at the car. It was quite clear to us that it was not possible for anybody of ordinary eyesight to tell the make of the car from that distance, and when we asked Mrs Jones she certainly could not do so on that occasion.

There were two other points which must have interested Detective Inspector Colin Wordley, who took the second, full, statement. First, Mrs Jones noticed, when she first saw the car, that the back door to the farmhouse was closed, as it only was when Fred and Mary were out. By the time she'd moved into the field for the second look, the door was open, and it was still open when the car had gone. It was clear that the person or people who had broken into Yew Tree Farm had driven there in the car which Gladys Jones saw.

The second point was about the dog, Skip. Mrs Jones' statement added: 'Whilst I had been in the garden I had not heard the dog barking, which he always does when strangers visit. He even barks at me, and I have known the dog for over twelve months.'

The dog had not barked. Moreover, the dog, it seemed, had been moved from one room to another. Fred Jones said he left it in the kitchen. Sergeant Potts found it in the scullery. Once again, the evidence suggested that whoever broke into Yew Tree Farm had some knowledge of the place, and was well enough known to the dog to move it without it barking.

Armed with Mrs Jones' information, the police started the search for more witnesses who might help with information about the blue car, probably an estate, probably a Ford Cortina.

The problems facing them were prodigious. In almost all the newspaper reports Yew Tree Farm was described as 'lonely'. Anyone who has been there testifies to the spookiness and loneliness of the place, but it is by no means remote. It sits in the junction of the A449, one of the biggest main roads in the area, and Lawnswood Road, a popular route to Wordsley, Kingswinford and Stourbridge. The track which leads from Lawnswood Road to the farm goes on through some fields and down to the Stour River. Though it is not a through route to anywhere, it was often used by courting couples or others who wanted to head into the countryside. It is also a public footpath.

The immediate problem confronting the police was the volume of traffic within yards of Yew Tree Farm, which built up to a climax in the early evening.

In May 1984, Mrs Ann Whelan and a friend, Jenny Powell, spent the afternoon outside Yew Tree Farm on both sides of Lawnswood Road, counting the number of cars which passed along the road. Between 3 p.m. and 5.15 p.m. they counted 266 vehicles going along Lawnswood Road towards the A449, and 385 going in the other direction. This meant that 651 vehicles passed by the farm on Lawnswood Road alone. Seven of these turned into the Yew Tree Farm track.

Ann Whelan and Jenny Powell weren't able even to start counting the number of cars which passed the farm along the A449 itself. Ann Whelan noted 'a continuous stream of traffic down that main road in both directions'.

There was a considerable build-up around 5 p.m. Between 4.30 p.m. and 5.15 p.m. in Lawnswood Road, 117 cars passed the farm on the way to the A449; 202 in the other direction. At one or two stages during this three-quarters of an hour the traffic to the main road was held up, and there was a tail-back in Lawnswood Road stretching as far as the farm.

There was of course an increase in car registrations between 1978 and 1984, and the figures for car movements in Lawnswood Road were probably marginally fewer in the former year. But clearly the newspaper boy had been murdered in broad daylight only a few yards away from heavy traffic movement in four different directions.

On the morning after the murder, police started to stop traffic and interview drivers. They set up a special caravan 'control post' at the farm with notices appealing to any motorist who may have seen anything which might help their inquiries to come in and make a statement.

Chief Superintendent Stewart also sent squads of policemen through Wordsley, Kingswinford and the adjoining areas, knocking on doors and asking if anything out of the ordinary had been seen on Tuesday, 19 September, at Yew Tree Farm.

The results were remarkable. The whole area had been shocked by the cruel murder of a cheerful and popular newspaper boy. There was an immediate determination to do everything possible to bring the killer to justice. First scores, then hundreds of messages poured into the caravan at the farm and into the murder inquiry headquarters at Wombourne.

Many of these reported cars seen in Lawnswood Road or on the A449 outside the farm. Most of these reports were so vague that they could be dispensed with at once. But police were surprised how many statements they were able to take from people in the area who had seen a car turning into the track at Yew Tree Farm during the afternoon of 19 September.

After the first week a pattern started to take shape. Without doubt, a blue car had been at the farm that afternoon. Most of the evidence seemed to suggest either that it was there continuously from as early as half past twelve in the afternoon, or that it returned to the farm on more than one occasion.

The statements which suggested one or all of these things, and which were taken in the first ten days after the murder, are as follows.

Robert and Janet Light were travelling to a Kidderminster carpet firm and passed the farm shortly before 12.25 p.m. Mrs Light, the more observant of the two, said: 'As we approached the farm drive, a blue car was reversing from the drive. The car stopped backing, and then continued out into the road to face Wordsley.' The car, she said, was a 'light blue estate car'. Mrs Light thought there were two white people in the car – but her husband thought there was only one.

Alfred Bishop, an insurance agent from Kingswinford, said that at about 1.30 in the afternoon he was turning off the main road into Lawnswood Road when 'almost immediately I was approached by a car which was turning left into the driveway of a derelict farm which I now know to be Yew Tree Farm. . . Regarding the car, I would say that it was blue in colour, and of a small to medium-sized model, possibly the size of a Vauxhall Viva. I cannot recall whether it was an estate car or an ordinary car.' Mr Bishop stressed that he wasn't sure that it was a Vauxhall Viva, and certainly didn't remember anything about the car's occupant or occupants.

Another witness also saw a blue Vauxhall Viva turning into the driveway of the farm – about an hour and twenty minutes after Mr Bishop's sighting. This was company director Roger Edwards, who lived in Hunters Drive, just a few hundred yards from the farm, Mr Edwards' habit was to drive each afternoon to a pub in Greensforge. On his way back from the pub that Tuesday (he reckoned about 2.50 p.m.) he turned off the A449 into Lawnswood Road. His statement to the police, which was given the day after the murder, went on:

'As I got into Lawnswood Road, I saw a pale blue car, I am certain a Vauxhall Viva, just in the act of turning left into the driveway of Yew Tree Farm. This vehicle had driven down Lawnswood Road from the opposite direction from which I was travelling. I noticed that the driver was a man, I would think in the age of fifty-five years. He was wearing a dark blue uniform with a single pip on the epaulette of his jacket. His hair was dark, but greying and somewhat wavy. The car was clean, no rust, and I feel this was a reasonably new car. I formed the impression that this man was either a police or fire officer due to the uniform he was wearing. He was not wearing any headgear.'

This driver, said Mr Edwards, was 'definitely on his own', but he would not know him again, or be able to describe him from such a fleeting glance. He had formed his view about the man's age by the fact that his hair was greying.

Mr Edwards' clear memory, especially his certainty that the car he saw was a Vauxhall Viva, impressed the interviewing policemen. They reckoned Mr Edwards an important witness, and noted his telephone number on the statement.

Mr Edwards' statement was quickly supported by two others. On 22 September, detectives on the 'knock-up' inquiry called at 60 Hamilton Drive, the home of Peter Hadley, a process manager. Mr Hadley was on holiday, and was sitting down to lunch with his father, Joseph Hadley. The police asked about Yew Tree Farm. Mr Hadley said he couldn't help. But when he returned to the table he remembered that he and his father had driven past Yew Tree Farm the previous Tuesday, and had seen a blue car in the driveway. The two men bolted their lunch and drove straight to the caravan at the farm.

Father and son confirmed each other's story. They had been for a drink and a game of snooker at lunchtime that Tuesday at the Constitutional Club at Kinver. They left the club at 2.50 p.m. and drove back to Wordsley, via Lawnswood Road. As they passed the farm entrance both men saw a blue car in the driveway. Neither could say whether it was a saloon or estate. It was parked on the righthand side of the track, near the hedge. Both men commented on it at the time, and they are fairly sure of the time, because, as Joseph Hadley put it: 'We arrived at my son's house at 3 p.m. and we were told off by our wives for being late for the meal that was prepared for us.'

13

Not very long afterwards, Frank Cogsell, a British Gas service engineer, also drove past the farm drive and saw a blue car parked in the track up against the righthand hedge. He was more certain about its type and make: 'I glanced in and saw a blue estate which I believed to be an Avenger estate.' He thought it was an Avenger estate because his brother had one of exactly the same colour. On reflection, and after being shown pictures, he thought it might have been a Ford Escort estate.

What time did Mr Cogsell see the car? He wasn't sure. He had been at a pub at lunchtime, and had visited a house to service the gas connection for about an hour and a half. He had then returned to his depot at Stourbridge before heading off again down Lawnswood Road. He put the time of the sighting at 'between 3.30 and 4.30'.

Anthony Cross, a highways inspector, could be more precise. He'd been to check the track at the side of the farm which was a public footpath. He wanted to see if there was a proper sign declaring it to be a footpath, so he parked his car outside Yew Tree Farm to have a close look. He didn't get out of his car while he looked for the sign, but he did notice, through the trees, a blue car, not on the track itself but in the open space between the track and the farmhouse. He could only see a few feet of the back of the car, but this enabled him to tell police officers he was sure the vehicle was an estate. 'It was either a Ford Cortina or a Ford Granada,' he said. He could judge the time almost exactly because, a few minutes after pulling off, he had noticed a road-sweeping truck emptying its waste. He had glanced at his watch to find it was 3.50 p.m., and he remembered thinking that they were late tipping at that time.

About twenty minutes later, Mrs Dorothy Southall was taking her granddaughter for a walk in her pram down Lawnswood Road. She reached the cottages at the top of the hill and pointed out two horses in a field.

'I only stayed in the position for a moment,' she said, 'but I did notice a vehicle parked in the driveway of Yew Tree Farm. The vehicle was behind a hedge, but I could see the top of it. I am certain that it was a van. It was mid-blue in colour, but it looked like a Transit or something smaller.'

Mrs Southall said she knew something about vehicles since her husband and her son had a haulage business, but it is worth noting that she was standing at least 300 yards from Yew Tree Farm. It is difficult for all but the most far-sighted person to tell more than the rough colour and shape of a vehicle from that distance.

There were two drivers who reported passing Carl Bridgewater as he cycled down Lawnswood Road. At almost exactly 4.15 p.m., Fred Edwards, the Water Board charge hand whose party of four we met with

14

Carl Bridgewater at the start of the chapter, drove down Lawnswood Road. He passed the boy as he climbed on his bike after a delivery, 'As I rounded the bend by the two cottages on the left,' said Mr Edwards, 'I noticed a light blue vehicle in the driveway of the farm. I could see the vehicle quite plainly. The boot of the car was nearest Lawnswood Road, in other words the vehicle had driven in the farm drive front end first.' Mr Edwards could not tell the make of the car, or whether or not it was an estate.

Mrs Margaret Heary, who lived at Kinver, also passed Carl as she drove along Lawnswood Road that afternoon at almost exactly the same time as Fred Edwards. As she passed the Yew Tree Farm drive she noticed 'a vehicle parked' in the driveway in exactly the same position as the car Mr Edwards saw. She had just passed her driving test and she was nervous in case the car reversed out into Lawnswood Road. The colour of the car was 'light, possibly blue. I am not able to say whether it was a saloon or an estate car, although I have the impression of a long roof on the vehicle,' she said. There was, she was sure, no one in it.

No less than three witnesses said they had seen a blue car in the farm track at 4.45 p.m., but all of them had the car facing in different directions. Wendy Stagg, a teacher, who was driving past, said she saw a blue estate car which looked as though it had reversed out of the track, and had stopped. Just by the car was a plum-coloured Allegro or Maxi car, and a man was standing in the road apparently talking to the driver of the estate. Edward Dickens said he glanced down the lane while passing in his car, and saw a 'medium-ranged car, probably a 1500 or 1600cc range, parked diagonally across the drive a short distance from the road with its nose facing towards the house'. And Mrs Geraldine Waldron, who was driving past with her aunt, Monica Ellison, remembers the time exactly because she put a joint in the oven at 4.50 p.m. the moment she got home, about five minutes away. 'I can say that I saw a car parked in the track which leads to the farm. The car was facing the roadway, and I remember that because I could see the radiator grill. The car was parked near the hedgerow at the bottom of the track. . . The colour of the car was medium to dark blue, it was definitely not a pale or light blue.' Neither Mrs Waldron nor her aunt could help further with the make of the car nor could they say whether or not it was an estate.

At 4.55 p.m., Brian Clarke was driving down Lawnswood Road in his Range Rover which gave him a specially good view over the hedges. Turning his head as he came to the farm, he found he had a 'very clear view'. 'I could see a motor vehicle in the driveway,' he said. 'I know this vehicle to be an Austin/Morris J4, owing to my trade. It was parked in the driveway and at an angle, and was medium blue in colour.' Mr Clarke said he also saw a man standing by the van with his back to the road. The man was of 'heavy build with light hair and shoulder length'.

There was only one other witness to a car in the track to Yew Tree Farm. He was considered by the police to be very important.

Terence Phelps, a builder from Stourton, was talking to a friend, Mrs Osborne, in Lawnswood Drive when Carl Bridgewater rode up with Mrs Osborne's paper. Mr Phelps then went inside for a cup of tea, and left the house at almost exactly 4.55 p.m. He drove straight down Lawnswood Road towards the junction with the A449. As he got to the junction, there was a tail-back of cars, and he had to slow down. As he got to the track by Yew Tree Farm, he almost stopped. He looked down the track, and saw a blue car with two or three men in it, slightly set back from the road, facing the road. The car was 'dark blue'. Mr Phelps was 'almost certain' it was an estate, something like a Ford escort.

He had never seen the men in the car before. He knew the Wilkes family, which farmed at Yew Tree, but none of the men were the Wilkeses. The only man he noticed at all was the driver, who had a head of 'thick dark hair' and was in his 'late forties'. He was wearing a light shirt and a tie.

This was the sum of the people who told police they had seen a blue car either in the track to the farm, or turning into it, or turning out of it in the four and a half hours between 12.30 p.m. and 5.00 p.m. on Tuesday, 19 September 1978. Of the fourteen people who made these statements, two (both before 3.00 p.m.) said they thought the car was a Vauxhall Viva (Roger Edwards was sure of it); three in varying degrees of certainty backed Mrs Jones's testimony that it was an estate car. None of these three corroborated any of the others as to the make of estate; one said a Ford Escort, two were not sure. Two others (Mrs Southall and Mr Clarke) said the vehicle was a van. The other seven were not sure at all, and were not prepared to hazard a guess. Taken together, these witnesses seemed to establish that there was a blue vehicle at Yew Tree Farm nearly all afternoon, since the gaps between the witnesses' times of sighting are very short. Other than that, they proved very little.

Very few of these people had seen any human beings at the farm. Roger Edwards had seen a man in uniform. Brian Clarke had seen 'a man of heavy build with light hair' at about 4.50 p.m. Leonard Bick was driving past the farm as early as 3.15 p.m. when he saw a man in the yard. 'One outstanding feature he had was the colour of his hair,' Mr Bick told the police. 'It was a blond, corn colour.'

Mrs Monica Ellison, out with her niece for a drive, had passed the farm at about 4.45 p.m. and had seen a man standing in the track. He was 'tallish, wearing lightish clothes'. She estimated his age as 'fiftyish'.

Who else had seen people at the farm or in the drive? Wendy Stagg had seen a person talking to the driver of the reversed estate car. Terence Phelps had seen two or three men in the blue car which was facing

16

outwards from the drive. Edwards, Clarke, Ellison, Stagg, Phelps, Bick. Their total identification evidence added up to very little.

What statements were there about people or estate cars seen *anywhere near* the farm on the afternoon of the murder?

Mrs Catherine Moyle, a housewife who lived in Tettenhall, had visited her parents at Woolaston. She thought the time was 'about 2.40 p.m.' when she saw a blue Ford Cortina estate car parked on the side of the main road – the A449 – opposite the farm and some distance north of it. Two men had walked out into the road in front of the car. One of them, dressed in a white shirt and tie, stocky and in his forties, looked straight at her. The other was a younger man. The police marked Mrs Moyle down as 'a good witness'. She was taken to police headquarters in Birmingham and shown police photographs. She singled out one of them as strongly resembling the older man she had seen in the road.

Nicholas Holden, a young man from Wordsley, had seen *two* blue Ford estates. One of them had been parked in Lawnswood Road on the same side as the farm, about halfway to the cottages on the hill. The other was turning into the A449 from Prestwood Drive, a bumpy lane which runs down near the farm to the River Stour. The second estate was driven by a 'solidly-built man of about 35 years with light brown hair and there was a male passenger with him'. He saw these two cars at 'about 3.00 p.m.'. Later, as he returned from a scrap dealer on the A449, Mr Holden said he saw the second estate again.

Mario Sabetta, a local restaurant manager, said he saw a car parked in Lawnswood Road about 100 yards away from the farm. As Mr Sabetta was driving towards the A449, the car was on the other side of the road. Two men came out from behind the car, and one of them, Mr Sabetta said, was carrying what looked like a shotgun. They went across the road and looked over the hedge on the Yew Tree Farm side of the road. When he first gave a statement to police on 26 September Mr Sabetta specifically said he could not remember whether the car was an estate or not. He thought it was a Ford.

Mr Sabetta gave a fairly close description of the two men whom he had seen moving across the road. The first was '27-28 years old, of broad build, with fair, wavy curly hair down to his shoulders'. This man was carrying a gun, which had a short stock and a long barrel. The other man was older, about thirty-five to forty, and taller. He was slim, with dark brown hair and long straight sideboards.

This happened not at the farm, but some way down the road. As he said later, Mr Sabetta didn't think it significant, and dismissed it as 'a rabbit hunting expedition' in an area where a lot of people had guns, and shot rabbits or foxes. The whole incident took place, he reckoned, at 3.25 p.m., about an hour before Carl was shot.

Terence Madeley, a painter and decorator from Wordsley, said he passed Yew Tree Farm almost every day in his van. He drove past the farm on the Monday and the Tuesday of the week Carl was murdered – and possibly the Friday before. On one of those days – *he couldn't remember which* – he'd seen a Ford Cortina estate pull out of the track by the farm and race away towards the A449. The car, he thought, was 'racing green' in colour. There were two people in it, of whom he gave a brief and cautious description. Since Mr Madeley was not sure – even in the same week of the sighting – on which day it had taken place, since he had the colour of the car as green, and since anyone turning wrongly off the A449 and realising their mistake might well use the farm track to turn round and head back for the main road again, his evidence at the time seemed insubstantial.

Even more remote was the statement of John Mills of Wall Heath who said he'd seen two men in a blue Cortina estate driving down the main A449 road at about 4.50 p.m. on the afternoon of the 19th. Mr Mills thought, though he was not sure, that the car had pulled out of Lawnswood Road into the main road.

By the end of the first week of the inquiry, and after hundreds of people had been questioned, only seven people had come forward with even cursory descriptions of people at or near the farm within an hour of Carl's murder. Of the seven, the police at once singled out Terence Phelps as outstanding. He had seen the newspaper boy that afternoon. Less than an hour later, he had seen the blue car in the mouth of the track, with two or three men sitting in it, one of whom he could describe reasonably well.

What other evidence had the police uncovered in that first week of inquiries? On 22 September, a single cartridge case from a shotgun was found at the corner of Doctors Lane, not far from the farm. Local papers brandished this as an important clue. 'A shotgun cartridge may have been thrown from the car of the fleeing killers of Carl Bridgewater, it was revealed today. It had been fired recently and could be from the murder weapon,' said the *Express and Star* on 29 September.

But that was all. Despite the enormous response from the public, there were very few clues.

On 27 September, eight days after the murder, Chief Superintendent Stewart took the always risky decision to publish an Identikit picture of the driver of the car Mr Phelps had seen in the Yew Tree Farm track. Mr Phelps had spent hours with the Identikit officers (and had looked through countless photographs of criminals at Birmingham central police station). The Identikit picture was published with a flourish in all the papers on the morning of 29 September. The local papers were the most enthusiastic.

'FACE OF A KILLER!' boomed the *Express and Star*. 'IS THIS THE FACE OF CARL'S KILLER?' inquired the *Birmingham Evening*

Mail a little more cautiously. The *Stourbridge County Express* asked 'DO YOU KNOW THIS MAN?'

The *Express and Star* reported that the Identikit was the result of a 'description given by a motorist who came face to face with the murder gang'.

'The killers,' the paper went on, 'were making their getaway when they were spotted. The man who saw them was stuck in a traffic jam at the end of the farm lane. . .

'The motorist's attention was drawn to the estate because it appeared to be hanging back, waiting to get on the Lawnswood Road.

'The driver of the getaway car is said to be in his forties, and his most distinctive feature is his head of thick dark hair. He may also have been wearing a dark jacket or tie. There was certainly someone else in the car with him – one and possibly two.'

The *County Express* quoted DCS Stewart as saying: 'He got a very good look at the man. I think it was all over and he was on the way out.'

This certainty that the men Mr Phelps saw were the murderers persisted for many weeks. It presented as fact the assumption that there had been 'three killers', and dominated all the police comments and the publicity for the next two and a half months. Detective Superintendent Eric Lycett, a senior officer in the inquiry, told the *Birmingham Evening Mail*: 'The killer will always be a prisoner in the hands of his two accomplices. His own frame of mind may deteriorate. How can he protect himself?'

The publishing of the Identikit picture brought the expected avalanche of information. Though the police welcomed the renewed public interest, they found, as they always do after the publication of an Identikit picture, that tracking down random phone calls about 'likenesses' was a heavy burden on the inquiry. In the first two days after the publication, the already overworked Wombourne headquarters received 700 calls from the public. Hundreds more police were drafted into the inquiry. They slogged round the 'informants' who thought perhaps their neighbour or the father of a girl at their daughter's school or even their uncle or their husband might be the men responsible. As so often, the exercise proved a failure.

Chief Superintendent Stewart said: 'We have got a lot of good stuff, but it takes a little time to get through it all.' (*Express and Star*, 30 September 1978.) He went on to say that he was still convinced that the 'murder gang' had close connections with the West Midlands, but may have fled the area.

Two days later, he told reporters: 'It is not a black picture by any means. I am optimistic, and my team is optimistic.' (*Express and Star*, 2 October 1978.)

To spur his optimism, Stewart called for a 'reconstruction' of the

19

events before the crime to try to jog witnesses' memory. Martin Flavell, a school chum of Carl Bridgewater, cycled round the newsagent's customers, ending up at Yew Tree Farm. No one came forward, despite another burst of publicity.

Stewart said: 'I am seeking a chink of light to enable me to make a breakthrough. I have so much information but all I need is that little break. It may be tomorrow, or a week tomorrow but I am hoping it will come.' (*Express and Star*, 4 October 1978.)

On that same day, local papers in the West Midlands reported a flurry of calls from people confessing to the Carl Bridgewater murder. They were all anonymous, and they all seemed to come from the same man. Senior officers remarked that cases of this kind always brought out 'phone nutters' but that this one was especially persistent.

Almost every day, DCS Stewart and his detectives tried a new tack to get more information from the public. They issued more detailed descriptions of the goods which had been stolen. These had been kept secret in the hope that the more unusual stuff might give the killers away if they didn't know the police were looking for it. No one responded. Chief Superintendent Stewart surmised that the 'three killers' (the trio was referred to almost every day despite very little evidence to suggest that the murder did involve three men) were closely related: 'There is a possibility we have not had the vital information we need because it could be a close-knit family unit who killed Carl.' (*Express and Star*, 14 October.)

That night Stewart took his wife out for the first time since the murder. He told newsmen: 'I still need one or two pieces to complete the jigsaw. They could come tomorrow or next week. But when I have these pieces, it will nail the killer.' (*Express and Star*, 15 October.)

In spite of the enormous number of messages, and the vast police force knocking up doors and following up the messages, the gaps in the jigsaw seemed to grow wider. A gun was found in the Stour, but a forensic report soon ruled it out as the murder weapon. Another reconstruction was staged. A blue estate car was left for half an hour with its tailgate up, just in front of the farm's door. The underworld bush telegraph, which was proving receptive, was phoned round once again. On 18 October, following information received, a gypsy caravan site near Wakefield in Yorkshire was raided by hundreds of police, and a father and two sons (perhaps a 'close-knit' family) were held for questioning. None of this produced that 'little break' Stewart was hoping for. He made two more attempts to get more information. On 10 October he launched a hunt for the 'courteous motorist' whom Wendy Stagg had seen talking to the driver of the estate which seemed to her to have reversed out of the farm drive. On 19 October he published two more Identikit pictures. These were made up by Mario Sabetta the restaurant manager, who had not seen a single person or even a vehicle at the farm, but had come across a car parked in the road 100 yards away, with two men, one with a gun, walking out from behind it, an hour before the murder. From this brief glimpse of the two men on the move, Mr Sabetta pieced together two Identikit pictures. They were published with the Identikit that had been put together by Terence Phelps and issued a fortnight earlier. 'Are these Carl's murderers?' asked the local papers, in headlines over the three pictures. The *Birmingham Evening Mail* was optimistic: 'This [the new Identikit pictures] means that the net is closing on the three men who blasted 13-year-old Carl. It has been drawn up with the help of an important new witness. He saw the man on the left carrying a shotgun leaving a similar blue Ford about an hour before the murder.'

In fact, as we have seen, Mr Sabetta was not certain even that the car was a Ford, let alone that it was an estate car 'similar' to the one seen in the farmyard by Mrs Jones.

On the day before these pictures were published, a woman rang Wombourne police station. Chief Superintendent Stewart felt that this anonymous caller might have had some genuine information about the killer. It was another of those 'phantom' calls which he believed was linked to the killing. He told the press the woman was 'mature and well-spoken'. It was possible, he said, that the murder involved a member of her own family. 'It could,' he said 'be the very thing I am waiting for.' (*County Express*, 20 October 1978.)

At any rate, the new Identikit pictures brought a new flood of phone calls and visitors to the police station all with 'information' which had to be checked out by an already overworked police force. At the same time, they were checking on all 7,000 registered owners of blue Ford Cortina estates in the West Midlands, and on every single shotgun licence over a wide area. Five hundred written questionnaires were handed out to the householders of Wordsley 'to close a small gap in our inquiries', as Stewart put it.

Mrs Janet Bridgewater, her grief growing as the weeks went by, was persuaded to make a public statement asking the families of the murderers to give them up. The public responded eagerly. By 16 November, fifty-eight days after the murder, the police of several forces, mainly Staffordshire and the West Midlands, had taken 5,000 written statements and had received 7,500 telephone calls. Stewart's 'chink of light' had not yet appeared.

Part of the problem in such a vast inquiry was to keep up with it. Several witnesses I spoke to seven years later told me they had been interviewed twice, sometimes by different police officers, the second pair of whom had no knowledge of the first interview. As the first two weeks of November passed without any vital new information turning up, senior detectives determined to get a closer grip of the evidence. They ordered a review of people who had been interviewed, especially those who had seen a car or a person in or near the farm.

Looking at the statements again, they were struck by the detailed re-collection of company director Roger Edwards who had seen a blue Vauxhall Viva driven by a man in uniform turning into the drive about an hour and a half before the murder. For a moment, their early cer-tainty about a Ford Cortina estate was replaced by an interest in a Vauxhall Viva. Another witness, Alfred Bishop, had also thought he'd seen what could have been a blue Vauxhall Viva turning into the drive.

Mr Edwards' statement had been taken by two detective constables from Chasetown, Staffordshire, Alan Mynott and Brian Withnall. They handed it in to 'the murder system', as it was known, and continued with their inquiries. In the second week of November, the inquiry was 'reac-tioned'. The two constables were given the Edwards statement back and told to trace the owner of the blue Vauxhall Viva. The only clue they had was the uniform. Off they trekked to every police, fire and ambulance station in the area – Wombourne, Brierley Hill, Stourbr-idge, Wolverhampton. They went to the local Water Boards, Gas Boards, post offices, Electricity Boards and even to the RSPCA and Securicor.

Everywhere the question was the same: is there an officer here who drives about in uniform in a blue Vauxhall Viva? Registration numbers were collected and fed into the police computer.

To their delight, they came up with one positive answer – and a name: Hubert Vincent Spencer, an ambulance liaison officer at Corbett Hos-pital, Stourbridge. He owned a light blue Vauxhall Viva. He drove it to and from work and around other hospitals in the area in ambulance officer's uniform.

Mr Spencer had been interviewed earlier in the Carl Bridgewater in-quiry. One of the very first 'phantom' calls which came into Wombourne after the murder had been publicised suggested that the police should talk to Mr Spencer, who collected antiques.

The job was assigned to Detective Sergeant David Wainwright and Detective Constable John Crowe of the Cannock police.

The two officers went to Spencer's house in fashionable Kingsley Road, Kingswinford. He was not in. They called again, and again. Still he was not in.

Finally, the officers made an appointment, for the evening of 24 Sep-tember, five days after the murder. This time Spencer was at home with his wife Janet and his daughter Janell. The officers explained that they were involved in the Bridgewater murder inquiry, and asked Spencer for an account of his movements on the previous Tuesday. Spencer an-swered at once that he worked at Corbett Hospital as an ambulance liaison officer and had been at work at the hospital all day the previous Tuesday. This could easily be confirmed, he said, with Mrs Barbara Riebold who was working with him that day as ambulance secretary. Mrs Riebold also lived in Kingsley Road, about twenty houses up from the Spencers. But Sergeant Wainwright, when he talked about the interview later, doubted that Spencer mentioned this. 'I don't think he could have told us that Mrs Riebold lived nearby,' he said, 'or we would have gone to see her there and then.'

Mr Spencer agreed at once that he collected antiques. This was plain enough anyway since his house was full of them. 'But,' he added, 'I am not a dealer.' The two officers apologised for the inconvenience and left.

'On reflection,' Sergeant Wainwright said, much later, 'it could be the case that the questioning of Spencer was not as deep as it was in some cases because it appeared that he could be easily accounted for.' DC Crowe said: 'He didn't show any alarm.'

Mr Spencer's statement to the officers was brief:

I am a married man residing with my wife and family at the above address. I am very interested in antiques, mainly clocks, and occasionally purchase things for my collection. I am not a dealer. I am employed by the West Midlands Health Authority as a station officer at Corbett Hospital, Stourbridge.

On Tuesday, 19 September 1978, I was on duty at the hospital from approximately 8.30 a.m. until approximately 5.10 p.m. I am the registered owner of a Vauxhall Viva saloon motor car, blue in colour, registered number LEA 605K.

The following morning, the two officers went to Corbett Hospital to take an even shorter statement from Mrs Barbara Riebold. She told them:

I am employed as the ambulance secretary at the Corbett Hospital, Stourbridge. I can confirm that Mr Hubert Spencer, who is the ambulance liaison officer, was at the hospital all afternoon on Tuesday, 19 September 1978, until he left at 5 p.m., or just after.

The officers walked out of the hospital. As they did so, they were followed by Hubert Spencer, running. As he caught up with them breathlessly, he asked the officers if they were satisfied about his movements the previous Tuesday, because, he said, there were others who could confirm that he was in the hospital all day.

'As we were quite satisfied at that point in time, we told Spencer it wasn't necessary,' said Sergeant Wainwright. 'He didn't appear to be over-anxious to me or particularly concerned.'

Constable Crowe, however, got a rather different impression. 'On reflection, he did appear to overreact when we checked with Mrs Riebold,' he said.

But the officers were satisfied. 'No record sheet was ever referred to by Spencer or Mrs Riebold, and we didn't ask to be shown any, due to our being satisfied,' was DC Crowe's account.

All this happened on 24 and 25 September in the week after the murder.

At that stage, Sergeant Wainwright and Constable Crowe had no idea that a statement had been taken by two other Staffordshire officers to the effect that a man in uniform driving a blue Vauxhall Viva had been seen turning into Yew Tree Farm on the afternoon of the murder. Had they known that, their inquiries might have been more rigorous.

Five weeks later, after the murder inquiry was 'reactioned', Constables Mynott and Withnall, who did know about the Viva turning into the drive for they had taken Mr Edwards' statement, were intrigued to find that Spencer and Mrs Riebold had already been interviewed as a result of an anonymous phone call, and even more so since he admitted being interested in antiques.

For a whole week that November they made what they later described as 'discreet inquiries' at Corbett Hospital and in the Kingswinford area about Hubert Spencer. The results of those inquiries convinced both of them and their superior officers that they might have come across the 'chink of light' for which Chief Superintendent Stewart had been praying.

To start with, they discovered that Spencer was not just an antique collector as he had pretended. He was in a small way what he had specifically said he was not, an antique dealer. In 1972, he and his friend Kenneth Farndon, who lived in a neighbouring street in Kingswinford, had rented a shop in Wordsley High Street and set up the first ever antique shop in the town. Ernest Perry, who rented the shop to Spencer, recalls that it was not a success. There was no formal lease for the shop and Perry remembers Spencer telling him after a few months that he and Farndon were losing money and would have to close down. Spencer asked if he could be let off the last three months' rent, which Mr Perry refused. He thinks Spencer did pay up in the end, and the premises were then let as a pet shop.

Secondly, the officers discovered that Spencer had a close link to Yew Tree Farm. Since he had been an ambulance officer in his native Smethwick he had worked part time for Hubert Wilkes, the farmer of Holloway Farm and Yew Tree Farm. He had led gangs of hospital and ambulance workers – all anxious to supplement their miserable incomes – to

Mr Wilkes' farms on summer evenings when there was too much work for the Wilkes' full-time staff.

In the course of this work, Spencer had grown friendly with the Wilkes family. He had also built up a close association with Yew Tree Farm and its tenants Fred Jones and Mary Poole. He was a frequent visitor to the farm both as worker and as guest. He used to borrow Jack Poole's gun to shoot rabbits on the farm. He had been inside thefarm-house on several occasions, and was known to admire the antiques in it. His name was in the old peoples' private telephone book.

So Hubert Spencer knew Yew Tree Farm inside and outside. He knew the farmer and he knew the old tenants. The detectives soon discovered that he often used a gun on the farm. Moreover, the farm was close to the hospital. If he wanted to avoid traffic on his journey between his Kingswinford house and the hospital at Stourbridge, Spencer would take the 'long cut' through the country, past the farm, and down the A449, and come back into Stourbridge by the Bridgenorth Road.

As they inquired further into Spencer's background the officers came across another remarkable coincidence. Hubert Spencer knew Carl Bridgewater. Shortly after his promotion to ambulance liaison officer, Spencer had moved from Smethwick to Wordsley, where he and his wife had bought a terrace house in a newly-built housing estate at Ascot Gardens. The number of their house was 21. At 25 Ascot Gardens, just two doors away in the terrace, lived Brian Bridgewater, his wife Janet, and their three children, Jane, Carl and Philip. When the Spencers moved into Ascot Gardens in 1970, Carl was five. When they left to go 'up in the world' to a semi-detached house at Kingswinford in 1975, Carl was ten. Carl's sister was exactly the same age as Spencer's daughter, Janell, and the two girls frequently played together. All the children, including Janell Spencer and Carl Bridgewater, went to the same school. The Spencers had to pass the Bridgewaters' house to get out of the cul-de-sac.

Nor was this all. There was another connection between Hubert Spencer and the Carl Bridgewater murder which arose from the weirdest incident in the whole weird story.

On 23 October, three days after the publication of the three Identikit pictures of the supposed killers, Bert Spencer, his wife and daughter visited Bert's brother Don at his home at Great Arthur Street, Smethwick – twelve miles from Kingswinford. It was raining. The two families decided to go for a drink in a local pub. This involved a walk from the back of Don's house through some scrub and woodland onto a dual carriageway, Telford Way.

The party which set out on the walk consisted of Bert and Don Spencer, their wives Janet and Valerie, and three teenage girls – the two Spencer daughters and a friend from the house next door. The party went to the pub and came back in the gathering gloom. Don Spencer told me himself what happened next:

'We walked up the footpath in the middle of the dual carriageway, Telford Way, and then we crossed over to go through the gate to the footpath. We had gone to the pub exactly the same way.

'As we were going up to the gate, one of the children, I can't remember which one, bent down and picked up a piece of cardboard which was lying on the pavement. It was a message that was addressed to someone called Bert, and had something to do with the Bridgewater murder. Bert insisted that we should all four take the card to the police station. We didn't think it was so important but he insisted, so we went.' (Interview with me 10 February 1984.)

Don Spencer was quite sure it was not his brother Bert who picked the paper up. He wasn't sure whether or not Bert had drawn attention to it before the child picked it up. At any rate, the children went on home, and the four adults walked down to Smethwick police station.

On duty there was Sergeant Philip Rich. Bert Spencer gave his name and address, handed over the card and said he strongly believed it might help police in their inquiries into the Carl Bridgewater murder. Sergeant Rich carefully read the card:

On one side, under the hugely printed name 'BERT', was the following message, all of it printed in block capitals: 'THAT CHAP WHO DISGUISES ISSELF WAS SEEN OVER THE FARM WHERE CARL BRIDGEWATER WAS SHOT. TED SAYS HE LIVES IN VICARAGE ROAD SMK. HE SCARES THE WOMAN. TAKE CARE. JOE.'

On the other side, in the same block capitals, was printed: 'HE SCARED DON'S MISSUS. 107 or 108 STONEY LANE UWP751R.'

Sergeant Rich asked the Spencers what they made of this curious message. The Spencers could not help. 'We didn't know anyone who lived at Vicarage Road or Stony Lane,' Don Spencer told me. 'We did remember that my wife Valerie had been scared once long ago by a bloke on Smethwick steps. He didn't assault her or anything, he just frightened her. But we couldn't see that that had to do with anything. We just couldn't make it out. It all seemed ridiculous.'

Sergeant Rich thanked the Spencers and they left. Much later, the sergeant testified to his own scepticism. In a sworn statement on 22 May 1980, a year and a half after the incident, he said: 'At this time it was raining heavily for some hours. I noticed, however, that the cardboard was completely dry.'

He kept the cardboard in his drawer until he went off duty early the following morning. Then, before going home, he conscientiously took the cardboard to the murder inquiry headquarters at Wombourne and handed it in.

As far as I can discover, and certainly as far as any published or released document about the case makes clear, no further inquiry was made at the time about this card. No one even checked the vehicle registration number which was printed on it. No one went to Vicarage Road or Stony Lane. No statement was taken from any of the Spencer family about it. Whoever had left the card out there in the open, so conveniently in Spencer's path, had obviously intended that these specific addresses and numbers should be followed up. They were not.

If inquiries had been made about the card, they would have revealed that the registration number belonged to a van owned at that time by Somerfield Laundries, of Smethwick. The van was driven by Harry Rushton, who worked for the laundry as a delivery man. Rushton lived at 76 Vicarage Road. His girlfriend, Janet Cotter, lived round the corner at 108 Stony Lane, where Harry often left his van.

Harry Rushton's laundry round took him out to the extreme west of the West Midlands area, and beyond. He had deliveries to make in Stourbridge and Stourton, and his run on Tuesdays took him within a mile or two of Yew Tree Farm. Harry's brother, Jim, had worked with Bert Spencer in the Smethwick ambulance service.

There was another remarkable fact which could easily have been uncovered. Hubert Spencer had spent his childhood and youth at Stony Lane, Smethwick. He was brought up at No.19.

Such facts, if they had been discovered, as they could have been by routine inquiries, might well have alerted officers leading the murder hunt. Harry and Jim Rushton might then have been interviewed. If so, the brothers would quickly have been ruled out as possible suspects. Neither man fitted any of the descriptions, nor did the laundry van remotely resemble any of the vehicles seen at the farm. Both men had regular jobs, and the records of their employers placed them at work during the afternoon of the murder.

If the brothers Rushton had been ruled out, the detectives might have returned to the piece of cardboard, puzzled. How on earth could such a serious document have been found by Bert Spencer and his family in such 'ridiculous' circumstances twelve miles away from his home?

Could Spencer have devised the card? The answer was yes, he could. He had lived for many years at Stony Lane and knew the area intimately. Jim Rushton, Harry's brother, was an ambulance man at Smethwick, who had worked alongside Bert Spencer, and had also been a member of the same judo club in the town. The families were close. Spencer had attended the christenings of Jim Rushton's children. Moreover, Harry and Jim Rushton had both visited Spencer's house at Kingswinford, when Spencer was redecorating his bathroom. Harry Rushton told me, many years later: 'I went to Spencer's house with Jim to collect some tiles and a washer. We travelled in the van whose registration number was printed on the card. We didn't stay long, and I hardly knew the man.' Jim Rushton agreed he had been friendly with Spencer. 'I always saw him as a pretty nice sort of bloke,' he said. (Interview with me, February 1984.)

The piece of card, conscientiously handed in by Sergeant Rich, was cast to one side, perhaps as the work of a crank, or as some strange quirk in a family quarrel. From 24 October, when Sergeant Rich handed it in, until 16 November, when the inquiry was 'reactioned', the card was buried in the mass of 'unseen' documents.

Indeed, the record suggests that the card remained buried there for far longer than that. But the card was indexed with the documents under Spencer, and it may well be that when Constables Mynott and Withnall came back to the murder inquiry headquarters with the results of their 'discreet inquiries' into the background of Hubert Spencer the card was noticed. If so, it would have disclosed another link between the ambulance officer and Yew Tree Farm.

Constables Mynott and Withnall were not a little excited by their discoveries. On 16 November they went back to see Roger Edwards again, and asked him for another detailed description of the man he had seen in the Vauxhall Viva. Mr Edwards could not help a great deal more, but when the constables reported back to the murder squad headquarters, Hubert Spencer at once became a prime suspect. Proof of this was the immediate promotion of one of Staffordshire's top detectives to take charge of the second interrogation of Spencer. Constables Mynott and Withnall were thanked and congratulated for their work. In their place were promoted Detective Chief Inspector Weslea Watson and Detective Sergeant Tony Holdway. DCI Watson was the number three in the entire inquiry – only Chief Superintendent Stewart himself and Superintendent Lycett were senior to him.

In the evening of 16 November, DCI Watson and Sergeant Holdway drove to Corbett Hospital to interview Spencer. All the other staff had left. Sitting there, in the empty reception area, they had an extraordinary conversation. It was recorded by DCI Watson:

At 6.30 p.m. on Thursday, November 16, 1978, in company with Detective Sergeant Holdway, I saw Hubert Vincent Spencer at the Corbett Hospital, Stourbridge.

I made known to him the reason for my visit, and said: 'Have you visited Yew Tree Farm?'

Spencer replied: 'Yes, I have. You have found out.'

I said: 'Why didn't you tell the officers?'

Spencer said: 'Well, to tell the truth, they didn't give me the chance. I don't want to cause any trouble for them, they seemed in a hurry to get away.'

I said: 'You could have contacted us.'

Spencer said: 'Yes, but if it came out I was working on the side I'd probably lose my job.'

I said: 'What work do you do on the side – dealing in antiques?'

Spencer said: 'Yes, I work on the farm for Mr Wilkes and I also have a spare time job as a barman.'

I said: 'Would revealing that lose you your job?'

Spencer said: 'Well, I think so, and of course the income tax people would be after me.'

I said: 'We are inquiring into a murder at a place where you have been.'

Spencer said: 'I appreciate that and I want to help.'

I said: 'You have been to the farm?'

Spencer said: 'Yes, hundreds of times.'

I said: 'You have been into the house?'

Spencer replied: 'Yes, I think two or three times about the gun. I was interested in buying it, I knew about it, and when Mr Poole died, yes, I went in once when he was alive and I think twice since.'

I said: 'You have been in the house?'

Spencer said: 'Yes, I went into the room, what you call it?'

I said: 'Living room.'

Spencer said: 'Yes. The other time I went through to where the foxes are. I would have loved those.'

I said: 'Who was there?'

Spencer said: 'At one time there was three – Fred Jones, Miss Poole and another woman, the other time just two.'

I said: 'You handled things in the house?'

Spencer said: 'I don't really think so.'

I said: 'You deal in antiques, you would have been interested.'

Spencer said: 'Well, I would have loved to own those foxes.'

I said: 'What attracted you to the gun?'

Spencer said: 'Well, I knew it was there and probably for sale. I think on one occasion it was with somebody else up Lawnswood Road.'

I said: 'You own a gun?'

Spencer said: 'I did until about twelve months ago.'

I said: 'Where is it now?'

Spencer replied: 'I sold it to Robert Thompson at 49 Kingsley Road. It was a twelve-bore. It's not at that address. It's kept at a cottage near a farm at Bridgnorth.'

I said: 'You were in the antique business?'

Spencer said: 'Yes.'

I said: 'With a partner?'

Spencer said: 'Yes, Kenneth Farndon of Mount Pleasant, King-

29

swinford – it's up on the right, the house with the white porch, I think it's the only one with a porch.'

I said: 'Where did you run your business from?'

Spencer said: '90 High Street, Wordsley.'

I said: 'I think it odd you didn't mention your connection with Yew Tree Farm to the officers.'

Spencer said: 'Well, they didn't want to listen to me, I didn't want it to get out about me working on the side. I'm doing a lot of work for Mr Wilkes on the farm.'

I said: 'You have a pale blue Viva car?'

Spencer replied: 'Yes.'

I said: 'Were you in Lawnswood Road on the 19th September, 1978, that was the day of the murder?'

Spencer replied: 'I don't think so. Were the roadworks going on in Wordsley then? I would have gone that way to and from lunch if they were.'

I said: 'What time do you have lunch?'

Spencer said: 'Sometimes twelve-thirty, but not later than two.'

I said: 'You have been to Yew Tree Farm in uniform?'

Spencer said: 'Yes, I think so.'

I said: 'There was a sighting of a man in a blue Viva in Lawnswood Road on the afternoon in question.'

Spencer said: 'You have someone who saw that?'

I said: 'It could be unconnected with the murder but we have to check it out.'

Spencer said: 'Of course you have, I would say I wasn't in Lawnswood Road that day.'

I said: 'You knew Carl Bridgewater of course?'

Spencer said: 'Well, you know that I used to live in the same area.'

I said: 'Three doors away.'

Spencer said: 'I don't think it was that close.'

I said: 'You were 21 and he was 25.'

Spencer said: 'I've been away from there three years.'

I said: 'He would know you, I suppose?'

Spencer said: 'Well, perhaps. I didn't recognise him.'

I said: 'Have you been concerned that some address of yours may be found at the farm?'

Spencer said: 'Well, to tell the truth I have been worried in case that little book had been taken. It had my name and address in it.'

I said: 'Yes, we know about that.'

Spencer said: 'You have got it then?'

I said: 'We know of it, yes.'

Spencer said: 'I was worried about that.'

I said: 'Why didn't you phone us up or make contact?'

Spencer said: 'Well, I should have done but like I said I didn't want to lose my job here.'

I said: 'We will want to see you again obviously.'

Spencer said: 'Yes, well, anything I can do. The civilians are investigating the murder.'

I said: 'How's that?'

He said: 'Well, surely whoever done it would have realised that those people were cripples and would have had milk and papers delivered.'

As Chief Inspector Watson and Sergeant Holdway returned to the murder inquiry headquarters that evening and pondered their interview with Hubert Spencer, their suspicions can hardly have been allayed. Spencer's excuse as to why he had not come forward with his knowledge of Yew Tree Farm and its interior must have shocked them. The whole of Wordsley and Kingswinford had been outraged by the crime. Thousands of people in the area had strained every muscle to assist the inquiry. Yet Hubert Spencer, who knew a lot about the farm, who had been there, in his own words, 'hundreds of times' had not offered to help even when police from the inquiry had visited his home.

His excuse that he wanted to keep his farm work secret from his employers was not very powerful. After all, as Spencer himself had told the officers, he also worked part-time as a barman, in full view of the public. This was at the Rose and Crown, Kinver.

His casual approach to his whereabouts during the lunch hour on the day of the murder must also have puzzled the officers. Since he obviously had been interested in the murder, surely he could have recalled whether or not he had taken the 'long cut' through the country on that day or whether he had gone the more direct route, through traffic. As Spencer himself admitted, he did travel the long way round by the farm when there were 'roadworks' – as he did when there were any other traffic hold-ups or even heavy traffic movement.

Further inquiries were necessary to check out Spencer's statement, and the detectives set about them vigorously.

Two days later, on 18 November, DCI Watson and Sergeant Holdway went to see Kenneth Farndon, Spencer's former partner in the antique shop at Wordsley High Street. He lived at 114 Mount Pleasant, Kingswinford, in the next street to Kingsley Road, where Spencer lived. Farndon had moved 'up market' from a terraced house in Wordsley to a detached house in Kingswinford in 1975, the very year that Spencer had moved in exactly the same way. Farndon had lived in the same estate in Wordsley, at 22 Marlborough Gardens, immediately next to Ascot Gardens where Spencer used to live and where the Bridgewaters still lived.

Kenneth Farndon agreed at once that he had been in partnership with Bert Spencer in the antique business at Wordsley High Street. He had put money into it, but Bert usually did the buying. Also, Bert had spent much more time at the business, since Farndon's work as a foundry worker prevented him from attending the shop more than occasionally. Since the shop closed, Farndon said, he had given up the business altogether, though he knew Bert kept up a little private buying and selling. Bert, he assured the officers, had never talked to him about any antiques at Yew Tree Farm he may or may not have wanted to buy.

Questioned further, Farndon said:

I do know he [Spencer] has been on the farmland shooting. I have been with him on one occasion. I don't own a gun, but he has a 12-bore barrel shotgun and in the past has had other guns. I haven't seen him with a gun for at least six months.

I remember either Bert or Janet told me that Bert hadn't shot at the farm for some time. They told me this since the murder.

I have never been to Yew Tree Farm house. The nearest I have been is some time ago, when I took my family with Bert's family. We had a picnic down the drive by the farm. Also of course as I mentioned I have been with Bert shooting on the land, but I have never been in the house.

Asked about his movements on the day of the murder, Farndon said he had been on holiday with his wife on his boat. He thought that on the crucial day he was at Stourport and mentioned a friend, Les Poole, who worked at Healey Mouldings, and who lived at Netherton Dudley. They had met, he said, while on holiday on the boat at Stourport.

Questioned more closely, Mr Farndon could not remember whether it was on the Monday or the Tuesday that he and his wife had gone on holiday. He thought it was the Monday. He knew he had arrived at York Street Basin, Stourport (about ten miles from Yew Tree Farm), at 7 p.m. He returned on the Friday. Mr Farndon told police that his wife kept a log of all the journeys they made in the boat.

Mr Farndon said he had never owned a shotgun. He had a gold-coloured Escort estate, which he'd left at Ashwood Marina, Wordsley, while he was away in his boat.

The next day the two officers were busy again on the same inquiry. They visited Robert Thompson, a self-employed builder, in his house at 52 Kingsley Road – the road where Bert Spencer lived at No. 42 and Mrs Riebold – the ambulance secretary at Corbett Hospital – lived at No. 82. Mr Thompson confirmed that he was a friend of Bert Spencer and said that Spencer had lent him his shotgun. He at once drove out to his cottage at Ditton Priors, near Bridgnorth, and produced for the police a

12-bore, single-barrel shotgun, which, he said, had been lent to him by Bert Spencer 'about twelve months ago'. He handed the gun over to the police. He told the police he had been at work at the private house of a Mr John Smith of Lower Gornal all the day of the murder, and named the man who was working with him, Eddie Morgan. He said he had never been to Yew Tree Farm and didn't own a car – though he did own a van and a truck. He had not, he said, discussed the Bridgewater murder with Bert Spencer.

Both the Thompson and Farndon statements were conscientiously followed up. Les Poole, the man whom Farndon said he met at Stourport, was seen by the officers on 20 November.

John Smith, the owner of the house at Lower Gornal where Thompson said he was at work all through 19 September was seen on 21 November.

Both confirmed the stories the two men had given.

The trail laid by Roger Edwards and his uniformed man driving the Vauxhall Viva had led to Bert Spencer, and Spencer's story had not been convincing. There were plenty of inquiries still to be made before he could be eliminated from police inquiries. Yet here, for some reason, the hunt suddenly seems to have stopped.

Chief Inspector Watson had told Spencer: 'We will want to see you again obviously.' Yet, according to the documents which the police released more than a year later, Spencer was not seen again, and made no further statements to the police. Mrs Riebold was not interviewed again about her statement that Spencer was definitely in the hospital all that afternoon. The hospital authorities were not approached to see if there were any other people in the entry hall who could remember Spencer's movements. Ambulance control at Smethwick were not approached to check on Spencer's recorded movements in September 1978, or on his expenses for journeys made outside his hospital. Spencer's wife and daughter were not interviewed about his movements that day. Anthony Wilkes was not interviewed about his knowledge of Spencer at the farm – nor was Fred Jones or Mary Poole. Mrs Farndon was not asked about the day she started her holiday, or about the logs she kept. From 21 November 1978, the whole inquiry seems to have ground to a halt.

No one has yet supplied to me or to anyone else any public explanation for this sudden stop. A year and a half later, the Director of Public Prosecutions, Sir Norman Skelhorn, wrote: 'Hubert Spencer was one of a substantial number of men seen by the police in the early stages of the investigation of the murder of Carl Bridgewater, and eliminated from the investigation.'

Eliminated from the investigation. How and why? The investigating officer himself, a chief inspector, had made it clear to Spencer on 16 September that he was *not* eliminated from the investigation. Not a word in all the documents released by Sir Norman Skelhorn suggest anything which could have eliminated Spencer from the investigation. On the contrary, the replies of those interviewed, especially of Spencer, suggested exactly the opposite – and must have deepened any suspicion the police must already have had. In the press, local and national, for the two weeks following the last available statement made in the Spencer inquiry, there is not the slightest hint either that Spencer was a suspect, as he clearly was, or that he or anyone else had been eliminated.

Whatever happened in the Spencer inquiry, however, it was not long before a dramatic event was to dispel all thoughts of the ambulance officer from the detectives' minds. On the evening of Friday, 30 November, nine days after the last recorded inquiry into Hubert Spencer's story, news came through to Wombourne of a robbery by an armed gang at an isolated farmhouse in the Worcestershire countryside, not an hour's drive away from Yew Tree Farm. Two men, one of them armed with a sawn-off shotgun, had burst into Chapel Farm, Romsley, near Halesowen. The farm lay in an isolated, unnamed lane, and got its name from its proximity to St Kenelm's church. It was inhabited, as was Yew Tree Farm, by old age pensioners, Jack Smith, aged eighty-three, and his three sisters, Mildred and Kathleen Smith and Mrs Henrietta Williams. The raiders, who were masked, demanded money. The old people refused, and put up a spirited resistance. They were pushed, and one of the old ladies fell heavily to the ground. The robbers escaped to a car, driven by a third man, and made off with no more than £300. Mildred Smith hobbled to the nearest farm and called for an ambulance. It took two of the pensioners to Corbett Hospital. The old people were released after treatment for shock and bruising.

The coincidences were astonishing. Three men, a shotgun, an isolated farmhouse, robbery with violence. The next day's *Birmingham Evening Mail* carried as its front-page headline: 'CARL LINK IN FARMHOUSE RAID?'

The report highlighted the links between the two farm raids: 'Police hunting armed raiders who struck at an isolated Midlands farmhouse last night were today investigating links with the murder of newsboy Carl Bridgewater. They believe the boy's murderers may have struck again.

'West Mercia police, who have mounted a massive hunt for the attackers, arranged an urgent briefing with murder squad detectives at Bromsgrove today to discuss links between the two cases.

'Chief Supt. John Barnett, who is leading the investigation, said today: "We shall be looking at every possibility, and the connection with the Carl Bridgewater shooting cannot be ruled out."'

At the 'urgent briefing' at Bromsgrove that morning the Staffordshire murder squad detectives were greeted with good news. A window

34

cleaner had seen what must have been the getaway car – a green Austin 1100 – as it raced away from the Romsley robbery. Indeed, he had seen two men running away from the farm to join the car. He had taken the number. The car belonged to a woman called Galvin, who lived in Birmingham.

Later that evening, more startling information was available. Linda Galvin had been interviewed. It seemed the car might have been driven by the man she lived with. His name was Vincent Hickey.

The name was flashed through the computers at Wombourne, with remarkable results. Vincent Hickey had already been interviewed in connection with the Carl Bridgewater murder! He had been taken in and questioned at Cannock police station in October because he had a criminal record and owned a blue Ford Cortina estate. He belonged to a close-knit family which had connections with the Birmingham underworld. He himself was serving a suspended sentence for deception connected with robbery. There was no time to lose. All other leads, including the inquiry into Spencer, were dropped. The hunt was on for Hickey.

CHAPTER TWO
Confessions

When police went to Linda Galvin's flat in Lower Beeches Road, Northfields, Birmingham, at tea time on 1 December 1978, Linda and Vincent Hickey were in bed. The doorbell went on ringing. Then the callers started banging on the door. Linda crept downstairs as Vincent hastily dressed. She shouted, 'Who is it?' When the reply came 'Police', she told them to wait a moment.

Vincent had no intention of waiting. He was out of the back window and running across the fields before Linda opened the door. He ran hard, avoiding the main streets until he arrived, breathless and exhausted, at the home of his Aunt Nancy. Nancy Godridge and her husband Les had been second parents to Vincent.

Vincent, who was twenty-five, had been in trouble almost all his short life. His childhood in South Birmingham and Redditch had been dominated by a strict, disciplinarian father, whom Vincent and his brothers would try to pacify with lies and make-believe. At the age of fifteen he went to a detention centre for stealing a car, and he had had a number of minor convictions since.

His life changed when he met his Uncle Joe, Nancy Godridge's brother, whom he adored. In 1975 he started work as an itinerant roofer – knocking on doors and suggesting that work should be done to the roof.

In November 1977 Vincent was working with three cousins – Nancy Godridge's son, Tommy Forbes, 49-year-old Reg Hickey, and Michael Hickey, Joe's son, who was then only fifteen. They 'scored' at a house near Rickmansworth, Hertfordshire, where an old man living alone handed over £130 in advance of work done on his roof. The money was promptly swiped by the delighted 'roofers'. They then discussed the exciting fact that the old man had taken the money from a bag which probably had a lot more in it.

Plans were laid for a robbery. Vincent decided that he wouldn't be necessary at the scene of the crime, and he made sure of a cast-iron alibi with Michael at a Birmingham club. Reg Hickey, Tommy Forbes and another man called 'Ginger' Thomas duly raided the house at

36

Rickmansworth and picked the old man clean of all his savings – a sizeable haul, worth several hundred pounds to each of the gang, including Vincent.

Unfortunately for the roofers, on their first visit they had left behind with the old man a piece of paper with their 'firm's' letterhead printed on it. It did not take the Hertfordshire police long to trace the letterhead to Vincent Hickey. They arrived at his house, where he lived with his wife Mandy, one cold morning in February 1978. Vincent quickly realised the game was up and offered a deal. He would give the police the names of his accomplices if they would charge him only with deception, not robbery. The police agreed at once. Vincent was charged with deception. So were Ginger Thomas and Tommy Forbes. Reg Hickey, however, who was already in prison for another offence, admitted the full robbery and was charged with it.

The Rickmansworth case was set down for November 1978 at St Albans Crown Court. Before it came to court, however, Vincent heard in the pub that the Staffordshire police wanted to talk to him about a quite different matter – the Carl Bridgewater murder.

He went voluntarily to Cannock police station. There he had his fingerprints taken. He was asked about a dark blue Ford Cortina estate car which he'd once owned. He told police he had got rid of the car the previous February, and it had been destroyed. He was then asked where he was on Tuesday, 19 September. He said at once where he thought he was. He assured the officers that he had no knowledge of the Wordsley area.

While his story was being checked, Vincent was held overnight – Saturday/Sunday, 14/15 October – at Cannock police station. Sometime that Sunday he was taken to an interview room by two detectives – Detective Sergeant Robert Lessemun and Detective Constable Ivor Millington – and asked to make a statement about the Rickmansworth robbery. He did so willingly. What he said did not differ from what he had already told the Hertfordshire police. The atmosphere at Cannock, Vincent recalled much later, was 'jovial'. Most of the discussion was about the abysmal form of West Bromwich Albion Football Club.

Vincent was released and driven by the police to the Night Out club in Birmingham where he met up with Linda Galvin. (He had left his wife and gone to live with Linda in August.) On the way, he chatted with the officers about the Bridgewater murder. Sergeant Lessemun, he recalls, said that the murderer came from Vincent's area and was 'running around with a gun'. (References here to Vincent's recollections are taken from a long statement which he wrote out in his own hand and sent to his mother, dated 6 July 1983.)

On 24 November 1978, Vincent's case came up at St Albans. He was charged with deception, and received a two-year suspended sentence.

Tommy Forbes and Ginger Thomas also got suspended sentences. Reg Hickey, charged with the robbery from which Vincent had had his fair and equal share, was sentenced to four years. The enormous value of 'grassing' – informing on accomplices in exchange for soft treatment by the authorities – was not lost on Vincent Hickey.

In the week after his court appearance, Vincent went back to roofing with Michael. It was a bad week, with little work and rotten money. Michael boasted to Vincent about a robbery he had taken part in on the day Vincent went to St Albans Crown Court. At the Dog and Partridge – a seedy pub in Selly Oak which was the Hickeys' headquarters – Michael had persuaded a couple of seasoned crooks, Jimmy Robinson and John Burkett, to take him with them on a full-scale armed attack on Tesco's store at Castle Vale. The robbers had got away with a sack of money, mainly in silver and copper, from the safe but it didn't amount to much. Michael was keen to have another go.

Vincent then had an idea. Two months previously he and Linda had swindled some old people on a farm at Romsley. The idea came from a coalman called Alan Murray, who also lived in Linda's flat. Murray had said that an old man had paid for coal from a tin which was full of money. Linda and Vincent promptly drove out to the farm. Linda knocked on the door and explained sweetly to the old people that she was the coal merchant's daughter. If they paid for *next* year's coal in cash, now, she said, they could avoid VAT. The old people cheerfully coughed up £350 from a large tin brimming with notes.

The lovers got clean away with their booty, but the image of the brimming tin haunted Vincent. Now, on 30 November, as he and Michael surveyed their miserable job and miserable earnings, he remembered the farm at Romsley. Why not rob it? There might be thousands in the tin.

Michael agreed at once and suggested they recruit Jimmy Robinson, who had masterminded the Tesco fiasco. Jimmy had a gun, and masks and gloves. The cousins drove straight to Weoley Castle, a neighbouring area of South Birmingham, and found Jimmy Robinson coming back from the pub. Robinson quickly took to the idea of the farm robbery, ran home, picked up his gun and masks, and joined the Hickeys. Off they drove to Chapel Farm, Romsley.

That robbery, Vincent mused grimly to his aunt and uncle on 1 December, had been a disaster from start to finish. Vincent assigned to himself the role of driver. Jimmy and Michael charged into the house wearing balaclavas, brandishing Robinson's sawn-off shotgun and shouting for money. The old people fought with great courage before they produced their tin. The robbers came away with only £200. Vincent nearly crashed the car in his anxiety to escape the scene, and the bungled getaway could have been seen by the driver of a van which had come up behind him. It now looked as though the police had got his car number. They would certainly have arrested Linda. He was in terrible trouble.

Three things then happened that Friday evening (1 December) to compound the wretched Vincent's panic. He phoned Roger Hill, a friend of Linda Galvin, and discovered that Linda was indeed being held by West Mercia police at Bromsgrove on suspicion of the Chapel Farm robbery. Alan Murray had also been rigorously questioned. Stephanie, Linda's thirteen-year-old daughter, had been put into council care for the weekend. Vincent begged Hill to do what he could to get Stephanie out.

Secondly, there was an urgent message from his mother, Ann Hickey, who wanted to see him in Redditch. He borrowed Les Godridge's car, and drove straight down. He met his mother in the car park of the Woodrow pub where she worked. She told him that her house had been raided by an army of police asking about the robbery at Chapel Farm. Instinctively, as soon as the police arrived, Ann Hickey had known her son was guilty. She refused to accept his half-hearted denials. In a rare outburst, she denounced him for betraying his mother, his wife and his girlfriend. She said she knew he was a petty criminal, but this was armed robbery. Mother and son parted in tears.

As he returned to the Godridges for the night Vincent pondered the third and by far the most sinister development. He had bought a lunchtime edition of the *Birmingham Evening Mail*. The headline shouted at him: 'CARL LINK IN FARMHOUSE RAID?'. Anxiously, he read the report which linked the robbery he had masterminded with the killing of the newspaper boy.

The 'link' stayed with him all weekend. He spent Saturday night (2 December) with his brother in Redditch.

On Sunday afternoon he travelled back to Birmingham and stayed with a friend in Handsworth. He kept ringing Linda's flat, but there was no reply. He was stricken with guilt that she was still in the police station for what he had done, but was too frightened to act on his own accord. At 7.30 on Monday morning, (4 December) he rang Roger Hill again, and begged him to take a taxi to Bromsgrove, which he promised to pay for, 'to see what is happening to Linda'.

Hill's brusque reply consisted of two words. But at 9.30, Vincent rang again, very agitated, to say that his family had appointed a solicitor to act for Linda, and again begged Hill to go to Bromsgrove. Some months later, Hill recalled: 'To the best of my recollection, his actual words after that were: "If it was any other charge, stealing cars or that, I would walk into the police station with a solicitor, but it is not. It's to do with the Carl Bridgewater murder and I will get fifteen years to life – but don't get me wrong, I had nothing to do with that."'

Les Godridge picked up Vincent in Handsworth on the Monday

morning (4 December) and took him to a café for a long discussion about his future. Les does not recall any mention of the Bridgewater murder. He remembers telling Vincent that he had two choices: either he gave himself up for the Chapel Farm robbery and served a sizeable prison sentence; or he left Birmingham altogether and tried to start a new life under an alias in London. There was no alternative. If he stayed in Birmingham, he was certain to be picked up. Meanwhile, Les agreed to run Vincent to the offices of George Brown, a solicitor. Les dropped him there early in the afternoon. 'I never saw him again as a free man,' he told me. 'When I dropped him at Brown's I still don't think he'd made up his mind what to do.' (Interview with me 2nd January 1986.)

Even before he reached his solicitor, Vincent ruled out flight as a serious alternative. Sooner or later he would be picked up. The fact that he had run away would be held against him. Anyway, he knew no one in London who would take him in. Reg Hickey and his friends would never forgive him for grassing on the Rickmansworth robbery. His family were disgusted with him. All Linda's friends were out to get him.

The alternative to flight, however, was to go voluntarily to Bromsgrove police station – a dreadful proposition. He had, after all, taken part in the Chapel Farm robbery, and would find it almost impossible to pretend otherwise. If found guilty, he was going to prison for the first time, and probably for a long stretch. Was there not some alternative? Might he not, perhaps, escape a prison sentence in the same way as he had done at St Albans – by grassing on the others in the robbery? *Perhaps* that might work, but, if he did so, would he not be denounced in turn by the others as the prime mover of the robbery and driver of the car? It was extremely doubtful, he thought, that any deal would be done which would allow him to escape a stiff prison sentence. The situation was far worse than it had been ten months ago over the Rickmansworth job. This time grassing on his accomplices was unlikely to get him very far.

He was trapped. Or was he? Was there perhaps something else, something more substantial that he might offer in return for dropped charges and even for bail? Well, there was the Carl Bridgewater connection. If he were to offer any information about the Carl Bridgewater murder then he might at least get Linda released, and walk out of Bromsgrove a free man. Then, perhaps, with Linda's strong connections in South Africa (she had a brother there), they could both jump bail and flee the country before the police could catch up with him. In a curious way the 'Carl link' with the Chapel Farm robbery was a stroke of luck for him. It put him in a position to offer valuable information – even if he had not got it.

He decided to go to the police. His solicitor made a call to Bromsgrove. An elderly articled clerk, Joe Roberts, drove Vincent to Bromsgrove police station. Long before they arrived, a reception committee was ready for them. When the Staffordshire police heard that Vincent Hickey was going to Bromsgrove, they moved quickly. Detective Inspector Fowlie, who had interviewed Vincent at Cannock on 15 October during the Bridgewater inquiry, hurried down to Bromsgrove. When Vincent walked into the station the first man he saw walking down a passage was Inspector Fowlie. If there were any doubts left about the relevance of the Carl Bridgewater business, and the opportunity it opened up for him, the sight of Inspector Fowlie dispelled them at once.

Mr Roberts and his client were shown into an interview room and confronted by two West Mercia policemen, Superintendent Deryk Knight and Sergeant Herbert Dickens. The superintendent started to ask questions about Chapel Farm. Where had Hickey spent the previous Thursday? What did he work at? Was he driving Linda Galvin's car that day? Did he remember a conversation with Alan Murray? Vincent answered (to most of them), 'No comment.' At the end of the interview, he was arrested on suspicion of deceiving the old people in September and for the robbery in November. He was refused bail, and locked up. Mr Roberts, the solicitor's clerk, went home.

As he reflected, in sudden loneliness, on the questions asked him, Vincent realised that any hope of ducking out of the Chapel Farm robbery had certainly vanished. It was obvious that Linda and Alan Murray had spilled the beans about the swindle in September. The connection with the robbery was overpowering. The police had all the necessary evidence. He was almost certain to be charged next morning. What could he do? He decided to offer a deal. He banged on the door of his cell and asked to see the CID officers again.

At 10.55 p.m. he was back in the interview room shivering and huddled against the electric fire. After some small talk about Linda and Stephanie, he came to the point – the Chapel Farm robbery. He lost no time in telling the police who was involved:

DCI Knight: 'If it wasn't you, who was it?'
Vincent: 'You know one of them.'
Knight: 'Who, Michael?'
Vincent: 'Yes.'

Vincent then pretended there were 'two other men' involved, whom he knew only by sight. He had merely lent them the car, and had not been involved, he said.

'They've been planning it for weeks,' he said about Michael and the 'two other men'. Then he paused and added: 'They've done other jobs as well. . . They did a robbery at Castle Vale about eight o'clock a week last Friday. Our Michael told me about it, he said it was just like something on the telly.

'They went into this place, one of them had a gun and two of them had pick handles. One of them dropped his pick handle, and the manager picked it up and swung it at his head. The bloke with the gun fired a shot at the manager. They used Linda's 1100; Michael borrowed it from her. In the papers they said it was a blue 1100 – they got the colour wrong.'

This was perfectly true. Michael Hickey, Jimmy Robinson and John Burkett had, as we have seen, carried out such a raid at Tesco, Castle Vale, on 24 November. The crime, which had terrified scores of shoppers in Tesco, had been widely publicised.

Superintendent Knight then asked: 'How long has Michael been knocking about with these chaps?'

Vincent replied: 'He met them in the Dog and Partridge two or three weeks ago and got talking to them. They'd done other jobs with another chap who'd dropped out and they wanted Michael to make up the team.'

Superintendent Knight then pressed for more information about the two older men. Hickey described one (Burkett) as a 'junkie', but couldn't help with his address. Of 'the other' (Robinson), he said: 'I could point out where he lives, or within a door or two.'

It was now well after midnight. Sergeant Dickens took up the questioning.

Sergeant Dickens: 'What other jobs have they done?'

Hickey: 'I think they did a job at a jeweller's shop because they had a load of silver bracelets.'

'Anything else?' asked the sergeant.

At this seemingly routine and innocent question Hickey paused. Then he said: 'Our Michael says the older one did the Bridgewater murder.'

Superintendent Knight could hardly contain himself. 'What's this?' he asked. 'Tell us about it.'

Hickey went on: 'Our Michael told me that he'd told him he'd done the Bridgewater murder and one day I was with them when Michael said to him about it. That he'd done the murder. And he got rattled which isn't like him. He's not the type who gets rattled easily, but he was then, and he said "turn it in" in that sort of voice.'

DS Dickens: 'Which is the one, the junkie or the other chap, the one you know?'

Hickey: 'The other chap.'

The interview ended at a quarter to one, with Hickey still refusing to name 'the other chap'. Hickey went back to his cell. The police decided to proceed cautiously. It was plain to them that Hickey was desperate to escape the robbery charges and was prepared to give any information, true or false, for that purpose. They decided, therefore, to increase the pressure to find out the identity of the 'other man' who, according to

Hickey, had been at Yew Tree Farm and at Chapel Farm.

The following morning, (Tuesday, 5 December) Vincent Hickey was taken once more to the CID office at Bromsgrove police station, where he was charged with the Chapel Farm robbery and with stealing £350 by deception. He was back in the cells within minutes, with nothing to show for a hard night's grassing on his cousin and his other accomplice.

He shivered there all day. He decided that he must give still more information. At eight o'clock in the evening he was back again in front of Superintendent Knight and Sergeant Dickens. The officers suggested that he might like to help them further in the Bridgewater business. Vincent agreed. He identified the 'other man' as Jimmy Robinson and offered to show the police where Robinson and Michael Hickey lived. Within the hour he was sitting in the back of an unmarked police car, heading towards Birmingham. Hickey directed the police to a block of flats at Weoley Castle, where he said Robinson lived. He wasn't sure of the address but he thought it was either No. 34 or 35. The police quickly confirmed that Robinson lived at No. 35. Vincent Hickey then directed the car to another block of flats in the middle of Birmingham, where, he said, Michael Hickey was hiding with his grandmother. Back the trio went to Bromsgrove, where Vincent was locked up once more.

By now the news of Hickey's statement had got to senior officers at Wombourne. They were greatly excited by it. Quick checks of the character of Jimmy Robinson suggested that he was a likely suspect, especially if, as Hickey had suggested, he had carried the gun during the Tesco robbery. Here was an armed robber, who had robbed a lonely farm with the help of a shotgun, being named as the Bridgewater murderer.

At four o'clock in the afternoon of 6 December, the day Vincent Hickey had pointed out Robinson's house to detectives, he was visited in Bromsgrove police station by Detective Chief Superintendent Robert Stewart, the officer in charge of the Bridgewater inquiry, accompanied by his two most senior officers, Detective Superintendent Eric Lycett and DCI Weslea Watson.

After introducing himself and his fellow officers, Chief Superintendent Stewart went straight to the point.

'I understand you have been saying things about who may be responsible for the murder,' he said.

'Well, it's nothing really,' replied Hickey. 'Only what I've heard.'

As soon as the officers asked for names, Vincent Hickey was ready to supply them.

'It's Jimmy Robinson and that other one,' he said. 'The one with the bad teeth. They know who he is.'

DCI Watson said: 'And Mickey, of course?'

Hickey replied: 'Well, yes, he had been involved with Jimmy and that other man. Someone has mentioned his name I think. Mickey has only been with them a short while. I think he replaced somebody on the team.'

Stewart interrupted: 'What are you saying, then?'

Hickey replied: 'I think they did your job. Mickey is very young, you know, and talks a lot. He told me Robinson had done the shooting. I didn't believe it, but then another time Mickey said it when Robinson was present. He went bloody mad.'

Hickey also said that he thought Robinson was 'capable' of the murder. 'He has the gun and that, hasn't he?' he offered helpfully.

This interview took only a quarter of an hour, but it was enough to convince the officers that Vincent's evidence was extremely important. Their excitement mounted an hour later when Vincent identified Pat Molloy, a friend and associate of Jimmy Robinson, as 'the man with bad teeth' who had taken part in the Bridgewater murder.

At once, the officers ordered the arrests of James Robinson, Pat Molloy and Michael Hickey.

Who was Robinson? He was born in Birmingham in 1934, and had emigrated to Australia with his family when he was sixteen. He started stealing from a very early age. Four and a half of his ten years in Australia were spent in prison. Soon after he returned to the West Midlands in 1961 he married and settled down to a regular job at Fisher Ludlow, a car components factory. In 1966 he was made redundant and started stealing again. In 1967 he was sentenced to another three years in prison for burglary. Soon after his release, his house at Tamworth, Staffordshire, was repossessed by the mortgage company, and his wife Doreen, who had stood by him through his long prison sentence, found herself and her children shifted out to rotten council housing.

'More and more,' wrote Robinson of himself in January 1982 in a long report addressed to Ann Whelan, 'to avoid the tense and unhappy atmosphere at home I took to spending days and nights in bouts of drunkenness and eventually was led again into a series of meaningless affairs, and generally led my wife a dog's life.'

His faithful drinking partner throughout all of this period was Pat Molloy, a carpenter whom he had met on a building site. Molloy was only six years older than Jimmy Robinson, but he looked old enough to be his father. Born in Ireland, he signed up for a short time in the RAF – but soon left for a life of petty crime. He did some long stretches in prison in the 1950s and 1960s, but had managed to avoid any serious conviction in the 1970s. Mild, passive and easy-going, Molloy was a foil to Robinson's impetuousness. He tagged along when Robinson went stealing but refused point blank to take part in any acts of violence. He was by all accounts an excellent carpenter and had no difficulty getting jobs. But he was happy to drift along in Jimmy Robinson's wake and to match his friend's remarkable capacity for draught beer.

In the summer of 1978, while Robinson was employed as a face-worker in a Midlands pit, his marriage finally broke up, and he went to live with a new girlfriend, Carol Bradbury. Carol Bradbury had herself returned from Ireland and a broken marriage there with her three children. She welcomed Robinson and Molloy into her council house in Weoley Castle. If Molloy was a huge eater, who never paid her a penny, he had his compensations. The children adored him.

The two men gravitated to the local pub – the California. Jimmy Robinson's account of the pub cannot be bettered.

'We soon realised that the Cali obviously suited us and we weren't long in acquiring what we thought were new friends, who were mostly petty thieves, con men, swindlers "fences", gas meter bandits, wife beaters etc. etc. You name it, the "Cali" had it.'

In particular, Robinson took up with a crook about his own age called John Burkett. The pair did what Robinson described as 'a few good jobs together, Molloy accompanying us on many of them, albeit as an honorary adviser due to his age, lack of athletic ability and general timidity'.

Not satisfied, perhaps, with the constant drinking bouts at the Cali, Molloy patronised another pub – the Dog and Partridge at Selly Oak. There he met Joe Hickey, described by Robinson as 'a very powerfully-built man in his forties, very cheerful and amiable and the only adequate description I can give regarding his drinking behaviour and manner of conduct in the Dog was that he "held court". Indeed *he*, more than the publican, was "The Gaffer" and most of the activity revolved around and through him.'

By the beginning of August 1978, wrote Robinson, 'Molloy and I had given up legitimate work and were screwing on a more or less permanent basis, along with John Burkett. John more and more was urging me to get a gun and have a go at the big money. I fell in with this idea after only the most fleeting caution, and any thoughts of possible consequences were pushed further and further aside at the thought of at last making a good few quid for only minutes or seconds of "work". Molloy didn't relish the idea at all, being of a fairly meek disposition. In fact, all the years I knew him. I never heard him argue with anyone, let alone resort to fisticuffs or violence.'

In early September 1978, Robinson bought a gun from a Birmingham criminal, Anwar 'Spider' Mohammad. He hid the gun in Carol's house under the floorboards, and didn't use it on his standard robberies. On the night of 18/19 September (the night before the Bridgewater murder) he robbed a Birmingham butcher's freezer (a favourite target for Robinson) and stayed up all night so that he could sell the meat in the early morning market. On 20 September (the day after the Bridgewater murder) he and Molloy went to Tamworth in a stolen car, got blind drunk, and robbed a Co-Op meat store in the early hours of the next morning. They drove back to Birmingham. As they parked their car at first light, they were stopped by a police car. Molloy made a run for it and got away. Robinson was arrested, and charged with stealing the car – and later with the meat robbery (there was meat all over his trousers). He was locked up in Winson Green prison on remand.

Robinson stayed in prison until 23 October when he got a nine-month suspended sentence for the Tamworth meat robbery and was released after Joe Hickey produced £40 to pay an outstanding fine for a separate offence. On his release, Jimmy Robinson went straight to the Dog and Partridge to celebrate, and to thank his benefactors. Before long he was planning his 'one big robbery' with John Burkett. The two men decided on a masked, armed raid on Tesco's store at Castle Vale on a Friday evening when, Burkett had discovered, the store's safe was open. Three men were needed – two to take the money, one to stand guard with the gun.

At the last moment, Molloy dropped out from the raid. At the Dog and Partridge, Michael Hickey, then only sixteen, volunteered to do the driving. He borrowed Linda Galvin's car and drove the two burglars down to the store. He and Robinson raided the safe while Burkett held several terrified shoppers at bay with the gun. When a manager chased Robinson from the shop, Burkett fired the shotgun over his head.

A week later, as we have seen, the Hickey cousins caught up with Jimmy Robinson as he walked home from the California after another heavy drinking bout. They propositioned him for the Chapel Farm robbery and he readily agreed. As always, he took the lead, storming into the farmhouse with his gun, and hitting at least one of the old people with it but not firing it.

When the three got back from Chapel Farm, Robinson and the Hickeys decided to keep away from each other and from their usual haunts for a day or two. So when Vincent Hickey went to Bromsgrove police station on 4 December Robinson didn't know about it. He wasn't at Carol Bradbury's house when Vincent Hickey took the police there on the evening of the 5th. On the 6th, he walked unsuspectingly into Harbourne Lane police station to report for bail. He was arrested and, to his surprise and shouted protests, frogmarched up the stairs to the interview rooms.

Detective Sergeants Ernie Robinson and Michael Hornby asked him about the Chapel Farm robbery, which he denied, and locked him up. Sometime after 11 p.m. they got him out of his cell and started firing questions at him once more.

In the early hours of the next morning (7 December) Jimmy Robinson agreed that he had done the Chapel Farm robbery, and promptly took the police to waste land not far from the Cali pub where he had hidden his shotgun. He then wrote out a statement confessing to the Chapel Farm robbery, and to associated offences, such as being in possession of an unlicensed shotgun. When the Bridgewater murder came up (the police say on Robinson's initiative but this is strongly refuted by Robinson who said the sergeants asked him about it first), Jimmy Robinson said he knew nothing about it.

The next day, 8 December 1978, was crucial in the murder inquiry. Jimmy Robinson was moved to Bromsgrove police station where he was formally charged with the Chapel Farm robbery, which he admitted. On the same day, police went to the home of John Burkett whom they also arrested and charged with the Tesco armed robbery. At Burkett's house they found someone they wanted badly: Pat Molloy. He was arrested for the 'Tamworth meat job' he had done with Robinson the day after the Carl Bridgewater murder.

Pat Molloy was driven with a blanket over his head, and at high speed, to Wombourne, where the Carl Bridgewater murder squad was waiting for him.

They were delighted at his arrest. They now had both the men implicated in the murder by Vincent Hickey – Jimmy Robinson and Pat Molloy. There was every reason to believe that Michael Hickey would be captured before long. There followed a series of long and probing interviews by Staffordshire CID officers of all three men in custody. From Thursday, 7 December, to Monday, 10 December, inclusive, Vincent Hickey, Pat Molloy and James Robinson were subjected to no less than thirty-six gruelling interviews. None of them was allowed to see family, friends or lawyers during all of this time. They were held in solitary confinement except for their interviews. In almost all of the cases, the police did not make contemporary notes. No tape recorders were used. The record which came down of the interviews was based on notes made by police officers after the interviews had been conducted. None of the police notes was agreed by the people they were interviewing. Details of what was alleged to have been said were not agreed by the three men when they later had a chance to see the police officers' statements. But the *substance* of what was said was never denied.

At first, the brunt of the interviews fell on Vincent Hickey.

On 7 December, in an interview presided over by DI Fowlie, Hickey tempted the officers with information, asking all the time what he would get in exchange for it. He again named Robinson and Molloy as the Bridgewater murderers, but he put his suspicion down mainly to 'a feeling'. He 'bet' the officers that these were the right men, without meeting their constant demands for something more positive.

DS Rogerson: 'If you get bailed, will you see us again for a statement?'

Hickey: 'Probably.'

Rogerson: 'What if you get remanded?'

Hickey: 'No way, fuck you, I won't say anything.'

Towards the end of the interview, Hickey did say something which alerted the officer's attention. He said that he had at some time in the previous weeks phoned his local police station at Bournville and named Robinson as Carl's murderer.

Hickey went back to his cells, and the police made inquiries at Bournville police station. There they found that someone at some time in the last few months *had* rung Bournville police station about the Carl Bridgewater murder. The call had been taken by Woman Police Constable Valerie McDonagh who had been on a three-month attachment to the CID office at Bournville. WPC McDonagh had made no note or record of the phone call, so she could not remember the date. The best she could remember was 'possibly the last week in October or the first week in November'. The caller, she said, had asked to speak to a sergeant. When no sergeant was available, he said: 'Tell your sergeant if he wants him, he is there now.' After a slight pause he went on: 'Look, it is about the Carl Bridgewater murder. You just tell him to get over. He will know it is me.'

WPC McDonagh did not pass this message on to her sergeant as the caller had suggested. Hundreds of calls had been received in different Birmingham police stations about the Bridgewater murder, especially after the release of the three Identikit pictures on 20 October. Moreover, if by some chance it was Vincent Hickey who had rung Bournville police station that night, he certainly did not put 'Jimmy Robinson's name in' as he alleged to the officers. The phrase 'he is there now' suggested someone in custody. This could not have referred to Jimmy Robinson in the last week of October or the first of November since Robinson was released on 23 October. Nevertheless, the coincidence between the call at Bournville and Vincent's statement impressed the officers, and led to another determined series of interviews with him the following day, Friday, 8 December.

The man chosen as chief interrogator was Detective Sergeant Robert Lessemun, who had taken Hickey's statement about the Rickmansworth robbery at Cannock on 15 October. Lessemun claimed he had got on well with Hickey on that occasion, and was therefore despatched to question him further. He went with Detective Constable Ivor Millington, who had also been present when Hickey gave his statement on the 15th.

Early in the morning, Lessemun and Millington collected Vincent

Hickey from Bromsgrove police station and drove him to Redditch, Vincent was glad to see someone he knew, and chatted freely in the car. His main problem, he told the officers, was that he had had a 'knock back for bail'. He was very put out at his treatment by the Bromsgrove police. 'I got the gun back for them,' he said. 'I told 'em where Robinson was and then they bloody charge me. . . I went in with me brief and put them onto it, and finished up being charged.' He needed help, he said.

He was put in the cells again at Redditch, and considered his position. The two officers from Staffordshire were not interested in Chapel Farm. They were interested only in the Carl Bridgewater murder. If they could help him, and Vincent Hickey had nowhere else to look for help, then he must convince them that he had information about the Carl Bridgewater murder. If the officers decided that he could not help them with the murder, his last hope of any sort of deal about bail or dropped charges was gone.

When the interview started in earnest at twenty minutes to one that afternoon (8 December), Vincent Hickey made his position clear at once. 'I'll sort it out if they give me bail,' he said.

DC Ivor Millington, who played the role of sceptic in the interviews while Sergeant Lessemun indicated he was looking after Vincent Hickey's best interests, said (as he kept saying throughout the interview): 'Vince, I have a funny feeling you know the answer.'

Vincent replied: 'I know something, but I don't know what to say.' And again: 'If I did [sort out the Bridgewater murder] I want no charges.' When Millington asked directly 'Were you involved?', Vincent replied: 'No.'

On and on went the interview, with the two officers stalking Hickey in a game which was well described by Sergeant Lessemun as 'cat and mouse'.

Vincent Hickey said he knew a lot about the murder but wouldn't say anything until he got a promise of bail and dropped charges on the Chapel Farm job. The officers said they could not possibly decide what to do about such things until they were convinced he *did* know something about the Bridgewater murder. Again and again they pressed him for 'a little thing'. 'Don't keep us dangling on a string,' Sergeant Lessemun insisted at one stage, accurately identifying the main intention of his prisoner.

Bit by bit, Vincent Hickey started to disgorge morsels of information about the Bridgewater murder. Often, infuriatingly, he promptly altered the information. For instance, he started by saying there were two cars on the job, one of which was a sky-blue Cortina estate. The colour of this estate quickly changed to dark blue. Another striking feature about Vincent's 'information' was that none of it could be checked. Vin-

49

cent would say nothing about the Cortina, for instance, except that it had been 'cut up'. He would say nothing about the 'other vehicle' except that it was a blue van with a white roof which had been impounded by the police at Redditch and was full of stolen gear.

About halfway through the interview, Vincent insisted on ringing DCI Knight at Bromsgrove. He told the inspector he could help the officers with the Bridgewater murder. In exchange he demanded an assurance that the Romsley charges would be dropped. Knight replied that if Vincent did help with information about Yew Tree Farm, he would be happy to submit a report to the Director of Public Prosecutions recommending leniency on Chapel Farm. But he stressed that if Vincent had in any way been involved at Yew Tree Farm, there was no hope of any immunity on the murder.

This seemed to pacify Vincent. When he again started to talk to the officers he was a little more helpful. The Yew Tree Farm robbers, he said, were looking for 'gold' – for 'sovereigns and spade guineas'. The officers looked a little blank. No one, as far as they – or anyone else – knew, had mentioned any gold or spade (George III) guineas at Yew Tree Farm. 'Well,' said Vincent, 'the kid was shot in the house – they were waiting for him.' This wasn't particularly powerful information either. Vincent pretended that the newspapers had reported that Carl Bridgewater had been shot in the driveway, but the officers knew this to be nonsense. Newspapers and television had consistently reported that the boy had been shot on a settee inside the farmhouse. They had even published pictures of the room where his body had been found. 'You haven't told us a single thing that makes me think you know,' said the exasperated Sergeant Lessemun.

Vincent retorted that the papers had claimed that the vehicle was parked in the drive. It wasn't, he said. Instead it had 'floated about', as he had done in Linda Galvin's car at Chapel Farm. Once again, the police were not impressed. Whatever the conflicting evidence of vehicles at Yew Tree Farm, there seemed little doubt that one vehicle used for the attack on the farm had been stationary in the driveway of the farm for some considerable time. With less and less patience, the officers pressed their demands for more information.

'The farmhouse has no hallway,' replied Hickey. 'You go through the back door and the living room's on the right.'

At last the officers showed a measure of respect for Hickey's information. 'How on earth did you know that?' asked Sergeant Lessemun.

'I know a lot more than that,' said Hickey, pleased at last to have roused the officers' interest. 'But give me what I want and I'll give you what you want.'

Inspired by one piece of information which they (wrongly) believed was not publicly available, the officers pressed on. What of the gun? 'It could be the same as the one used on the Romsley job,' said Vincent. Plainly fishing to see if he was on the right track, he then asked the officers if the gun retrieved from Jimmy Robinson had been the murder weapon. The officers said they did not yet know.

Hickey told them that the gun, which he said he'd seen, had a 'silver engraving' on its side, which it had not.

As the game of cat and mouse continued, Vincent complained that he was feeling ill, and went outside for a drink of water. As he was drinking, Sergeant Lessemun asked: 'You were on that job, weren't you, Vince?'

Hickey nodded in the affirmative.

Lessemun asked: 'Were you the driver?' Hickey answered: 'Yes.' He started shaking and reeling, and the officers took him back to his cell. It was twenty past three in the afternoon, 8 December 1978.

Jubilantly, the officers rang Wombourne. Hickey had collapsed, and admitted his involvement. Senior officers should come right away. Less than an hour later, Chief Superintendent Stewart and DCI Weslea Watson were in Redditch police station, examining the voluminous notes which DC Millington and Sergeant Lessemun had put together.

At a quarter to six, Hickey was brought up again from the cells. He was sobbing and shaking – 'in a terrible state', according to DCI Watson. He asked again to be 'out' of the Chapel Farm job if he gave information on Bridgewater. Stewart replied firmly that he was not in charge of the Romsley inquiry, and could give absolutely no assurances as far as the Bridgewater murder was concerned. He could, he insisted, only talk of doing deals when he knew the extent of Vincent Hickey's involvement.

But Hickey would say nothing more. After an hour and a half of fruitless bargaining, he was taken back to the cells.

Two and a half hours later, at ten to nine in the evening, he was confronted again by Sergeant Lessemun and DC Millington, neither of whom were at all happy at having raised the expectations of their chiefs, only to see them speedily dashed. They were determined to get to the root of Vincent's involvement. They were, they told him, 'sure that he had had something to do with the murder'. The mere fact that he had accurately described the location of the living room in the farmhouse was enough to prove that. After another hour or two of questions, in the course of which Hickey said nothing new, the officers suggested it was time he made a statement about the Bridgewater murder. Vincent tentatively agreed, and was taken upstairs yet again, this time to face DCI Fowlie, who had been waiting all day for something positive to happen.

Sergeant Lessemun told Inspector Fowlie: 'Vince has decided to make a statement telling his side of the story.'

Hickey said: 'Yes, I can't live with it, I wanted to tell someone before.' He then told the officers that he had already confided to his uncle, Joe Hickey, that he had had a part in the murder.

As the officers prepared to take the statement, Hickey returned once again to a familiar theme: 'What's going to happen to me?' he asked. 'If I'd got bail today it would have been something to show the way.' As the inspector started to ask questions, Vincent backed away. 'Look, let me go back down,' he said. 'I can't make a statement. . . I want out before putting people in.' He started making his own way back to the cells, when Lessemun and Millington caught up with him, remonstrating with him. Hickey offered them a small crumb of comfort. 'If I do sort this out, it'll be to you two,' he said. The officers left him at twenty past midnight – some sixteen hours after his first interview had started.

It seems certain that the police were convinced by Hickey's confession of guilt. DC Millington's 'funny feeling' had, they felt, been vindicated. But they had little hard evidence. There was no signed statement. Vincent had told them very little they could check, and even less which would not have been guessable by anyone who had followed the murder in newspapers and on television. His description of where the living room was in relation to the back door of Yew Tree Farm did impress them, but everything else seemed speculative, insubstantial.

The officers made two checks. There had been a van at Redditch impounded with stolen goods. But it was grey, not blue, and did not have a white roof. They approached Joe Hickey who told them Vincent had never mentioned Yew Tree Farm to him, or to anyone else he knew. He apparently convinced the officers that this was yet another of Vincent's 'blinds'. The next morning, they went again to see Vincent. He seemed better and more cheerful. In a relatively short interview that morning he went on saying that he had been involved in the murder. Asked how he had got into the farmhouse, he said he was 'too fat to get in the window' and that he 'walked in'. Again and again he returned to the Chapel Farm robbery and his demand that the charges there be dropped in exchange for information about the boy's murder.

'You said the van found at Redditch was blue,' said DC Millington. 'We've been told it was grey.'

Hickey replied: 'It *was* grey.'

Both the murder vehicles had changed colour!

'You're being crafty, Vince, I can see that,' said Sergeant Lessemun.

Hickey said: 'Remember what I said about the footballer, making 'em think you're going one way then going the other. That's what football is all about, being crafty.'

There was worse to come the following morning (Sunday, 10 December) when once again the officers saw Vincent at Redditch police station. 'I've made up my mind – no statements,' was Hickey's greeting to them.

After some more fencing, the pugnacious DC Millington snapped: 'All right then, just tell me what happened to the lad's paper bag?'

Hickey replied at once: 'I can't.'

'Why not?' barked the constable.

''Cause I wasn't there,' Hickey replied.

There was a pause. 'That's a turnabout,' said Sergeant Lessemun.

Yes, Hickey replied, it *was* a turnabout. He had been 'messing the officers about' in the hope he might get bail on the Chapel Farm job. When the sergeant and the constable said they just didn't believe him, and referred to his hysteria the previous Friday, Hickey said he was acting. 'If you switch your mind, it's easy,' he explained. He still insisted that Jimmy Robinson was the man they wanted but he stressed that he himself had nothing to do with the murder and certainly wasn't making any statements or signing the policemen's notes of the interviews.

When the two detectives went back that same Sunday afternoon at twenty to four – Vincent's seventh interview in three days – they found their suspect even more exasperating. He agreed to make a statement on the Romsley robbery, and even encouraged the officers to write out a statement incriminating Robinson in the Bridgewater murder. When they had written it out, however, he refused to sign it. Once more they left him, stymied. Though they had been convinced by Vincent's histrionics on the 8th, they had nothing to corroborate them. Every time they checked something he'd said, it proved to be wrong or common to anyone who knew anything about the case.

As they went through their notes once again and puzzled over them, the corroboration they'd been searching for suddenly arrived. An exultant phone call came through from Wombourne. Pat Molloy had confessed to being at Yew Tree Farm. He'd named three men who'd been with him – Vincent Hickey, Michael Hickey and Jimmy Robinson. Yes, yes, it was *not* just a 'verbal' as Vincent's confession had been. Pat Molloy had *signed a statement*.

Pat Molloy, as we've seen, was arrested at John Burkett's house on 8 December and taken to Wombourne police station, the headquarters of the Bridgewater murder inquiry. He was charged that evening with the Tamworth meat robbery which he had committed with Jimmy Robinson on 20 September.

The Tamworth meat robbery was not a serious offence. Molloy and Robinson had made about one hundred pounds out of it. No violence or arms had been involved. Robinson, as we've seen, was convicted on 23 October of the robbery and given a suspended sentence. If Molloy had been charged only with the Tamworth job, he could expect to be free again before long.

He was in far less trouble, ostensibly, than were Robinson and Vincent Hickey. He had deliberately steered clear of the two armed robberies at Tesco, Castle Vale, and at Chapel Farm. Indeed, on the evening of the Castle Vale robbery, he was so keen not to take part that he left Birmingham altogether. He was, moreover, quite happy to admit the Tamworth meat robbery, and any other in which he might have been engaged. It had been his habit in the past, when caught, to admit what he'd done and plead guilty.

Molloy's whole approach was entirely different to that of Vincent Hickey. Whereas Vincent did not really want to help anyone unless he could help himself, and had openly expressed his distrust of policemen, Pat Molloy was anxious to do everything he could to please everyone.

At 6 p.m. on the evening of Saturday, 9 December (when Molloy had been in a cell without contact with anyone for twenty-four hours), he was visited there by two Staffordshire detective constables, John Perkins and Graham Leeke. Like their colleagues Lessemun and Millington who were working on Vincent Hickey at Bromsgrove, Perkins and Leeke were a seasoned team. Unknown to Molloy, another officer was also involved. Detective Constable John Robbins sat outside the cell out of sight but well in hearing taking notes of what was said inside.

The constables introduced themselves, explained they were making inquiries into the Carl Bridgewater murder, and cautioned Pat Molloy.

'I'd like to help you,' said the Irishman. 'But I don't know anything about the matter.'

Perkins replied, immediately: 'We believe you do. You're involved with men who have committed a similar burglary at Romsley.'

Molloy admitted to that at once, but continued, in answer to question after question, to deny any connection whatever with the murder at Yew Tree Farm. He had, he said, never been anywhere near the farm and didn't even know where it was. A typical passage went like this:

> Perkins: 'I can see you're thinking, Pat. You're not protecting the killer are you?'
> Molloy: 'I don't know the killer.'
> Perkins: 'Are you frightened of someone?'
> Molloy: 'I've got no one to be frightened of, have I? I've done no murder, I wouldn't do it, I wouldn't do it.'
> Perkins: 'Pat, if you only broke into the farm, tell us, and tell us who killed the boy.'
> Molloy: 'I don't know, do I?'
> Perkins: 'Pat, you're too old for this game. If you're shielding someone who killed this boy, you are not helping yourself. What if he kills again?'
> Molloy: 'I wouldn't protect him.'

Leeke: 'Think what the parents of this boy have been through. Good God, he was only delivering a paper, he wouldn't have shopped you, he wouldn't have recognised any of you again. Why kill him?'

Molloy: 'He wouldn't have recognised me because I wasn't there.'

Again and again, the officers insisted that Molloy had been in on the Yew Tree Farm robbery.

Perkins: 'Well, you are in trouble now, me old Pat.'

Molloy: 'It wasn't me. I didn't do it.'

Perkins: 'You did, Pat. There's nothing so certain. I'm not saying you shot the lad, but I'm saying you were in on the screwing.'

Molloy: 'You don't want me to admit something I haven't done, do you?'

Perkins: 'Of course not, that's no good to us. We only want you to tell us if you did it, or if you know who did it.'

Molloy: 'I would, I would.'

Leeke: 'You appreciate what a terrible crime this was?'

Molloy: 'Yes.'

Leeke: 'Well, if you were on that job, as I suppose you were, and if you didn't shoot that lad, then you must be a complete idiot to defend one of your mates.'

Molloy: 'No one will believe me. I never did it. I was not there. I would not do such a thing.'

Perkins: 'Well, someone did.'

The firmer Molloy's denials, the more certain the officers became:

Leeke: 'The more I listen to you the more I think you were on that job.'

Molloy: 'I wasn't, Sir.'

Leeke: 'Now you were there, me old Pat. What happened to the gear from the screwing, Pat?'

Molloy: 'What screwing?'

Leeke: 'The one at Yew Tree Farm.'

Molloy: 'I don't know. I wasn't there.'

Leeke: 'Are you sure? You don't look very sure to me.'

Molloy was keen to help, but kept repeating hopelessly: 'You wouldn't want me to admit something I didn't do, would you?' or 'I can't admit anything I haven't done, can I? I told the police all that I've done, I've been honest.'

These pathetic answers infuriated the officers. They believed they were talking to a child murderer, who was prevaricating. They grew angrier.

Molloy: 'I've admitted lots of things to the police. I would have admitted this too.'

Perkins: 'I'll bet you would. You've only admitted the others to get us off your back. That's as old as the hills, that trick.'

Molloy: 'It's no trick.'

Perkins: 'Not bloody much, it ain't. You think we'll be satisfied with a few good screwings and robberies and that, but what you don't appreciate is that for a murder we're more particular.'

Molloy paused, went to speak but said nothing.

Leeke: 'You're thinking again, Pat.'

Molloy: 'Too right, I am thinking, what you'd be thinking if you were me.'

Leeke: 'Only guilty men have to think. If you're innocent, you've got nothing to think about.'

Molloy: 'I am innocent.'

Leeke: 'I don't believe you, Pat.'

Molloy: 'I am, please believe me. . .'

Leeke: 'I wouldn't believe you if they paid me.'

The interview went on at the same intellectual level for about two and a half hours. Finally, the officers left the wretched Molloy, shaking and gibbering, in his cell. At eleven o'clock, slightly more than an hour later, they were back again. They had no more information, but they started off exactly where they had left off:

Perkins: 'Look, if you deny all knowledge of the farm and it's ever proved that you were at the pub with this lot dinner time and you all disappeared in the afternoon and any evidence is found to put any of your crew at the farm, then you're in real lumber.'

Molloy: 'I realise that, Sir.'

Perkins: 'But do you?'

Molloy: 'Of course I do.'

Leeke: 'This is murder, Pat, not some fiddly screwing. If you did the screwing and not the murder, why don't you tell us what part you played yourself? Only one has pulled the trigger.'

Molloy: 'I know what you mean, Sir.'

Leeke: 'I hope you do.'

Molloy: 'As I keep saying, my conscience is completely clear. I didn't do it, and I wasn't there at all.'

Leeke: 'For a man with a clear conscience, your face doesn't give that impression.'

Confessions

Molloy: 'I'm a worried man.'
Leeke: 'Why?'
Molloy: 'Because this is a serious matter.'
Leeke: 'Not if you're innocent.'
Molloy: 'I am innocent but I am still worried. You all think I did it, and that worries me.'
Leeke: 'We're having a right game now, aren't we?'
Molloy: 'Yes, but don't get the wrong idea, please don't get the idea we did it, please believe me, please believe me.'
Leeke: 'It's no use repeating that phrase "please believe me" – you don't look a bit genuine.'

The same theme was taken up by DC Perkins:

Perkins: 'There's no way we can believe you, Pat. There's something in the way you act and the way you reply to our questions that makes me convinced that you've got some part in this.'
Molloy: 'What do you mean?'
Perkins: 'You always pause before you answer our questions.'

To round off this part of the interrogation, DC Perkins asked Molloy to look him in the eyes and tell him he wasn't on the job. Pat Molloy did so, promptly. DC Perkins said he still didn't believe him, and would be coming back to question him the next day. It was now very late, just after one o'clock in the morning, Sunday, 10 December.

That Sunday was not a day of rest for the unfortunate Irishman. At half past eleven in the morning the persistent Constables Perkins and Leeke were back in his cell, with the persistent Sergeant Robbins outside in the passage with his notebook.

Perkins wasted no time in getting back into the groove he'd carved the previous day.

'Well, Pat, you've had a chance to think,' he said. 'Is there anything else you'd like to say about the murder or the burglary?'

'No, Sir,' replied Molloy. 'You must believe me now that I didn't do it.'

This time, however, Perkins did have something else to talk about. At once he spoke about 'Robinson and Hickey'. 'If you are involved in this murder,' he said, 'you are going to feel pretty confident that they are not going to grass you up.'

Molloy replied: 'I wasn't there, Sir, so I can feel pretty confident, can't I?'

Perkins: 'But if they did admit being involved, then that would leave you in a terrible position.'

Molloy: 'Yes, but I'm in a terrible position now.'

Perkins: 'Why?'

57

Molloy: 'Because I'm suspected of murder.'

Perkins then turned on the heat.

'Come on, Pat, you were almost there. You were just on the brink of telling us what you know. You've done that a few times now. You want to tell me, I know you do. You realise that you've got to look after yourself, nobody else. Forget Hickey and Robinson, look after yourself, you're on the brink of telling us what you know. Why not tell us the lot, Pat? Come on.'

To which, like a stuck gramophone record, Molloy answered: 'I can't because I don't know anything, I wasn't there.'

Perkins and Leeke left, but before Pat Molloy could get his breath back, his cell was once more full with police officers – this time more senior ones: Detective Sergeants Dennis Walker and John Robbins – he who had been taking notes of all the other interviews – were at him again.

'I've no need to tell you what all this is about,' said Sergeant Walker, to which Molloy wearily replied: 'I know only too well.'

But the sergeant was referring to new circumstances, something substantially different in the case against Molloy. 'You haven't got as many friends as you'd thought you'd got.'

When Molloy muttered that he still had some friends, Detective Sergeant Robbins chimed in: 'Now look, Pat, this is no bullshit. You've reached a stage now where you're in need of help and whether you like it or not we're the only people who can help you. Remember, you haven't got to say anything.'

To which Pat Molloy gave a strange reply: 'Well, look, I've told the others I know nothing at all and if the others have told you I was there, they were telling lies.'

The interview continued:

Robbins: 'I think it's time, Pat, that you started to think of your own welfare.'

Molloy: 'Yes, I suppose you are right, Sir.'

Walker: 'Pat, all you're doing is digging a deep hole for yourself. The more lies you tell, the deeper this hole is going to get. In fact, it will get so deep that you will be reaching up and asking for help. Now, I personally think that you were involved in this incident at Yew Tree Farm and that you were afraid of your accomplices and you are trying to cover up.'

Molloy paused, and said: 'I've been asked the question so many times that I'm getting confused and I wish you'd believe that I didn't do it.'

Walker: 'Well, I think you're lying and the sooner you tell the

58

truth the better you'll feel about this whole business.'

The officers walked out of the cell.

This short interview was a turning point in the interrogation of Pat Molloy, and is worth some study.

What was the new element which Sergeant Robbins introduced when he referred to the 'stage now' which Molloy had 'reached' which made him 'in need of help'? The recorded interview mentioned nothing new against him. As far as Molloy knew at that time, the only reason he was suspected of being at Yew Tree Farm on the day of the boy's murder was because he went around with Jimmy Robinson. Jimmy had been involved in Chapel Farm, but since no one suggested that Pat Molloy himself had been involved in Chapel Farm or the Tesco robbery, there was, on the face of it, little for him to worry about. All the hours of interview by DCs Perkins and Leeke had not produced a single piece of evidence which connected Molloy to Yew Tree Farm.

Though DCs Perkins and Leeke had referred often to Robinson and Hickey they had not, according to their official record, told Molloy the most damning evidence against him: namely that Vincent Hickey had named him as one of the murder squad, along with Robinson and Michael Hickey. Throughout all the records of all these interviews, nowhere does Leeke or Perkins say that Vincent Hickey had put Molloy in the frame (which he did, as we have seen, on 6 December, and which led to Molloy's arrest on the 8th).

It is almost beyond belief that the two officers did not use this vital piece of evidence when pressurising Molloy to tell the truth about Yew Tree Farm. If they did not say, 'Look, Pat, Vincent has told us you were there', then perhaps they ought to have done. For that was the reason they started talking to Pat Molloy in the first place.

At any rate, by the time Sergeants Walker and Robbins came on the scene on the afternoon of 10 December, the notes suggest that Molloy *did* know – either from the sergeants or the constables – that somebody had named him. 'If the others have told you I was there, they are telling lies,' he said. Why should Molloy say such a thing unless the police had told him that 'the others' were naming him? Certainly, when he came to write and talk about those interviews, that was his understanding of what was going on. He insisted later, on many occasions, that the police made it perfectly clear to him that the chief reason they suspected him was that Vincent had named him.

At any rate, the interview with Walker and Robbins clearly had a remarkable effect on Molloy. He was considering its full impact when he was confronted in his cell again a few minutes later (at 3 p.m.) by Walker and another, more important, officer in the inquiry. This was

Detective Inspector Jeffrey Turner who had masterminded the Molloy interrogation from his upstairs office at Wombourne police station. As each set of notes was made up of the interviews, they had been taken up to Inspector Turner for him to study, and for urgent and anxious conferences in his office, which seemed to continue right round the clock.

This was the first time that the Inspector had met the Irishman, but he started with a familiar refrain:

Turner: 'You have not told anyone that you were at Yew Tree Farm when the boy was shot.'

Molloy: 'I wasn't there, Sir, I don't know anything about it.'

Turner: 'I know you were at the farm, Pat. Why do you think we are here?'

Molloy: 'If anyone has said anything about me, it must be because they want to protect someone else.'

Turner: 'Do you think someone would put you in for a murder like this if it isn't true?'

Molloy: 'Only to protect someone else.'

Turner: 'It is a tremendously serious thing to accuse anybody if they haven't done it. Mind you, we are accusing you now, so you must realise we are confident you are involved.'

Molloy: 'Won't anyone believe me? It is nothing to do with me.'

Turner: 'I don't believe you because I know you were on the job. Why don't you tell the truth and get it off your chest?'

Molloy: 'You just want me to admit it to make it easy for you. You just want the job cleared up.'

Turner: 'Patrick, we would not be doing our duty if we accepted a false admission from anyone just to clear the job up, and leave the killer free. You must realise how important it is for us to find those responsible.'

Molloy: 'I wish I could help you, Sir, but I can't.'

Turner: 'You can't or you won't?'

Molloy: 'I can't, Sir, believe me.'

Turner: 'You can help if you want to, Pat. What's the problem? Did you pull the trigger?'

Molloy: 'I did not, Sir. You don't expect me to admit to something I haven't done.'

On and on this went, the same tough questions, the same (entirely false) assurances that the inspector *knew* Pat Molloy was on the job. Once again, though there is nothing in the record to prove it, it is impossible to read these passages and imagine that Molloy did not know that he had been placed 'in the frame' of the murder by one at least of 'the others'. As the questions grew more and more repetitive and more and

60

more insistent, Molloy sank into long silences. Believing these to be 'significant', Inspector Turner piled in with questions about 'threats of violence', allegedly from those who were responsible for the murder. Then he stormed out of the cell.

Sergeant Walker, who was left with Molloy, remembered that the suspect was utterly 'shaken, licking his lips'. He asked for a glass of water, and got one. After a long pause, he was recorded as saying: 'I need some advice, Sir. Do you think I could see the boss?' The sergeant replied that it would take a bit of time to contact Chief Superintendent Stewart. He asked if there was anyone else Molloy would like to see. 'Could I see the chap with the beard on his own?' asked Molloy. Almost at once, the bearded DC Perkins arrived in the cell. Walker left, and joined DC Leeke in the passage outside.

Then they heard this extraordinary conversation:

Molloy: 'I need advice. I need help. I'm in a terrible mess.'

Perkins: 'Pat, the only advice I can give to you is to be honest and straightforward. It's up to you.'

Molloy (dropping his head and sighing): 'I was there at the farm when that lad got shot, but I didn't know about the gun until after. I was told that it was Jimmy who did it, and it was an accident.'

Perkins: 'Are you saying that you were involved in the burglary, but took no part in the murder?'

Molloy: 'Yes, Sir, that's right. I was upstairs looking for something of value. I was upstairs and heard a bang. I knew that it was a gun being fired. I went downstairs. They were still in the room. I heard Jimmy say it went off by accident. Then I ran out.'

DC Graham Leeke burst into the cell. 'You know Graham, Pat, don't worry,' said DC Perkins soothingly, and Molloy continued:

'I am worried. I'm terrified of the others. They have threatened me with personal injury.'

Leeke: 'Who are the others, Pat? Do you mean the persons that are on the job with you?'

Molloy: 'Yes, Sir.'

Leeke: 'Well, who are they? We need to know the complete story.'

Molloy: 'Vinny Hickey and his relation Mickey and Jimmy.'

Leeke: 'Do you mean Jimmy Robinson?'

Molloy: 'Yes, Sir.'

Perkins: 'Tell me about the car, Pat, the one you took to the farm.'

Molloy: 'There was a blue Cortina estate and a van Jimmy borrowed

rowed from someone at the Dog and Partridge. It had a white top.'

Leeke: 'How did you travel, Pat? Who did you go with?'

Molloy: 'I went with Vinny Hickey – he drove. Mickey, his relation, came with us. I sat in the back.'

Leeke: 'How did Jimmy get there?'

Molloy: 'Jimmy drove the van. We parked them away from the farm and walked down to the farm.'

DC Perkins took up the questioning. Molloy said that from where they'd parked the cars the four had walked down to the farm in twos. Jimmy Robinson had then broken into the farm through a window and let the others in. Molloy had gone upstairs into a bedroom, and searched through a chest of drawers, stacking the drawers on top of each other after he'd gone through them. He didn't find anything or take anything.

Suddenly, he'd heard a shout that someone was coming. He hid for a while, then he heard a bang and ran downstairs. The three others were in the sitting room, arguing and shouting. He heard Jimmy say: 'It went off by accident.' He saw the body of the boy on the settee, shot through the head. The interview continued:

Perkins: 'What happened then?'

Molloy: 'I was appalled and felt sick.'

Perkins: 'Did you see the gun then, Pat?'

Molloy: 'I never saw it.'

Leeke: 'How did you get away, Pat?'

Molloy: 'Well, I heard some coming and going of motors earlier and when I ran out both of them, the van and the Cortina, were there at the top of the drive.'

Molloy went on to say that he had left in the Cortina with Jimmy and Vinny, and Michael Hickey had driven the van away. He didn't see the gun on the way out either. Asked about the stolen property, Molloy said: 'I never had anything at all, Sir.' He didn't know where it had been dumped either. Molloy then said he was frightened, and commented: 'I have been threatened by Vinny and Jimmy. I was told never to admit anything to do with this job, but to turn others in and the police would be satisfied.'

DC Perkins then got out pen and paper and took down a statement, dictated by Molloy. In full, the statement which became by far the most important document in the case, read as follows:

I, Patrick Molloy, wish to make a statement. I want someone to write down what I say. I have been told that I need not say anything unless I wish to do so and anything I say may be given in evidence. I need to tell you the truth, you wouldn't understand the pressure that I have been under. I am terrified of the others, I have been threatened with personal injury. I know they will deny it but even so I must tell you the truth. I was at the farm when that lad, the paper boy was killed. I was upstairs searching for something of value, anything, money or coins.

Four of us had gone to the farm. There were two motors, a blue Cortina Estate, which I went in with Vinny HICKEY who was driving and his relation Mickey. I sat in the back. Jimmy ROBIN-SON drove a van, I think it had a white top, it belonged to someone in the Dog & Partridge, he borrowed it for the job.

We arrived at the farm first and waited for Jimmy who arrived shortly afterwards. We parked both motors away from the farm and walked down to the farm. We didn't all go together, me and Vinny walked down first. We waited and the others joined us. Jimmy broke in through a window and loosed us in. They went downstairs and I went upstairs by myself.

I searched the bedrooms I remember taking the drawers from some furniture and after searching them I stacked them one on top of the other. I had been drinking and cannot remember the exact time that I was there but whilst I was upstairs I heard someone downstairs say be careful someone is coming. I hid for a while and after a while I heard a bang come from downstairs. I knew that it was a gun being fired.

I went downstairs and the three of them were still in the room. They all looked shocked and were shouting at each other. I heard Jimmy say, 'It went off by accident'. I looked and on the settee I saw the body of the boy. He had been shot in the head. I was appalled and felt sick. I just ran from the house.

I heard someone outside messing about with the cars earlier, there was some coming and going of the cars and when I ran out both the van and the Cortina were at the top of the drive to the farm. Mickey HICKEY drove the van away, I don't know where he went to. I went with Jimmy and Vinny, Vinny drove back to Selly Oak, he dropped me off first by the Plough and Harrow. I went to a cafe opposite and had something to eat. I only had a cup of tea though, I couldn't eat, I was still too shocked.

We all met at the Dog & Partridge and after closing time we went to do the farm. I didn't know much about the job but it was Vinny's. I didn't know that a gun was going with us, I wouldn't have gone. I think it took us about half an hour to get to the farm. After the job, I've been told since, Mickey dumped the property but I don't know where. Since the job I have been threatened by

Vinny and Jimmy. I was told that if I was arrested I must not admit anything to do with this job but to turn some others in and the Police would be satisfied. I can't state my sorrow sufficiently about the murder of that boy.

I have read the above statement and I have been told that I can correct, alter or add anything I wish. This statement is true I have made it of my own free will. P. Molloy.

After all four pages had been signed by Molloy, DC Perkins asked four or five other questions. How had the boy's head been lying after the shooting? Molloy leaned his body over to the right, and lowered his head onto his right shoulder. Asked who moved the boy's bike, Molloy said: 'I don't know, Sir, I never saw it.'

It was shortly after half past five in the afternoon, 10 December 1978. Constables Perkins and Leeke left the cell and walked upstairs with the signed confession.

Within the hour, the big chiefs of the inquiry were at Wombourne, reading the statement.

At a quarter to seven, they trooped to the cells – DCS Robert Stewart, Superintendent Eric Lycett, DCI Weslea Watson and the two constables, Perkins and Leeke. Stewart asked Molloy if he had told the truth in his statement. Molloy said yes, he had. He denied he'd fired the gun, and said he knew nothing about the stolen property.

'Are you all right?' Stewart asked.

'Well,' mumbled the Irishman miserably, 'it is not a very comfortable position to be in. I can't be very happy in a position like this.'

As the officers left the cell after only five minutes with Molloy, they must have felt a sense of jubilation and relief. Eighty days of relentless inquiry had at last brought results. Pat Molloy had cracked under interrogation. The story he told corresponded in several crucial respects with the initial information from Vincent Hickey. He too had said there were four people at Yew Tree Farm and that they had travelled in two vehicles – a Ford Cortina and a van. Both Vincent and Molloy had said that the vehicles had been parked well away from the farm – to begin with, at any rate – and that the robbers had walked down to it. The coincidences seemed to lead to the inescapable conclusion that the four men named by Molloy were the gang who murdered Carl Bridgewater.

After a hurried discussion, DCS Stewart decided that the two other men in custody at Bromsgrove – Vincent Hickey and Robinson – should be confronted at once with Molloy's statement. He gave orders that Robinson should be moved that night to Droitwich, and he, the two chief inspectors (Watson and Jarvis) and Superintendent Lycett piled into a car to meet him there.

They saw Robinson at ten past nine. After a few preliminaries,

Stewart dramatically produced Molloy's statement. 'Read this then,' he suggested. Robinson read it, and declared at once that it was 'fucking rubbish', and 'a load of bollocks'. He could not explain why Molloy should have made such a statement. He thought it conceivable, though unlikely, that Molloy and the two Hickeys had somehow gone on their own to Yew Tree Farm with his gun, without telling him.

Stewart, Lycett and Watson left soon afterwards, but DCI Jarvis stayed behind. Accompanied by other officers of the murder squad, Jarvis questioned Robinson until a quarter past two the following morning. Robinson remained firm that he had 'never been near the farm'. He broke down more than once, shouting and weeping that he had not killed the boy, and had no idea how he had been shot, or by whom. Confronted with the coincidences between what Molloy and Vincent had said, and the fact that a barmaid at the Dog and Partridge, Helen Johnston, had heard him talking to Molloy about the murder, he denounced them all as 'liars'.

Meanwhile, at Bromsgrove, Sergeant Lessemun and DC Millington, whom we left depressed by Vincent Hickey's sudden refusal to continue with a confession, went to see him again. 'Vince, things aren't looking too good,' said DC Millington. Gradually, they let him have the news that a signed statement implicated him in the Bridgewater murder. Hickey refused to believe it. At about midnight, DI Fowlie came into the interview room with a copy of Molloy's statement. Hickey read it, and threw it on the table in front of him, using exactly the same phrase as Robinson had done a few miles away at Droitwich. 'That's a load of bollocks,' he said. And later: 'It's not true.' He became derisive, almost jocular. 'I'm not being fitted up for murder,' he said. 'You think you know who done it. You will come and tell me you're sorry when you find the real murderers. You coppers are animals, putting innocent people behind bars.' Defiantly, he insisted that he had never been anywhere near Yew Tree Farm and that a dreadful mistake was being made.

Vincent did not get to bed until 1 a.m. When he was roused the following morning he once again replied cockily and aggressively to the officers' questions. 'That's bent – you'll soon find out,' he told DI Fowlie and his men. They gave up after only a few moments.

Robinson was given a much harder time. All day of Monday, 11 December, he was questioned at Droitwich, mainly by the Birmingham officers whose official duty was to ask about other robberies he had committed in Birmingham. The conversation always returned to the Bridgewater murder. Robinson freely admitted several other robberies, describing them in great detail. He begged the officers to believe that he had nothing to do with the Bridgewater killing. The more sceptical and rough the questioning, the more desperate Robinson became. At one stage he was on his hands and knees on the interview room floor, literally praying to be left alone on the murder charge. On another, he offered to confess to the murder, but protested he could give no details since he had never been to Yew Tree Farm or anywhere near there.

The firm denials of Robinson and Vincent Hickey for a time slowed the momentum of the inquiry. It was obvious that there were to be no easy confessions, followed perhaps by pleas of guilty. Instead it looked as though the police evidence would have to be tested in a trial. Patrick Molloy's confession was of course powerful evidence, which, taken together with Vincent Hickey's initial interviews and confessions, might almost be enough to convict the two men. But the statements on their own were weak. No details seemed to be corroborated by independent facts or evidence.

By the late morning of 11 December it was clear to Chief Superintendent Stewart and his other officers that Jimmy Robinson and Vincent Hickey were not going to confess to the murder, and would contradict Pat Molloy's statement. At once, they decided to return to their main source, Molloy, for further questioning. The job was taken out of the hands of the constables who had spoken to Molloy in the first place, and handed to two very senior officers: DCI Weslea Watson, third in charge of the inquiry, and DCI Colin Wordley, who had been at Yew Tree Farm by seven o'clock on the evening of the murder and had accompanied Brian Bridgewater to the mortuary to identify his dead son. Watson and Wordley were extremely well-informed on all the evidence which had been gathered at the farm and elsewhere and they set themselves, without prompting, to gather from Molloy any information which would prove that he had been at the farm on the fatal evening.

No doubt Pat Molloy realised that he had now reached a point of no return. He had admitted to being at Yew Tree Farm on the evening of 19 September. There was no ducking the fact that he had signed a statement saying he was there. It was no use going back to his original denials. Indeed, anything which suggested that that was what he wanted to do, anything which antagonised the police officers, was now extremely dangerous. For unless the officers believed his story that he was at the farm they might not believe that he was upstairs when the boy was shot. If they thought he was deceiving them, they might conclude that he was trying to escape responsibility for the murder. He might find himself accused of a most horrible murder, with his own statement irrefutable evidence against him. The interview which followed, and which went on, with a break for lunch, for more than four hours, was therefore crucial not just for the officers to get the information they needed but for Pat Molloy to give it to them.

DCI Watson, who conducted most of the first interview, started cheerily by asking Molloy how he felt. 'As well as can be expected,' the Irishman answered. 'But I was restless.'

The questions started with the meeting of the four men 'on the day of the farm job'. Molloy repeated that they had met at 'the Dog'. Asked if he wanted to enlarge on how and when the plot was laid, Molloy looked down and stayed silent. Later, however, he supplied the names of six men – Dave Waller, Joe Hickey, his mate Albert Chatterly, Bill Williams, whom Molloy described as 'a scaffolder', Jimmy and Johnny Smith, whose addresses he guessed. All of these, he said, were there at the Dog and Partridge on the 19th as the four men plotted their raid on Yew Tree Farm. Most of these men had already been interviewed. None of them could recall seeing either Pat Molloy or Jimmy Robinson in the Dog and Partridge at any time that day.

What had Molloy to say about the vehicles, and the journey to the farm? Every question was specific. Every answer was vague, and hedged about with qualifications:

Watson: 'How did you get to the farm?'
Molloy: 'In the car.'
Watson: 'Who was driving the car?'
Molloy: 'Vinny, I think.'
Watson: 'What kind of a car was it?'
Molloy: 'I think it was a Ford Cortina.'
Watson: 'Who else was in the car?'
Molloy: 'Mick, a relation of Vin's.'
Watson: 'Anyway, you got into the car. Do you remember it?'
Molloy: 'A Ford Cortina Estate, I think, I'm certain it was one with a folding seat. . .'
Watson: 'Can you tell me which way you went?'
Molloy: 'I couldn't tell you which way they went. I don't remember much of the journey.'

After saying he was wearing every-day clothes, which had all since been lost, Molloy went on to discuss Jimmy Robinson's clothes:

Watson: 'Do you remember what Jimmy was wearing?'
Molloy: 'He had a different pair of trousers on every day. He had his trousers washed every day.'
Watson: 'Does he always wear trousers?'
Molloy: 'He had jeans on the Tamworth job.'
Watson: 'What would he be wearing then at the farm?'
Molloy: 'I should imagine he was wearing trousers.'
Watson: 'What about the upper clothing?'
Molloy: 'It wasn't very cold this day, so I suppose he wore shirt sleeves.'
Watson: 'What about headgear?'

Molloy: 'It would be a woollen cap. He always wore caps. . . It was a red one with white flecks.'
Watson: 'Do you remember anything about the journey?'
Molloy: 'It's vague.'
Watson: 'Too vague to remember anything?'
Molloy: 'I remember getting out of the car and walking to the place.'
Watson: 'Did you put anything on?'
Molloy: 'No, but all the others put caps on.'

Molloy went on to say, as he had in his statement, that the two vehicles were parked one behind the other on the road about a hundred yards from the farm. All four men, he said, walked to the farm. Asked why they parked the vehicles so far away, he replied: 'I don't really know.' Asked to describe the van in greater detail, he said: 'It was a transit van, dark blue or black. I think it had a white top, but I'm hazy about that.' He was hazy about everything:

Watson: 'When you went to the door, was Vince carrying any-thing?'
Molloy: 'A bag, I think.'
Watson: 'You were with them, and were going to do a burglary, were you, or was it a tie-up job?'
Molloy: 'A burglary, I think, but I don't really know what they had planned.'
Watson: 'What happened at the door, then, when you and Vince were there?'
Molloy: 'It was very vague. . .'
Watson: 'Why did they park the vehicles so far away?'
Molloy: 'I don't really know.'
Watson: 'Was there anything around the back door?'
Molloy: 'I just can't remember anything.'

Asked about the farmhouse, Molloy said he got to the stairs through a hallway. He thought there were plaques on the walls (which there weren't at Yew Tree Farm). When he talked about what he did in the bedroom upstairs, at last there was a little something to interest the chief inspectors:

Molloy: 'I pulled the drawers out of the sideboard type of thing.'
Watson: 'How did you do it?'
Molloy: 'I pulled them out one at a time, and had a look at them. I don't know, but I think I put them on top of one another; that's the usual way I do it.'

Watson: 'Why do you do that?'
Molloy: 'It's tidier.'

How long had Molloy been in the room, searching it? Only five minutes, he thought. Then he heard a door opening – he thought it was the front door. He heard a loud bang, and rushed downstairs. There was 'somebody on the settee' – he couldn't see who it was.

Watson: 'Who was in the room?'
Molloy: 'Jimmy, Vinny and Mickey.'

Molloy then said he had never seen the gun, so he couldn't describe it.

Every question was met with the same imprecision and evasion. It was obvious that Molloy was trying hard, and was anxious to please, but he was not succeeding.

'You are telling us a story that puts you in the best light,' insisted Inspector Watson. 'There's more that you can tell me and I'm asking you to consider that.'

The officers left for lunch.

If they had hoped that the interview would improve after lunch, they were sadly disappointed. Watson began by telling Molloy it was 'obvious' he was being far from truthful about the affair.

Molloy started earnestly once more: 'Well, I'll go through it once again from when we arrived at the house; that's the most important part. What happened at the pub is true and the vehicle part is true.'

He then paused, and started again.

'The door was locked when we got there and someone went round the back.' He paused again, and Watson waited.

'Well?' he asked after some time.

Molloy: 'You understand that I have been threatened about saying anything about this, and the reason is I know too much.'

Watson said: 'I understand that.'

In truth, however, the Irishman's explanation was difficult to understand. If Molloy was indeed frightened of Robinson and the Hickeys, and if they had been engaged with him in the murder, his main interest was to get them convicted of murder and himself of some lesser matter, carrying a much lower sentence. Having named them, there was no advantage at all in holding back on the details of the raid on the farm.

It seemed more and more as though Pat Molloy's problem was not that he knew too much, but that he knew too little. He stumbled on: 'I'm very hazy about the details of the house, you understand that. I was upstairs when I heard someone say someone was coming. I thought I told you about that. I heard some muttering then I heard the bang. When I went downstairs, there was two of them there, and one of them had the gun.'

When Watson asked for more details, Molloy said Michael and Vincent were in the room, and Michael was holding the gun.

Only an hour or so earlier, when Watson had asked Molloy who was in the room immediately after the murder, the Irishman had replied: 'Jimmy, Vincent and Mickey.' Now suddenly Robinson had vanished from the scene.

'Where was Jimmy?' asked the chief inspector.

Molloy replied: 'I don't know where he was exactly, but I think there was somebody upstairs.'

Having cut down the murderers from three to two in a couple of hours, Molloy quickly contradicted himself once more. In the previous day's interview, just after he signed his confession, DC Leeke had asked him: 'You haven't mentioned the boy's bike. Someone moved it. Who was that?'

Molloy had answered: 'I don't know, Sir, I never saw it.'

Now, a day later, he said: 'There was a push bike there, I suppose it was that young chap's. I nearly fell over it.'

Watson: 'Where was it?'

Molloy: 'Sprawled on the ground about five yards from the doorway. I stepped over that.'

Watson: 'Why did you mention the bike?'

Molloy: 'Just because I nearly put my foot through it, and nearly fell over it.'

Then Molloy added that 'it was said' that the bike had been 'hidden' – 'put behind a hedge of something'.

DCI Watson switched subjects:

> 'What about the dog, do you remember that?'
>
> Molloy: 'I can't really say about the dog.'
>
> Watson: 'You remember somebody having a go at the door, do you?'
>
> Molloy: 'I don't. I wasn't by the door all the time. I was walking around the house some of the time.'
>
> Watson: 'What did you see when you walked round the house?'
>
> Molloy: 'I can't really be sure of that.'
>
> Watson: 'How did you get into the house?'
>
> Molloy: 'Through the door, it was opened from the inside.'
>
> Watson: 'Who by?'
>
> Molloy: 'Jimmy.'
>
> Watson: 'What about a dog, did you hear that? It's been in the papers.'
>
> Molloy: 'Yes, I saw it in the papers, or I think I did. I don't want to confuse you.'

Confusion, however, seemed to be the central feature of his answers.

He was hesitant, uncertain, vague. This last salvo on the dog seemed to have a dramatic effect on him. It was almost as though he *had* read about it in the papers, and was shocked that he could not help the officers about such an obvious feature. There followed this remarkable exchange:

> Molloy: 'Suppose I wasn't there at all?'
> Watson: 'Whatever makes you say that now?'
> Molloy: 'Do you think I was there?'
> Watson: 'I do.'
> Molloy: 'How do you know I was?'
> Watson: 'Well, you have said so yourself.'
> Molloy: 'Yes, I've made a statement about it.'
> Watson: 'I don't know why you should say that now. You're not messing us about, are you?'
> Molloy: 'No, I was there. I just don't know how I'm going to come out of all this.'

The interview then picked up again, though Molloy really had nothing of any interest to tell the officers. Once again he told them he knew nothing about the gun, nothing about the car, nothing about the property taken from the farm and had only a 'hazy recollection' of the van. He told the detectives, to their consternation, that he didn't think Jimmy's sawn-off shotgun was the one used at Yew Tree Farm, and the gun, which he now pinned firmly on Michael Hickey, did not seem to be sawn-off at all. He said the property was in 'plastic bags' down at the feet of the people in the car, and Michael had had the gun in a black plastic bag. The interview petered out. The following morning, Tuesday, 12 December, the chief inspectors again questioned Molloy. But it was the same litany of specific questions and vague answers.

On 13 December senior officers in the murder inquiry were locked all day in an anxious conference. The initial enthusiasm after the Molloy confession had dimmed. As the notes from all the interviews since the confession came in, several problems loomed large. The denials of Jimmy Robinson and Vincent Hickey had been consistent. True, there were one or two hints in the notes of Robinson's answers which could have suggested he knew something about the murder, but the officers themselves knew what pressure he had been under, and how unreliable their notes might seem when subjected to cross-examination in court. The fact was that Robinson and Vincent were denying the murder, and almost certainly would continue to do so though they had not yet produced an alibi which could be properly tested. Michael Hickey had not yet been found. But by far the worst development had been the reaction of Molloy. Only the most optimistic officer could see anything positive

71

in his answers. His equivocation seemed ridiculous in the light of his confession. He had confessed to involvement in this, the biggest crime in the area for many years. Yet here he was quibbling about the details.

Even in the short period of two days he had contradicted himself not on minor matters but on the central features of the crime. In his first confession to DC Perkins he said he had been told that Robinson had done the shooting, and that Robinson had said, as Molloy came down the stairs, 'It went off by accident.' Robinson had been standing with the other two in the room where the murdered boy lay on the settee. Yet only a day later, the story had completely changed. In his interviews with Inspectors Wordley and Watson, Molloy said that when he came downstairs only the two Hickeys were standing in the room, with Michael holding the gun. In this story, Robinson was upstairs looting the bedrooms, as Molloy had been. Thus the central question: 'Who pulled the trigger?' had two different answers from the man who said he was an eye-witness.

There were other contradictions. Molloy had told DC Perkins he never saw the boy's bike. He told Watson and Wordley he nearly stepped on it as he came out of the house. He told Perkins he had 'never seen' the gun. He told Watson and Wordley that he saw the gun quite clearly, that it was out of its bag, 'bare' and was able to speculate whether it was sawn-off or not.

Even when they took away the contradictions, the story did not match what the police already knew about the case. There was no one at the Dog and Partridge who could remember Robinson and Molloy in the pub in the midday opening time of 19 September.

Of course it was helpful that Pat Molloy had mentioned a blue Ford Cortina estate as the vehicle in which the robbers travelled to the farm. But the most common feature of all the press and television reports of the case was that a blue Ford Cortina estate was involved. It was interesting that Molloy and Vincent Hickey had mentioned a van, and had described it. But Molloy could not give a single clue as to where either of these vehicles could be found.

Molloy's story seldom fitted the independent evidence already garnered. Whatever could be concluded from the sightings of the cars in and around the farm, there was little doubt that a blue car was parked in the driveway of the farm itself, backed up against the door, at the time of the murder. Molloy's cars were parked about 100 yards away apparently in the road. There were no witnesses at all, as far as the police could see, who had seen two vehicles parked in this way within 100 yards of the farm. The closest any car had come to the farm, in Molloy's account, was at the top of the drive when he came out of the farm. But who had driven these cars to the top of the drive? Here was Molloy running downstairs when he heard the bang, there were the two (or three) men in the room with the boy; here was Molloy feeling sick and running out-side to the top of the drive where he got into one of the cars which had been miraculously driven there presumably by the men he had left be-hind in the room.

What about the Identikit pictures, and the two or three men seen in the car by Terence Phelps, the builder? Molloy had said that three men had driven away from the top of the drive in a Ford Cortina estate. That fitted Mr Phelps's story. It was also suggested to Molloy that he looked like one of the people in the Identikit pictures, which is arguable. Molloy insisted that Vincent Hickey was driving. Vincent Hickey at that time had a full beard, and was, according to Molloy, wearing casual clothes. He was twenty-five. Mr Phelps had described the driver as a man in his forties, in collar and tie, with dark hair and clean-shaven. Molloy said all the other three wore caps. *Nothing fitted.*

'Suppose I wasn't there?' Molloy had said. Suppose he wasn't? Sup-pose he had collapsed under the pressure of interrogation? Somehow a real effort, involving more than just interviews in his cell, had to be made to find out once and for all whether Molloy was involved in the murder and whether he could provide a single piece of evidence, apart from his confession.

They decided to take Molloy to the farmhouse. This was an unusual and in some ways dangerous course. For if Molloy did say or remember anything, it could be argued later in court that he had been prompted to do so. However, Molloy was not the main police suspect, and his in-formation was vital for the officers to be certain he was telling the truth.

Accordingly, at a quarter past eleven on the morning of Thursday, 14 December, Molloy was visited in his cell by two more police officers whom he had never seen before. In charge was Detective Chief Inspec-tor Richard Wood from Stafford police. His sergeant was Derrick Wys.

In an unmarked police car driven by PC Scott, the three men drove to the Dog and Partridge, Selly Oak.

Chief Inspector Wood had asked Pat Molloy to indicate the route he and his three companions took to Yew Tree Farm on the day of the murder and to point out anything he recognised on the way. Molloy replied: 'Yes, I don't know which way we went. I had a lot to drink and was very hazy. I had had a lot to drink. I don't remember anything about the journey. I might even have had a sleep on the way.'

So PC Scott made his own way out to Wordsley, while the inspector and Molloy passed the time in conversation.

Wood: 'Who had decided to do the job? There must have been some discussion in the pub about it?'

Molloy: 'No, I was having a drink with Jimmy. The other two were in there but they weren't drinking with us. I went with Jimmy. He must have known what was on.'

Wood: 'I thought you said you went in the car?'

Molloy: 'Well, Jimmy went off. He must have gone to fetch something from home.'

Once again, Molloy's story changed. 'I went with Jimmy,' he told Inspector Wood, when he had told everyone else he had gone with the Hickeys. When Wood caught him out in the contradiction, he contradicted himself yet again. For if Jimmy had 'gone off to fetch something from home', how could he have followed the Hickeys to the farm, as Molloy's earlier accounts suggested he did?

Wood was expressing his surprise that in the course of the journey that afternoon no one had said anything about what they were going to do, when the car came into Wordsley.

'Is this area familiar to you?' Wood asked.

Molloy replied: 'No, I don't know it.'

'Very well,' said the perplexed inspector. 'Anyway, keep looking around and tell me if anything appears familiar.'

The car then went along Lawnswood Road past Yew Tree Farm and into the A449. After about a mile, it turned round and came back past the farm. It eventually parked in sight of another farmhouse. Wood broke the silence.

'Have you seen anything yet that strikes a chord with you?' he asked.

Pat Molloy answered: 'No, not yet.'

They then went back into Lawnswood Road and towards the farm. As the car approached the farm, Wood said to the driver: 'Pull in there for a few minutes and let us talk about the journey.' He showed the driver the track leading to the back of Yew Tree Farm and said: 'You can turn round there.' So the car went into the track, drove down to the back of the farm, and parked by the outhouses.

In the shadow of the farmhouse which he said he had robbed three months earlier, and in the course of which robbery a most awful murder was committed, Pat Molloy then had the following conversation with the inspector:

Wood: 'You have had a good tour around the general area. Have you seen anything at all which could help you to recall the afternoon of the murder?'

Molloy: 'No, I wish I could. It would help me now, wouldn't it?'

Wood: 'What do you mean?'

Molloy: 'Well, if I could remember more about it, you would know I was telling the truth.'

Wood: 'That would depend on what you told us, but in any case I would have thought you must have remembered more than you have indicated. Can you remember where you left the car, for instance?'

Molloy: 'Yes, I think we parked it on some sort of roadway and walked to the house.'
Wood: 'How far did you walk?'
Molloy: 'I would think about 100 yards.'
Wood: 'Where was the van?'
Molloy: 'I did not see it but Jimmy must have parked it somewhere near because he was walking just behind us.'
Wood: 'Can you describe in as much detail as possible what happened after that?'
Molloy: 'Well, we walked up to the door and there was nobody in, and somebody, I think it was Jimmy, went round the house and got in through a window and he opened the door and let us in.'
Wood: 'Is that as you remember it?'
Molloy: 'Yes, but I think somebody tried to force the door.'
Wood: 'What did they use?'
Molloy: 'I think it was a nail bar or something.'

This 'nail bar' had been mentioned in conversation by Molloy himself a couple of days earlier. On that occasion he had simply told the police that Jimmy Robinson had a nail bar. Now he was saying the nail bar had been used to 'have a go' at the farmhouse door. It was all quite useless to Chief Inspector Wood who knew from the evidence of the scene-of-crime officer Sergeant Potts that the instrument used on the farmhouse door had been a spade. It was lying beside the door, and showed signs of the same crimson paint.

The conversation continued, with Chief Inspector Wood finding it increasingly difficult to disguise his scepticism:

Wood: 'What happened when you entered the farmhouse?'
Molloy: 'I went upstairs.'
Wood: 'Just like that? Didn't anybody say anything, tell you what to do or what you were looking for?'
Molloy: 'I think it was coins. I went to this bedroom.'
Wood: 'Why do you say coins? Did someone tell you?'
Molloy: 'Yes, I think it was Vinny, yes, Vinny.'
Wood: 'So you went upstairs to look for coins in a bedroom? Can you describe it?'
Molloy: 'I don't remember much. I was very fuzzy. There was a chest and a bed.'
Wood: 'I can well imagine there would be. Was there anything else?'
Molloy: 'I can't say.'

Molloy then told the story again of how he had taken the drawers out of the chest, and stacked them, of how someone else 'might have come up' (he was not sure about that), about how he heard the bang, and went downstairs.

Wood: 'When you went downstairs, can you remember what you saw?'

Molloy: 'I can't remember much about it. I saw the lad. He was on the settee. I looked at him. He was slumped on the settee.'

Wood: 'What do you mean slumped on the settee?'

Molloy: 'He was slumped like this' (indicated by leaning over to his left side).

Wood: 'Are you sure? Was he exactly like that?'

Molloy: 'Yes, slumped over' (again leaned to his left).

Wood: 'You could see that, could you?'

Molloy: 'Yes, I looked at him. I didn't see any marks on him. I didn't look long. I was gone.'

Chief Inspector Wood of course had not been present at the earlier interview when Molloy had shown police how the boy was 'slumped on the settee'. Then he had leaned his head on his *right* shoulder and leaned his sitting body towards the *right*. On this occasion, he leaned to his left. In fact, the dead body of Carl Bridgewater had not been slumped at all, but lying full length on the settee, on his right side, his head resting on a bolster, with a vast gaping hole in the left side of his lower head and neck. His legs were dangling on the floor. No one who had seen such a ghastly sight could fail to remember it clearly.

Wood went on:

'Can you remember anything about the room? Where the door was, the position of the settee, what else was in the room?'

Molloy: 'No, I was fuzzy. Just the lad on the settee. It was terrible.'

Wood: 'What were the others doing at this time, what was said?'

Molloy: 'They were just standing. Mickey had the gun. I hadn't seen it before.'

Wood: 'You had travelled in the same car, had you not seen it then?'

Molloy: 'I don't think he had got it then. I think it was Jimmy's. He must have had it.'

Wood: 'But you are quite sure that Mickey was holding it when you went into the room having heard the shot?'

Molloy: 'Yes, I think he had it.'

Wood: 'What happened then?'

Molloy: 'I went out. I was first out. I remember treading on a

bike just outside the door. It was lying on the ground, not by a wall
or anything.'

Wood: 'What was the bike like?'

Molloy: 'I don't know. I didn't fall. I just stumbled over it.'

In his first interview after his confession, Molloy had said that he had
never seen the newspaper boy's bike. To DCIs Watson and Wordley
he'd said he'd *nearly* fallen over it when he came outside the farmhouse.
Now he was saying he *did* step on it. The significance was that there was
slight damage to two spokes on one of the bike's wheels, as though it
had been stepped on (though it had also been thrown over a wall).

The conversation continued:

Wood: 'What did you do then?'

Molloy: 'I went back to the car. I was first. They came after.'

Wood: 'Did you all get into the car, that is the three of you?
Where was Jimmy?'

Molloy: 'I don't know. He must have got in the van. I didn't see
him.'

Wood: 'There must have been some panic at this stage. What
was said when you were all in the car?'

Molloy: 'I don't know. They just threatened me about it.'

Wood: 'Had the other two anything with them, a gun or any
property from the house?'

Molloy: 'I didn't see the gun. I think Mickey had two bags.'

Wood: 'What was in the bags?'

Molloy: 'I don't know, they were just ordinary bags. I think one
was yellow and the other a dark one.'

Wood: 'What did he do with them?'

Molloy: 'I think he had them down at his feet. He was in front.'

Wood: 'They were not very bulky then.'

Molloy: 'No, he had them between his feet.'

Wood: 'Was there anything else?'

Molloy: 'No, I don't think so.'

There were more contradictions. Jimmy 'must have got in the van'.
But in his very first confession statement, Molloy had Michael driving
the van away on his own. Again, the list of property which was stolen
from Yew Tree Farm on 19 September included, for instance, a copper
warming pan, a tantalus and other bulky items such as a teapot and fire
tongs. These could certainly not have fitted into two shopping bags. Indeed, one of the stolen items was itself a large green shopping bag, with
loops, which also seemed to have escaped Molloy's attention.

Wood went on:

77

'Where was the car when you came out of the house?'

Molloy: 'Where we had left it.'

Wood: 'On the road about 100 yards away?'

Molloy: 'Yes. I don't remember. I think it was.'

Wood: 'You don't seem to remember very much, bearing in mind what happened.'

Molloy: 'I have told you. I had had a fair lot to drink. When I do I get very fuzzy and can't remember about anything.'

Wood: 'But nothing like this had happened to you before, had it? You had gone along on a job you knew little about. A young boy had been shot and killed, and two men had threatened you, presumably if you didn't keep quiet about it. Whatever condition you were in when you went to the house, I would have thought these events would have brought you up with a jolt.'

In answer to this very reasonable question, there was, according to DCI Wood and Sergeant Wys, 'a long pause' during which Molloy became a little dejected. Then he said: 'You would think so, wouldn't you, but I can't remember and I wish I could.'

Inspector Wood may or may not have noticed that in another crucial respect Molloy had changed his story again. In answer to DC Perkins, soon after his confession, he had talked about a 'coming and going of motors' while he was still in the farm, and about his rejoining the Ford Cortina at the top of the farm drive. This coincided with Terence Phelps's statement that he saw a blue car in the track with two or three men in it at about 5 p.m. But now all that had been abandoned. Instead, Pat Molloy and the Hickeys walked to their car a hundred yards away down the road. Three men, one with two shopping bags crammed with loot, and another carrying a bag with a gun in it, had walked down the road to rejoin their cars. But not a single witness out of hundreds of people who had been in Lawnswood Road that afternoon and who later came forward had seen anything like it.

The whole of this extraordinary conversation had taken place *in the Yew Tree Farm drive itself, in full view of the imposing farmhouse.* Chief Inspector Wood asked yet again: 'Can you remember anything at all about the house? What did it look like?'

Staring at Yew Tree Farm, Molloy replied: 'No, I can't. I have no idea, really. I don't think this means anything to me. But the road up there (indicating Lawnswood Road) seems to ring a bell, but I can't say why.'

Immediately the police car drove up Lawnswood Road towards the cottages. When they got to the bend of the road, Molloy looked around him and said: 'I don't know, it could have been.'

Wood: 'What do you mean? This could be where you parked?'

Molloy: 'I don't know, there is something about it.'

Lawnswood Road is a narrow road, constantly used by traffic. It is not wide enough to allow two cars to pass one another if cars are parked on one or other side, even if the parked cars have one set of wheels on the pavement. The evidence collected from people in cars in Lawnswood Road on 19 September included several statements of people who remembered waiting to pass cars stopped or parked in different places in Lawnswood Road. Not a single witness, however, had seen a blue car and a van parked together in Lawnswood Road for any time that afternoon.

Apparently without any further relevant conversation, the police and the prisoner made their way back to Wombourne, and Molloy was locked up again.

Inspector Wood's report of the experiment at Yew Tree Farm must have plunged his senior officers in further gloom and doubt. What were they to make of the wretched story which Molloy was telling? Leaving aside all the times he had contradicted himself and changed his story, how could anyone even start to believe that he could not remember any detail of his attack on Yew Tree Farm even after he had sat outside the farm? There were several such details which would have clinched the matter: if Molloy had mentioned a car parked right up against the farm door, for instance, as Mrs Jones had remembered seeing it; if he had remembered one single item stolen; if he had remembered anything convincing about how the goods were taken away; if he had remembered a single identifying feature of the gun, or even who had carried it; if he had remembered that someone had used a spade to try to open the back door; if he had remembered that someone on the day of the murder had thrown (or placed) many of the goods they had taken all round the farm grounds; if he had remembered a single distinguishing feature of his journey to or from the farm. If he had remembered one aspect of any of these matters the murder would have been solved.

But he had remembered nothing about any of it. The only piece of evidence which he had apparently given spontaneously which seemed to correspond to evidence which he could not have known about was his description of his method of searching drawers. It was true that in one bedroom upstairs at Yew Tree Farm the drawers had been taken out of the chest and piled on top of one another; this unusual feature of searching had been remarked on by the scene-of-crime officer Sergeant Potts only a few days after the murder. But this hardly compensated for his failure to mention a single other relevant matter.

The officers discussed the alternative explanations for Pat Molloy's astonishing behaviour. It was possible of course that he had been so drunk at the time of the raid and so shocked by what happened that he was now suffering from a form of amnesia. This could account for his original denials, and for his later vagueness. It was just conceivable that he had rushed out of the farm in terror and disgust without taking any notice of his surroundings or of what his colleagues were doing.

Perhaps Molloy needed his memory jogging again, in another way. The next morning, Friday, 15 December, Chief Inspector Wordley went again to the Irishman's cell. His mission this time was to tell his suspect what he was doing on the morning of the murder, in the hope that this would release some information about the afternoon.

The result was disastrous. Pat Molloy brightened up when he was told where he was on the morning, but he still couldn't remember where he'd been or what he was doing on the afternoon. In the morning, he said, he'd been driving with Jimmy Robinson and Carol Bradbury in a Ford Cortina. It was 'an oldish one, brown or I think it could have been a whitish colour, which I don't think it was'. But the Cortina used in the afternoon for the Yew Tree Farm job, he thought, was 'a bluish colour'. How he and Robinson managed to transfer Cortinas between morning and afternoon he had no idea.

Chief Inspector Wordley left after twenty-five minutes, encouraging Pat Molloy to think again about the 19th. Molloy did so and wrote out some notes about it. When Wordley returned in the afternoon, Molloy proudly handed over his notes. The officer seized them eagerly and read through the first of the four pages. They dealt in meticulous detail with the visit to the hospital where Carol Bradbury had just had an operation, and the return journey to Carol's house. Halfway through the second page, Molloy wrote that he and Robinson left the house at about 11 a.m. The whole of the rest of the notes read as follows:

> I believe me and Jim went out an hour or two later to the Cali for a drink, but i cant be certain of that. Jim had repaid me £10 he owed me that morning.
>
> I have some hazy thing in my mind that we both went to Selly Oak on the 22 Bus and got off in harborne lane. I think i walked back 30 yards or so to see if the car was still there, and it was. And i believe it was there for most of that week. I believe Jim carried on to the Dog Pub, and i think i went to the Plough and Harrow on the corner of Harborne Lane where i usted to meet some Irish Friends, Joe Murphy may remember me being there, also his friend Steve. I also did meet in there (Irish Tony) Tony Teeny, of Weoley Castle area; also Chriss Tierney of 20 Shenley Weoley Castle I always had a drink with this man. So perhaps he would remember me being there, As i remember Jim said he sold the meat for £100 to be shared with two others since Jim was the Paymaster in these deals. i am saying what he told me who he was going to pay out to. The reason I am telling this is to help place the

whereabouts of me and Jim that day especially the afternoon and evening. Their names being John Burket and Dave Haughton. This could prove important, as regards what time and place Jim Payed them their share.

I can distinctly remember Now where the Payments was made. John Burket called to the house for Jim he had a cup of tea and he said David Haughton and his mate Arther were at the Stonehouse Pub.

I think the three of us namely me, Pat, Jim and John went to the Stonehouse in car of Johns about 11.30 A.M. where we met these two men after about an hour John suggested a game of cards. The four of them decided to play Poker. Draw Poker first and then Stud Poker. I did not play as i dont play cards of that nature, Jim had a streak of luck, Arther was the first to Pull out of the game, I believe he lost about £6 The other three carried on until about 2.15 P.M. By that time Jim had cleaned out Dave Haughton of his share of the meat money. John Burket lost heavily as well. I believe Jim won close to £80 Out of his winnings he bought everyone in the Pub a drink which come to £7 at closing time we went our different ways. Me and Jim walked home to Carols home. The other three went in the car in the direction of Northfield area where they lived. There was some dinner prepared for us and the other girl at school.

Chief Inspector Wordley finished reading, and looked up. 'This is of course different to what you have previously told us,' he said. It also contradicted itself. First, it said that Molloy and Robinson had gone to the Cali. Then, there was this 'hazy thing' in Molloy's mind that they had gone by bus to Selly Oak, and had split up, Molloy for the Plough and Harrow, Jimmy for the Dog and Partridge.

Then the whole story changed again. Suddenly, John Burkett had gone to Carol Bradbury's house, and had taken Molloy and Robinson to another pub, the Stonehouse. There they had had a game of cards with 'Dave Haughton and his mate Arther'. The game of cards is described in detail, with Molloy even remembering who won what. Then the players left the Stonehouse and walked back to Carol's house.

The notes had *two* stories of what the two men had done in the middle of the day on the 19th. Plainly, they could not have been in the Cali, the Plough and Harrow, the Dog and Partridge, and the Stonehouse at the same time. Worse, both stories contradicted Pat Molloy's signed statement, in which he said that he and Robinson had met the Hickeys that lunchtime at the Dog and Partridge.

'Could you have gone to the Dog later?' asked Wordley.

Molloy replied: 'That is what I can't remember. I can't remember much about the afternoon for sure.'

The notes did not take the matter an inch further. Wordley and his colleagues checked the various stories with the various witnesses, Dave Haughton, his mate Arthur, the landlord of the Stonehouse pub. All these (and others too) remembered the card game at the Stonehouse. All insisted that it could not have been on a Tuesday. The two barmen remembered the game of cards well. Yet they assured the police that the game could not have been on a Tuesday since they were never both on duty on a Tuesday.

Not a single detail of the stories about the pubs could be corroborated. Nor was there a single word in the support his story. Perhaps, then, Molloy was increasingly terrified of the consequences of ratting on his mates, and feared either for himself or for his family.

Both possibilities were given one more airing by the murder inquiry's third-in-command, Chief Inspector Watson. On 16 December, two days after his extraordinary visit to the farm, and the day after his further interviews with DCI Wordley, the Irishman was visited once more in his Wombourne cell by Chief Inspector Watson, alone:

Watson: 'Are you all right?'

Molloy: 'Reasonable, I suppose.'

Watson: 'You have been a bit neglected. We have been busy otherwise.'

Molloy: 'I am sure you are.'

Watson: 'Anything else come into your mind since Mr Wordley saw you yesterday?'

Molloy: 'Not really. Nothing I can think of.'

Watson: 'You appear to be very frightened to me.'

Molloy: 'Well, the position I'm in and the kind of people that are involved, I may have reason to be, wouldn't you think?'

Watson: 'Have you really been threatened then?'

Molloy: 'Yes.'

Watson: 'Who by?'

Molloy: 'Well, like I say, you know who I am concerned with, don't you? I'm thinking they could perhaps get at my children. Do you?'

Watson: 'I don't really think they would do anything, but of course you know what they are capable of. Have they said anything about your children being harmed if you talk?'

Molloy: 'Not in as many words, but you never know. They are a bad lot.'

Watson: 'All the more reason why you should tell the truth about the whole situation. We can get it sorted out then.'

Molloy: 'I wish I could help you. I've been trying so hard, but I just can't get it clear. I'll keep trying.'

Shortly after the murder

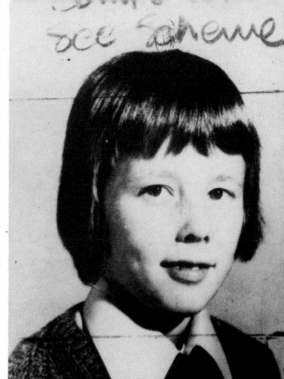

Carl Bridgewater

Carl's schoolfriend helps to reconstruct the scene of the murder

Chapel Farm, Romsley

Hubert Wilkes (centre). Michael Howard is to his

The police identikit picture of the murderer

The public house, The Dog and Partridge, fro
which so much evidence was drawn

CARL MURDER

HAVE YOU SEEN THIS MAN?
TELL THE POLICE
WOMBOURN 4611, 3661 OR 6624

Express & Star

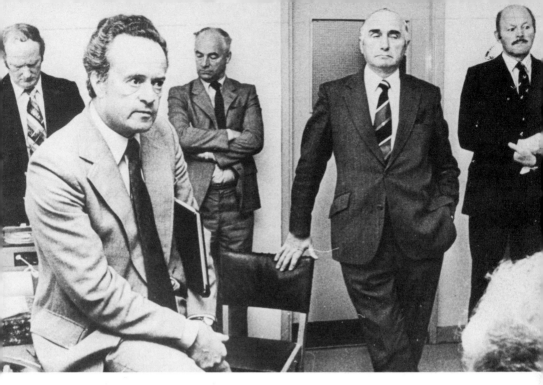

Detective Chief Superintendent Bob Stewart (left) and Assistant Chief Constable Harry Bailey

Helen Johnston, Anwar 'Spider' Mohammad, Brian Sinton and David Kane: vital prosecution witnesses

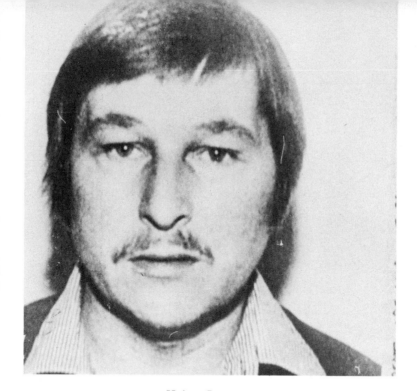

Hubert Spencer

Dennis Eaton

John Burkett

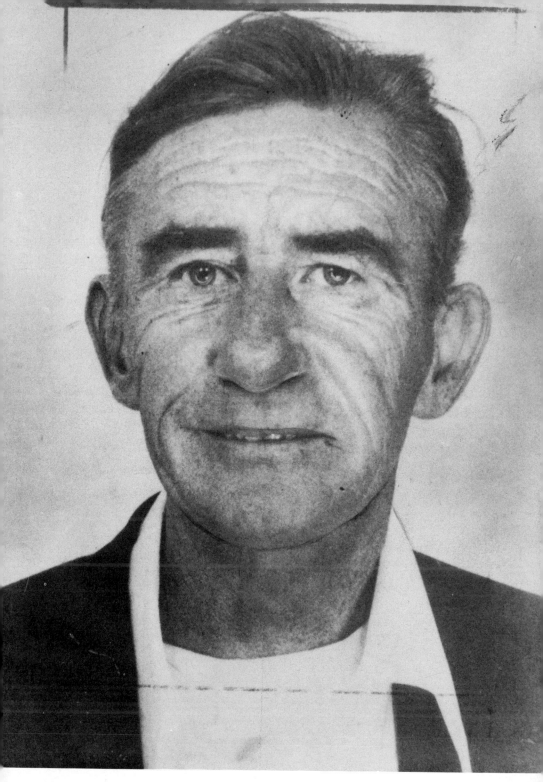

Pat Molloy

James Robinson

Michael Hickey

Vincent Hickey

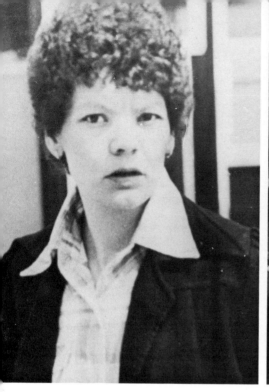

Carol Bradbury

Susan Bennett

Catherine Guy

Linda Galvin

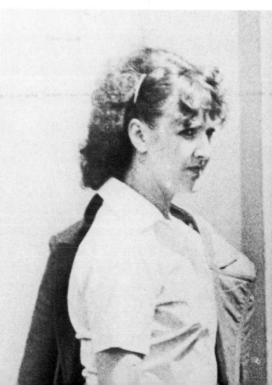

Michael Hickey (left) and Vincent Hickey protest their innocence, four years after
their sentences

Ann Whelan, Michael Hickey's mother, at Yew Tree Farm

Stopped short by the same dumb ignorance, Chief Inspector Watson tried his other tack:

> Watson: 'Did you fire the gun at Yew Tree Farm, Pat?'
> Molloy: 'Did somebody say I did?'
> Watson: 'Well, you know, it's been suggested by someone.'
> Molloy: 'Yeah, by Vincent Hickey. He would – to protect his own.'

According to DCI Watson's account of this interview, Pat Molloy then started looking at a poster of the three Identikit pictures issued two months previously. He asked for a pencil and drew in on the lefthand picture a beard. 'That could be Vinny, couldn't it?' he asked the startled inspector.

'Is it?' asked Watson, (the lefthand Identikit picture described a man in his forties. Vincent Hickey was twenty-five).

'I would say so,' said Pat Molloy.

Watson said: 'The one on the right could be you, I suppose.'

Now it was Molloy's turn to be surprised. 'Well, do you think so? Well yes, maybe.'

Watson made one last thrust. 'You are being very suggestive,' he said. 'Why don't you come clean and tell me about it?'

But Pat Molloy was back in his shell again. 'I wish I could,' he muttered. 'Don't you think I would get it sorted out if I could? But I can't.'

Watson left with those last two words ringing in his ears. *'I can't.'* What did he mean by that? Was he really suddenly worried for his children when he had abandoned them without a penny several years ago? Had he really been threatened with reprisals if he talked? If he had been, was it not greatly in his interests to ensure that any possible tormentors were locked up for countless years on a murder charge? Had he not already committed the central sin of grassing? So *why?* was he holding back?

'I can't.' The words could mean so many things. Their most obvious meaning was that Pat Molloy was not able to provide more information because he had not got it. Almost every word that he had uttered since his confession on 10 December suggested that he had *no information* about the farm or the robbery. One conclusion followed from that. He had not been there. He had been 'put in the frame' by Vincent Hickey's desperate attempt to get a pardon on the Chapel Farm robbery, and out of a mixture of revenge and despair had agreed to implicate others whom he thought might have done the murder, but had not.

Molloy was not charged. For the next four days he was left alone in his cell while the police sought to clinch the case against him from the fourth of the Yew Tree Farm raiders he had named: Michael Hickey.

Michael Hickey was sixteen years old, and he was frightened. For much of the last few years he had been pretending to be far older than his age. Now, suddenly, he was a boy again. As a child he had been devoted to both his parents and couldn't understand why they were not devoted to each other. His mother, Ann Hornigold, had been born into a prosperous confectioner's family in Norfolk. She had come to Birmingham to a job as a hotel receptionist when she was twenty-five. There she met Joe Hickey, a driver for Cadbury's. Their relationship was stormy. Michael was born in December 1961. In 1970, Ann finally left Joe and took Michael to Tamworth where they lived in a small council house.

They lived together without any contact with Joe Hickey for more than three years. One day on a visit to her mother's house in Birmingham, Ann discovered that Michael had been to see his father. She was furious and forbade him to do it again. 'In retrospect, all wrong,' she wrote much later in a letter to me. 'I should have explained my reasons and beliefs, but it was too late, I suppose. I now automatically became the nagging Mum, and Joe Hickey became the big spender, showering his particular brand of "love" on Michael.'

The more she banned her son from seeing his father, the more he did so. He started playing truant from school to visit his father in the daytime. Birmingham social services department intervened, and suggested that Michael might go more often to school if he lived with his father. This was agreed, but it didn't work. Michael spent more and more time away from school and eventually left, at the earliest possible moment.

He enjoyed the company of his father, especially in the pubs. From 1974, when Ann married a customs officer called Fred Whelan, Michael lived in Joe's house, and in the company of Joe's mates. At fifteen, he was a regular at the Dog and Partridge where his size successfully disguised his age. He had a steady girlfriend, Karen Smith, who had his baby in July 1978. He was close to his cousin Vincent. Early in 1978, Michael was convicted of deception after a roofing expedition, and fined £80. At sixteen, he was slipping rapidly into the netherworld of petty urban crime.

He was constantly seeking to prove himself among the regulars at the Dog and Partridge. He drove Jimmy Robinson and Johnny Burkett to the Tesco robbery at Castle Vale. During the robbery itself he was terrified, but once it was over he soon regained his self-assurance. A few days later, when Vincent suggested a robbery at Chapel Farm, Romsley, Michael agreed to go. It was Michael, not Vinny, who joined Robinson in the actual raid.

Michael had been proud of his bearing and manliness at the two robberies, and had held his head high in the Dog and Partridge. But on 6 December, exactly a week after the Chapel Farm robbery, his world started to fall apart. Strolling into the Dog in the evening, he was told by the landlord that Vinny had been arrested, and that his father wanted to see him.

When Joe Hickey came into the pub at one o'clock in the morning, he asked his son what he had been getting up to with his cousin. After some prevarication, young Michael admitted to his father that he had been on two armed robberies in the past fortnight.

In a detailed account two years later, Michael wrote: 'Then my Dad just started to cry and said: "don't you realise you are going away for a long time for what you've done?" I just kept on saying: "I know Dad, I'm sorry".' In reply, Joe Hickey told him to pack his bags and get off to his aunt's house at Wisbech, near Peterborough, until the family could find out how bad things were for Vinny.

His stepfather, Fred Whelan, drove Michael to Wisbech. The lad told his aunt he had come for a short holiday. Every night he would steal out to a call box to ring his father. The news was always bad. Huge squads of police had raided his flat, and the homes of all his family and friends. Both father and son were surprised at the level of police activity after two ordinary robberies. One night, Joe Hickey gave his son the explanation. Michael wrote in his 'report' later: 'My Dad said on the phone that the police knew I did Tescos and Chapel Farm, and they were now asking questions about a newspaper boy's murder. My Dad asked me if I knew anything about this murder. I said I knew nothing about it until he said it on the phone.'

Joe Hickey urged his son to wait until he had spent Christmas at his aunt's, but then to come back to Birmingham and give himself up to the police.

The plan was forestalled by the police. On 19 December, when Michael was still in Wisbech, buying Christmas presents, his cousin Michael Parsons came with the news that squads of Birmingham police had arrived at his aunt's house and were waiting for him there.

Somehow, Michael slipped through the police net and escaped to Peterborough where he caught a train to Birmingham. He arrived late at night, and went to see his girlfriend at her mother's house. He was let in for a moment to gaze for the last time at his sleeping baby. He was pressed to leave, and wandered out again into the freezing night. He went to his father's house, but Joe Hickey wasn't in and Michael was thrown out of there too. He made his way to the house of a friend, who let him in. He slept till late the following day, when his father burst into the house. 'The police are outside, so get your coat, son,' said Joe Hickey, who was weeping. Michael was arrested by DCI Watson, and taken at once not to Bromsgrove or to Bournville Lane, where he was wanted for the Chapel Farm and Tesco robberies, but to Wombourne, where he was wanted for the murder of Carl Bridgewater.

He had already made up his mind to confess to the Romsley and

Tesco robberies, and did so swiftly. He told Sergeant Brian Harrison and DC Davies about both robberies in meticulous detail. The officers showed a certain impatience. DCI Watson warned Michael he was in Wombourne police station. What interested the officers there was not a couple of two-bit robberies but a child murder. Michael Hickey began as Robinson and Molloy had started: 'I didn't go to no farm. I know nothing about it. . . I keep telling you I know nothing about it.' The sergeant and the constable dwelt on the coincidences between the robberies: the two farms, the fact that one of the men who was at Yew Tree Farm had named the Hickey cousins. Michael was not impressed. 'I've nothing to worry about. It wasn't me. I wasn't there, and I don't know why you're involving me.'

Sergeant Harrison was indignant. 'And you can sit here,' he said 're- maining quite calm and collected, being accused of such a serious matter and showing no sign of remorse. Do you know what I mean?'

Hickey: 'No.'

Harrison: 'You show no emotion at all. Do you feel sorry for the little lad who got shot?'

Hickey: 'Yes, but it wasn't me. I wasn't there.'

Harrison: 'I know that if it was me sitting in your shoes being accused of this thing, I would be worried. You're not.'

Hickey: 'Nothing worries me. I've no reason to worry. It wasn't me.'

The interview ended.

Michael Hickey thought his ordeal would soon be over, that he would be charged with the two robberies and moved from the cramped cells at Wombourne to a prison. But for the next two days (21 and 22 Dec- ember) he was interviewed almost continuously by a host of police offi- cers, all of whom told him they were absolutely certain that he had killed Carl Bridgewater. Through three interviews on the 21st and no less than five more on the 22nd Michael Hickey remained quite firm. He had not been at the farm. He had no idea where the farm was. He could not help with any detailed questions about the gun or anything else be- cause he knew nothing about the murder.

'I will tell you something, Mickey,' insisted Detective Sergeant Leslie Leek (not to be confused with DC Graham Leeke, who had interviewed Pat Molloy), 'you are either a very good liar or there is something wrong in your head that you have convinced yourself that you don't know any- thing about it.'

To which Michael replied: 'I am not either of those. I'm not barmy. If I'd been there, I'd remember it.'

Gradually, his resistance began to crack. He started to shout and swear. (Leek: 'How did the gun go off?' Michael: 'I don't know. I wasn't fucking there.') During the last of the five interviews on the 22nd Michael broke down altogether.

DI Turner had been concentrating on two themes. The first was that Michael Hickey was denying he was at Yew Tree Farm because he had pulled the trigger. The second was the statement of Pat Molloy. Until that interview, Michael Hickey had not seen the statement and whenever it was mentioned had indicated that it could not exist. At about 7.30 in the evening, Inspector Turner produced the statement. Michael read it and described it in the very same words of his cousin Vincent and of Jimmy Robinson: 'That's a load of fucking bollocks.'

He was greatly affected by the statement. Inspector Turner drove home his advantage by taking the boy's mind back to his family, and his beloved father:

Turner: 'Do you think Joe thinks you have done it?'
Hickey: 'I don't know. He asked me and my mother asked me and I told them I don't know fuck all about it.'
Turner: 'Perhaps your father believes that you did do it; he probably knows you best of all.'
Hickey: 'Well, I didn't do it, I wasn't there. I only wish I knew where I was.'
Turner: 'Why should someone say you were there if you were not?'
Hickey: 'I don't fucking know.'
Turner: 'It staggers me, Michael, that you can sit there how you do and take this in your stride almost as if it is not happening. Do you think if you keep saying you weren't there it will all go away?'
Hickey: 'Why has that bastard said that, why has he said I was there?'
Turner: 'There is only one reason, that is because you were there. I can only conclude that you deny having been there because you are the one who pulled the trigger.'
Hickey: 'I wasn't. Why can't you believe me?'
Turner: 'I don't believe you. I have told you repeatedly. Look at the statement, what does it say? "I went with Vinny Hickey and his relation Mickey. . . Mickey drove the van away. . . Mickey dumped the property." You are in it up to your ears, Michael, and you have not had the experience to know how to handle it now.'

According to the police version, Michael then put his head in his hands and burst into tears, shouting and swearing abuse at Molloy and complaining that his Dad was upset.

The inspector and his colleagues tactfully left the room, only to return a few minutes later.

Turner: 'Do you feel better after that outburst, Michael?'
Hickey: 'No, I just want to sleep.'

Then DI Turner delivered the *coup de grâce*: 'I think you want to tell us about being at Yew Tree Farm.'

'I don't,' Michael replied. 'I wasn't there. I want to go to sleep.'

The officers retired. Three days of intensive interviews in which every possible effort had been made to impress on the lad how desperate was his position had failed utterly in their objective. Convincingly and coherently, Michael, just turned seventeen, had denied any involvement in the murder. He *was not there*, he said. And he could not understand why anyone should have said he was.

Disappointing though Michael Hickey's replies must have been for the officers, at least they had all four suspects under lock and key. Pat Molloy had suggested he was scared to talk while even one of the men he had named was free, and able to strike at Molloy's family and friends. So when the news came in that after long interrogations Michael Hickey was not admitting anything, the tireless Inspectors Watson and Wordley decided to visit Molloy in his cell to see if he would now talk more freely about Yew Tree Farm. Watson broke the good news:

'We have got young Michael Hickey in. We arrested him last night . . . is that any relief to you?'

Molloy: 'It helps.'

Watson: 'We've got to sort it out now, as you appreciate. There was an indication that it might alter things when he was arrested, so what is your situation now. Does it alter things?'

Molloy: 'Well, it doesn't really, unless he tells you something.'

Watson: 'You have said to Mr Wordley and myself that Michael was the person holding the gun when you walked in the room.'

Molloy: 'Yes.'

Watson: 'Is that an insinuation that Michael fired the gun?'

Molloy: 'Yes, I suppose so.'

Watson: 'Can you enlarge on that any?'

Molloy: 'No, not really.'

Watson: 'You have no doubt about Michael holding the gun then?'

Molloy: 'No. I've said that in my statement.'

Watson: 'You didn't. In fact, in your statement, and I'm coming to that, you in fact said that Jimmy had the gun.'

Molloy: 'What I meant is I knew Jimmy had a gun. I'm sure that's what I meant to the question at the time.'

Watson: 'We have to be clear.'

Molloy: 'I was probably referring to the fact that Jimmy had a gun.'

Watson: 'Yes, we know that Jimmy owned a gun.'

Molloy: 'Yes, that's indisputable, that is.'

Watson: 'Let me remind you what you said in your statement. You said the three of them were in the room. What are you saying now, as you've contradicted yourself?'

Molloy: 'I've said both things, haven't I?'

Watson: 'Which is correct then?'

Molloy: 'I just don't know.'

Watson: 'So either could be correct?'

Molloy: 'Yes.'

The picture which Molloy had painted so vividly in his statement only eleven days previously was now completely distorted. Interrogation by the officers had produced a contradiction. In the statement, Jimmy was holding the gun. In later interviews, Jimmy wasn't there, he was upstairs. Then Michael was holding the gun. Now that Michael was in captivity, Molloy was not so sure. Either version could have been correct. Or neither.

The inspector left. Five minutes later, perhaps after an effort to control himself, he was back again with the same patient questions, which were answered with the same pathetic and obsequious uncertainty.

Who was in the cars when they travelled back from the farm? At least Molloy had been consistent on that. In almost every interview up till then he had said that Michael Hickey had driven the van back, while the other three had gone back in the car. Now he said that Jimmy Robinson drove the van back.

'You told us different than that – why?' asked Watson. To which Molloy hung his head yet again and muttered that he had been confused. The questions came on faster, and the answers came on vaguer. What was the colour of the car on the 19th? Molloy wasn't sure. 'Brownish', perhaps, or 'muddish' or 'bluish'. Was it an estate? He couldn't be sure.

On, then, to the period just before the four men met up to go to Yew Tree Farm. Molloy had said he had been in the Dog playing cards. Then he decided the card game was in the Stonehouse. But the officers had found out that the card game at the Stonehouse had not been played on the 19th at all. The day-off arrangements of the barmen, who remembered the game, made it clear that the game could not have taken place on a Tuesday. Molloy thought they were wrong. He said there might have been a barmaid there.

Watson was moved to ask: 'Are you enjoying this? You seem to be avoiding every point that's being put to you.'

The Irishman hung his head, and made no reply.

'You are confusing us,' Watson insisted.

'Not deliberately,' said Molloy.

89

'I am not convinced,' said the inspector finally, 'that you have told us all that you can tell us, and you will have to tell the truth sometime.'

Respectful as ever, Molloy answered quietly: 'I've tried to remember and I shall keep on trying.'

Perhaps to reassure himself, Watson fired a last desperate question at his most helpful suspect.

'You *were* there?' he asked.

Molloy's reply was very strange indeed.

'I shall,' he said 'be pleading guilty to being there.'

Watson left. He did not return.

This was the eleventh interview which police had had with the Irishman since he signed his confession. In every one of them he had shifted his position. At first, the police assumed he was frightened of his accomplice who was still free. Yet now Michael Hickey was caught, Molloy was even vaguer about the murder, even more infuriating with his contradictions.

It was an uneasy Christmas break for the officers in charge of the inquiry. All four of their suspects, it is true, were behind bars. Three of them – the Hickey cousins and Robinson – were charged with other serious offences which would ensure their custody for a long period. As far as these three were concerned, there was no rush for a decision. But there *was* a problem with Pat Molloy.

Molloy had been charged with the meat robbery at Tamworth in September – for which Robinson had already been given a suspended sentence. Robinson had walked free from the court over the meat robbery, and Molloy would probably do so as well. Molloy had been in custody since 9 December. Unless he was charged with something more serious, it was likely that his lawyers would apply for bail and give Molloy the chance to escape. Obviously with the signed confession safe in their hands, the case for a speedy murder charge on all four men named in it was very strong.

The chief problem was lack of evidence. Yes, Robinson had a shotgun but there was no proof it was the gun used at the killing. Yes, none of the men could say where they were on 19 September, but the date was a long time ago and they might simply have forgotten. Yes, Molloy had confessed, but his statements since were full of such monstrous contradictions that his confession could be torn to shreds in even amateur cross-examination. Yes, Vincent Hickey had confessed – though not in a statement – but he was now denying it, and there was an obvious motive for his confession.

Moreover, Jimmy Robinson and Michael Hickey had, even on the evidence of the police's own accounts of the interviews, denied any connection with the murder from first to last. If Molloy's evidence was to count against the others, it would have to be corroborated by something else. That something else was sadly missing.

Whatever discussions took place between Detective Chief Superintendent Stewart and his top officers that Christmas weekend, they moved swiftly as soon as it was over. Boxing Day was on a Tuesday. On Thursday, 28 December, Pat Molloy was taken from his cell to Wombourne Magistrates Court and charged with the murder of Carl Bridgewater. The news was splashed across all the newspapers the following day. 'Police officers are now certain,' announced the *Express and Star* that day, 'that four men were involved in the murder.'

The papers went to the Director of Public Prosecutions. On 9 January 1979, Vincent Hickey was taken from Bromsgrove and charged with the murder. Nearly a month later, on 7 February, Michael Hickey and James Robinson were also charged.

The four suspects were now facing trial. Could a credible case be made against them?

CHAPTER THREE
Alibis

The Bridgewater Four, as the four suspects quickly became known, might well have been the Bridgewater Five. For several days after his arrest on 8 December 1978, John Burkett was also a prime suspect. Indeed, to some investigating officers he seemed the most likely of the five to have pulled the trigger on the newspaper boy. Burkett was the man with the gun at the Tesco robbery, and had fired it. He was known as a 'wild man'. Vincent Hickey had named him in his 'confession', though Pat Molloy had not.

Fortunately for John Burkett, however, he and his family could remember where he had been on 19 September. He and his wife had visited his mother in Weoley Castle, Birmingham. There were several witnesses to this, and Burkett was dropped as a suspect.

In the days immediately after their arrests, none of the other four suspects could remember a single convincing detail about their whereabouts on the 19th. In itself, this was not surprising. All four were drifters, without any fixed address. None had permanent jobs. All spent long periods of the day drinking. Their memories were fuddled with booze.

Long before his arrest, however, Vincent Hickey *had* given an account of his whereabouts on the 19th. He had been questioned by police at Cannock on 15 October. If it could be shown that he had lied about his alibi, he was in serious trouble.

On 15 October, Vincent assured police that he had spent the bulk of the afternoon of the 19th in the Dog and Partridge pub. This had been supported at the time with the pub's licensee, David Bruce. He told police that 19 September had been a special day. One of the pub's most regular and popular customers, Dave Waller, had had a phone call that afternoon to tell him his wife had given birth to a baby. There had been a great deal of celebration for the rest of the afternoon and evening. Some customers had been in the pub continuously from eleven in the morning to eleven at night.

'I cannot say for certain whether young Vincent Hickey was there,' Mr Bruce told detectives on 15 October. 'It would have been unusual for him not to be there at lunchtime. I can only say that Vincent Hickey probably was there. I cannot remember specifically, as there were about fourteen people there.

'Vincent comes every lunchtime and if we stop late after hours for a drink Vincent always stops as well.'

Joe Hickey, Vincent's uncle, told police on 15 October that he had gone to the Dog and Partridge at about 12.30 on the day of the murder, and left at about 3.00. 'The usual crowd was in there, including Vincent,' he said. 'I left the pub at 3 p.m. and went home, so I left Vincent playing darts.'

This was confirmed by at least two other Dog regulars at the time, and undoubtedly helped the police at Cannock in October to rule out Vincent Hickey. His 'confession' in December however, sent large squads of police combing South Birmingham for Dog and Partridge regulars to see whether their memories had been at fault.

Perhaps the most vital witness was Dave Waller, who had become a father on 19 September. On 11 December, when Molloy, Robinson and Vincent were being held in police cells without access to friends or lawyers, Waller was approached by two Staffordshire officers as he was drinking in the Dog and Partridge. Like other regulars there, Waller had himself been in trouble many times and had served time in prison.

The officers asked him to come to Wombourne police station to help them with their inquiries. He refused, but changed his mind when they started to threaten him. He was held at Wombourne from half past twelve until nine in the evening. 'They kept coming into my cell – eight of them – and beating me up – telling me to say the Hickeys weren't in the pub at three o'clock. I refused.' (Interview with me, published *Daily Mirror*, 21 July 1983.)

The next day, 12 December, the wretched Waller was picked up in the street and taken again to Wombourne where he was locked in a cell for more than fifty hours. Again and again different sets of interviewing policemen accused him of lying to protect the Hickeys, or promised him protection against the Hickeys if he was frightened of telling the truth. During the course of those two days at Wombourne, Waller says, he was kicked in the testicles and his head was repeatedly smashed against the wall. To his credit, however, he stuck firmly to his story. There was no doubt in his mind that both Vincent and Michael had been in the pub on the afternoon his baby was born.

Twice more – on 15 December and on 31 January – Waller was hauled off to Wombourne. He was not charged with any crime. He claimed then and later that he had been falsely imprisoned and assaulted. He immediately sued the Chief Constable of Staffordshire in the county court on both grounds. The police put up a show of resistance. But in 1980, long after the Bridgewater case was over, they paid Dave Waller

£1,000 in final settlement of his claims but without admitting liability. Further evidence of the tactics employed by the police with the regulars at the Dog came from James Patrick Smith, another professional thief who knew the Hickeys. In a statement made at Sudbury prison long after the Bridgewater case was over, James Smith said:

> I was seen at Wombourne police station and at Bournville Lane police station both before and after Michael Hickey was arrested in Christmas 1978. I was not always seen by the same officers. The police appeared to think that I had evidence that the four defendants had definitely committed the murder in question. The police had obviously heard that I went around with Jimmy Robinson and Pat Molloy. Once the police realised I was not involved in the crime in question, they asked whether I could say that I had seen the four defendants together. I told the police that I had only seen them in the Dog and Partridge public house, Selly Oak, and even then they were not together. The police told me that if I would tell them that I had seen the four together at any time before or at the time of the murder case, we could get away with murder. 'You know you are waiting to go to court. If you can help us, you won't even have to go to court for these charges.' They said they did not want any lies. They said: 'If you can put your finger on anything that can make it concrete with the Hickeys, there is a lot of reward money left.'

James Smith, however, did not change his story. He had *never* seen the Hickey cousins in company with Molloy and Robinson. *Nor could the police find a single witness who had ever seen the four men together.*

In one respect, however, the persistent interviews with regulars at the Dog and Partridge extracted some new information. Dave Bruce, the licensee, decided to change his evidence of 15 October that Vincent Hickey 'probably' was in his pub on the afternoon of the murder. After a series of long interviews, Mr Bruce finally made a statement on 19 December, as follows:

> Since making the statement I have thought the matter over more fully and discussed it with my wife, and I am now certain that Vincent was not in the pub during that particular afternoon. . .
> Vincent and Michael Hickey – they came in during the lunch time – but left well before closing time. I did not actually see them leave, and I did not know what vehicle they were in.

This statement did not last long. The more the police questioned other regulars at the Dog and Partridge, the more it became clear that the Hickey cousins *had* been in the pub that afternoon. Dave Waller said they had. Jim Smith said they had. Tommy Vallance said they had. Ronald Brookes said they had. In the end, after another about-turn, even Dave Bruce said they had. The fact that the Hickey cousins were in the Dog and Partridge for the early part of the afternoon of the murder, probably until 3 p.m. and maybe even a bit later, was established beyond doubt.

Very much the same happened with Jimmy Robinson and Pat Molloy. As soon as the two men were arrested, police started inquiries among the regulars at the California, whose clientele was, if anything, even more anxious to help than at the Dog and Partridge. Unhappily, there was nothing to mark 19 September – as Dave Waller's baby had marked the 19th at the Dog. The manageress of the Cali, Patricia Rogers, could say no more than that Jimmy Robinson and Pat Molloy were in the pub most days before Robinson was arrested, but she could not remember the day. Mrs Rogers recommended that the police speak to Tony Keevins who was reckoned as an expert on the Bridgewater murder. Similar advice was freely given by another California regular, Melvin Rarily. Almost all the Cali customers were very forgetful about the 19th.

There was, however, one episode which *did* fix 19 September as an important date in the lives of Jimmy Robinson and Pat Molloy. Carol Bradbury, in whose house both men were living, had come out of hospital that day after a minor operation on her fallopian tube. The police asked Cali regulars whether or not they recalled any conversation in the pub about that.

One of them did. She was Carol Wilson, who drank at the Cali most lunchtimes. She remembered Jimmy Robinson talking to her on the day that he had brought Carol home from hospital. She had no doubt that at 'about 1.30' she had chatted to Jimmy about the journey back from hospital and about Carol's health. She could not remember the time they left. She had left the pub at ten minutes to three but couldn't remember whether the two men were in the pub at the time. This evidence was never challenged. Jimmy Robinson was outraged that none of the other Cali regulars came forward to prove his story that he and Molloy were in the pub until after closing time. But considering the circumstances and the pressure from the police, he could be grateful that one witness, who did not waver at any stage, placed him and Molloy in the California at least at 1.30, and probably considerably later.

So it was that at a very early stage in their inquiries, and despite the most extraordinary efforts to prove the opposite, the police conceded that the Hickey cousins were in the Dog and Partridge until about 3 p.m. and that Robinson and Molloy were in the California until about the same time. What happened then?

At no time did anyone say or even hint that they had seen the four men meet somewhere that afternoon. Without such evidence, the alibis to three o'clock created an immediate difficulty for the police. Molloy and Vincent, in their 'confessions', both suggested that the four men had travelled in two cars to Yew Tree Farm. On several occasions, the police 'test drove' between the Dog and Partridge or the California to Yew Tree Farm. On one occasion, the police reported the journey took twenty-seven minutes; on another, a more sober forty-five.

If the more sober figure is accepted (and I have never been able to do the journey in less than three-quarters of an hour; once it took nearly an hour), the prosecution case rested on the two pairs of men leaving different pubs at closing time, meeting up, and getting to Yew Tree Farm at least by the time Mrs Gladys Jones saw the car in the farm at four o'clock, and preferably by the time Mario Sabetta said he saw two men – one with a gun – in the road near the farm at 3.25. This left only a very few minutes for any journey between the pubs, any meeting or any discussion between the four men about where they were going and why.

However, it was possible, just, to make that journey. Any successful alibi depended on what happened after closing time. Here the men's stories divide, and have to be considered separately.

Jim Robinson and Pat Molloy

In his first interview on the day after his arrest, Pat Molloy gave the police the alibi which he and Robinson staunchly insisted on all the way through to their trial, and afterwards.

DC Perkins asked him: 'Where were you on the day of the murder?'

Pat Molloy replied: 'I went for a drink at the Cali on the dinner time and left at about three, then I went to my digs.' His 'digs' of course were at Carol Bradbury's maisonette at 35 Wolston Croft, Weoley Castle.

Asked if anyone had seen him at his digs, Pat replied that Carol Bradbury had seen him there, and she had been there all the time.

Jimmy Robinson was much less specific when he was first asked about it. All his days, he pointed out, seemed to merge into one, and it was quite absurd for him to pretend he could remember one out of the pack, after a period of nearly three months. After a while, as though to jog his memory, the police told him that Carol Bradbury had come out of hospital on the day of the murder. Jimmy brightened up immediately. He described in detail how he and Molloy had fetched Carol in an old car he had stolen, and taken her some of the way back home. He had been nervous in case the car was recognised in the Weoley Castle area, so he dumped the car in a car park and insisted that they got a bus the rest of the way. Carol was furious. Robinson, in his rush to sell his stolen meat that morning, had forgotten to bring a clean set of clothes which she had asked for. She felt scruffy and degraded as she climbed into the bus.

The trio got back to Wolston Croft about 11.30 a.m. Jimmy had 'made up' a chair near the fire for Carol. Jim and Pat had then gone out to the Cali for their usual lunchtime boozing session. They had returned in the afternoon to the maisonette. Carol was in bed, and spent the rest of the afternoon there. Robinson explained (and there was no argument about it) that he had carried out a robbery the night before (18 September) and had not slept a wink. He said that he and Pat were exhausted and both slept soundly that afternoon – Jimmy alongside Carol upstairs, Pat in a chair by the fire, downstairs.

Both men, therefore, out of contact with one another, told the same story about where they were when Carl Bridgewater was being shot at Yew Tree Farm.

Carol Bradbury's life, meanwhile, had been turned upside down. From the moment Vincent Hickey had pointed out her house to the police, she was constantly visited and questioned by plain-clothes officers.

At first, she did not realise how serious the case against Jimmy was. She was visited on 7 December, the day after his arrest, and told Jimmy was at Harborne police station. She went there, but could not see him. At Harborne she gave a short statement to the police in which she told of her relationship with Jimmy and of his arrest for the Tamworth meat job the previous September. She was not asked, and did not say anything, about 19 September.

On 9 December Staffordshire police came to her door and asked her to go with them to Wombourne police station where they said (wrongly) they were holding Jimmy Robinson, Carol was anxious to see him. After arranging for the baby to be looked after for an hour or two, she went willingly. When she got there, however, she found herself being interviewed for hours on end. The police told her to her horror that Jimmy was a suspect for the murder of the newspaper boy, and it was vital for her to remember where he was on 19 September.

She arrived at Wombourne police station at ten in the morning and was not allowed home, in spite of constant pleas about the baby, for twelve and a half hours. 'They kept on and on about this date,' she told me in an interview in October 1985. 'September 19th, September 19th. Could I remember what happened on that day? Of course, just like that, I couldn't. I was scared. They locked me up for hours on end in the dark and told me to rack my brains and remember.'

Eventually, a friendly policewoman came to the cell. Did Carol not have something in her handbag which might remind her of the day? she asked. Carol emptied her handbag. A hospital appointments card fell out, revealing to Carol's intense relief that 19 September was the day she had been discharged from hospital.

She then gave a long statement, which went in some detail into the events of 19 September.

> At about 9 a.m. on September 19, the sister or nurse came and said I had a visitor. It was Jimmy and Pat. They had come to take me home. I saw the doctor at 10 a.m. and some minutes later left with Jimmy and Pat. They had an old dark blue van parked round the corner. Jimmy drove. I sat by him, and Pat sat on the floor at the back.
>
> When we got to Selly Oak, Jimmy parked the van and said it was stolen. We three caught the No. 22 bus home. I went straight to bed. Tracey [Carol's oldest daughter] went shopping with the baby.
>
> Jimmy said that he had to go out and he and Pat left. This would be between 11 a.m. and 11.30 a.m. I don't know where they went to. I dozed off and some time later, certainly after the pub shut at 3 p.m., it could well have been after that, they both came back. I don't know where they had been. I never asked.
>
> I stayed in bed all day. I felt very weak and drowsy. I remember that he came to bed and slept by me for about a couple of hours before he went out on the booze again at about 7.30. I was very hazy about the time.

Carol left Wombourne police station that Saturday evening with an overwhelming sense of relief. She had been able to remember 19 September because of the lucky coincidence of the hospital appointment. She could be quite certain now that Jimmy Robinson had nothing to do with the murder of Carl Bridgewater. When the murder had first been mentioned, she had been incredulous. Robinson was indeed a wild man, and a professional thief. But he was very fond of children, and happy in their company. This was one of the reasons Carol had been so fond of him. 'The kids loved him,' she says. Her daughter Tracey, who when I talked to her many years later was herself a mother with a tiny baby, enthusiastically supported her mother's judgement.

Carol Bradbury's statement on 9 December suggested a complete alibi not just for Robinson but also for Molloy.

If Jim had come back from the pub and had slept with Carol for a 'couple of hours' before going out at about 7.30, he was not likely to have taken a forty-five-minute drive to Wordsley, robbed Yew Tree Farm, and murdered Carl Bridgewater at 4.15. If Molloy was with Jim, as Carol also stated, then Molloy too was in the clear.

The police, however, had not finished with Carol Bradbury. They wanted to see her again and again. Carol remembers that miserable Christmas ruined almost every day by visits from different sets of police officers from Staffordshire or from Birmingham. On 22 December she was taken in again for another statement. She stuck to her original story about the afternoon of 19 September:

> Jimmy went out with Pat for a drink and then came home. I had gone for a lay down, and he came and went to bed with me for a couple of hours. He was in bed with me for about two hours and he did not get up until about 7 p.m. The children told me that *Star Trek* was on when Jimmy got up.

Molloy was charged on 28 December, Vincent Hickey on 9 January. Both had incriminated themselves. But what of Jimmy Robinson who denied all knowledge of the murder and of Yew Tree Farm? Did he have an alibi, as Carol's earlier statements had suggested? Robinson himself, protected now by his solicitor, Tony Fryer, was saying with increasing confidence that he and Molloy had spent the afternoon of 19 September partly at the California pub (as the police now accepted) and partly at Carol's flat.

Police inquiries were redoubled.

Once again, on 24 January, Carol Bradbury was taken to Wombourne police station. Once again, unprotected by friends or lawyers, she was subjected to a long interrogation. Once again she made a detailed statement, even longer than the one she had made before Christmas.

In minute detail, she went through the story of her collection from the hospital, the journey home partly by car, partly by bus, and her arrival home with Robinson and Molloy at about a quarter past eleven on the morning of the murder.

The statement then went on:

> After about ten minutes from the time when we got home, Jimmy left with Pat to get the papers. He came back alone after about ten minutes. . . He was in too much of a hurry to go to the pub, the California pub up the road. He went to fetch me the papers, that's why he came back into the flat before going to the pub. He came back without Pat. He was alone. He glanced at one of the papers and after a few minutes he asked if I minded if he went to the Cali and that he would stay with me that night. He left shortly after.

Carol said she had then sent her eldest daughter Tracey out to buy some meat, peeled some potatoes and relaxed. When Tracey came back she fed the baby, and cooked a meal:

I put Jim and Pat's dinner in the oven. That would have been about 2.50 p.m. Then I told Tracey that I was going upstairs to have a sleep. The next thing I remember was that Jim came up to me in bed. He had a big bunch of flowers with him.

Here, Carol says, the interview was broken off for some time while the police warned her. 'They told me that it was very serious for me if I said anything wrong in my statement,' she said. 'They told me they had interviewed the people where Jimmy bought the flowers at the florist opposite the California, and they had suggested that it might have been the Wednesday of that week when he bought the flowers. They said if Jim had bought them on the Wednesday, then I'd be wrong to say he came with them on the Tuesday. They kept telling me not to say for certain it was the Tuesday when Jim bought the flowers, though I was sure he'd bought them on the day I came out of hospital.' (Interview with me, 5 October 1985).

So Carol Bradbury's 24 January statement went on:

I would like to say now that I am confused about the afternoon, I don't want to say anything that I know is not true. The trouble I have in trying to remember is that the days when we were all at home were very much the same. I don't really remember one after-noon from another. The problem is that some days when Jim and Pat went to the pub, sometimes they would come back about 3 p.m., and sometimes 5 p.m. or 6 p.m.

After this, as though to heed her own warning, Carol Bradbury said nothing more about the afternoon. Her statement continues with what happened at tea time.

At tea time about 6 p.m., I think that it may have been about 7 p.m., Tracey said that Jim got up at 7 p.m. and then he was on about going out.

There was no reference in this statement to *Star Trek*, as there had been in the previous statement. *Star Trek* that Tuesday evening started at 6.54 p.m. just about the time that Carol Bradbury and her daughter both said Jim got up. If he had indeed 'got up' he must have been lying down somewhere, and the most likely place was Carol Bradbury's bed. However, this was not very important any longer. For Carol Bradbury's fifth statement seemed to detract from all her others up to that time. Whereas before she had seemed quite certain that Jimmy Robinson was with her on the afternoon of the murder, now she could not be so sure. The alibi, for the moment, had gone.

Before the statement ended, however, there was a further reference to flowers. While describing the following morning – Wednesday, 20 September – Carol said that she had made Jim and Pat some breakfast before they went to the pub. She went on: 'I now remember that Yvonne Burkett came round to my flat on the Wednesday with a bunch of flowers. I really only think this though.'

The police had heard about flowers from three other people. Among the many friends and neighbours of Carol Bradbury and Jim Robinson whom they interviewed was Mrs Violet Collins, who lived in the same estate. Police first went to see Mrs Collins on 23 December, the day after Carol Bradbury's long third statement. Mrs Collins said:

I have given a lot of thought to the time when Carol Humphreys [Carol's married name], Jimmy Robinson's wife, came out of hospital the second time. I remember being on my balcony overlooking the phone box at Barnes Hill at about 3.30 one afternoon. I saw Jimmy Robinson carrying a bunch of red and white flowers. I called down to ask him how Carol was and he said: 'She is all right'.

I honestly can't remember if I saw Jimmy with the flowers on the Tuesday or the Wednesday or even the Thursday after Carol came home. That would be either the 19th, 20th, or 21st September, 1978.

I am not able to say which definite day I saw Jimmy with the flowers, I know it was certainly after Carol had come out of hospital. I am afraid I just cannot help you at all. I thought about the day quite a lot since you asked me but I am not sure which day it was.

Mrs Collins' encounter with Jim and the flowers, she concluded, happened on the Tuesday, the Wednesday or the Thursday. It could not, in fact, have been on the Thursday since, from the early hours of that morning, Jimmy Robinson was in police cells, after being arrested for the Tamworth meat robbery.

So Mrs Collins saw him with flowers on the afternoon of the Tuesday or the Wednesday. Which?

One answer came from police interviews with Yvonne Hards, John Burkett's girlfriend, whom Carol knew as Yvonne Burkett. Yvonne Hards made five statements to the police between 19 December and 22 February. On the morning after the murder, 20 September, she said she and John Burkett had set out to see his sick mother. She had bought flowers for the old lady, but on the way to her flat had called in to see Carol Bradbury who had come out of hospital the previous day. She gave Carol the flowers. In her first two statements, this fact was said casually and not questioned. But in her fourth statement – given on 15

February – she was pressed for more details:

> John and I went in, and Carol was in the house with her 12-year-old daughter, and also the baby. Jimmy Robinson was definitely not there. Knowing that Carol had recently come out of hospital, I gave her the flowers. I recall that there were already some fresh flowers in the house. What type I cannot remember.

Yvonne Hards said exactly the same in her fifth and last statement, which she gave on 28 February.

'I recall that there were already some fresh flowers in the house.' This was on the Wednesday morning, the day after the Bridgewater murder. These flowers must have been bought before the Wednesday morning. The probability was that they had been bought the day before – the day Carol came out of hospital; and that it was these flowers which Mrs Collins had seen in Jimmy Robinson's hand as he came along the road under her balcony. Yvonne Hards' evidence backed up the alibi. It strongly suggested that Mrs Collins saw Jimmy with the flowers on the Tuesday – at precisely the time Carl Bridgewater was being shot some twenty miles away.

The defence never saw Yvonne Hards' statements. Most of the statements made to the police by witnesses were, as is normal, formally made available to the defence. In practice, there were so many statements – some 7,000 – that the defence lawyers never got round to looking at them.

But in the Carl Bridgewater case there was an additional, and remarkable, restriction. It was presented to the defence in letters to all four solicitors as late as 1 August 1979, just two months before the trial. The letter, signed by Mr Chance of the Director of Public Prosecutions Office, went like this:

> I enclose a list of names and addresses of persons who have made statements in the course of the investigation but are not prosecution witnesses. This list has been requested by the solicitors representing one of the accused, and it is of course right that it should be supplied to the solicitors for all the accused. In the interests of justice, I am not prepared to make available the statements of those persons indicated by a X on the list.

The one solicitor who had bothered to ask for this list was Tony Fryer.

The ban by the DPP was extended on 9 August when Mr Chance wrote again to the lawyers advising them of six new names, including two vital alibi witnesses, who should now be 'marked X'.

No one at the DPP's office then or since has been able to explain what were the 'interests of justice' which prevented the defence from seeing these statements. As we shall discover, the most common feature of the starred statements was the support they gave to the defendants' case, especially the alibis.

At the time the law on such matters was vague. There was a general 'flexibility' which allowed the prosecution not to disclose statements. In December 1981, however, two years after the case, the Attorney General, Sir Michael Havers, issued a set of detailed guidelines for the disclosure of 'unused material' (including all unused statements) to the defence. The general rule was straightforward: 'All unused material shall normally be made available to the defence solicitor if it has some bearing on the offence(s) charged and the surrounding circumstances of the case.'

The prosecution had a 'discretion' not to disclose such material in five cases: i) if the witness might be intimidated into changing his statement; ii) if the statement is believed to be wholly or partially untrue; iii) if the statement favours the prosecution, but there are good grounds for believing the witness might change his statement 'due to feelings of loyalty and fear'; iv) if the statement is neutral, and there are good grounds for believing it might be changed; v) if the statement is 'sensitive', for such reasons as national security, intimidation of witnesses or domestic strife.

The guidelines made it clear that if there was any doubt about the matter, the balance should fall in favour of disclosure.*

It is difficult to argue that the statements which were withheld from the defence in the Carl Bridgewater case could possibly be covered by any of the five exceptions.

In 1985, Michael Hickey's solicitor, who was then Jim Nichol, as part of his work for a petition to get the case sent back to the Court of Appeal, applied to the Director of Public Prosecutions for sight of the statements which were made to the police, but which were not used at the trial. The DPP immediately agreed. Jim Nichol also asked if he could see the 'starred' statements which the DPP had denied to the defence before the trial. Again, the DPP immediately agreed. 'There was no question raised about it,' Mr Nichol says.

One reason for the change of heart may have been that the Attorney General's 1981 guidelines, if they had operated in 1979, would certainly have obliged the prosecution to hand over most of the statements they in fact withheld.

The 'starring' of Yvonne Hards in particular meant that crucial corroboration of the 'flowers' alibi was denied to the defence.

---

* Archbold, *Criminal Pleading, Evidence and Practice*, 1985, pp.328-31.

There was still further evidence of the 'flowers' alibi. It came very early on in police inquiries. Its source was Mrs Susan Bennett who lived two doors away on the same walkway as Carol Bradbury – at No. 39 Wolston Croft. Police went to see Mrs Bennett on 16 December 1978, and asked her about 19 September, the day Carol came out of hospital.

Mrs Bennett remembered the day very well. Carol's daughter, Tracey, had come to her in the morning 'in a panic' because Carol's baby was sick. She had tended to the baby. Mrs Bennett said:

> I never saw Jimmy at all that day. I'm certain about that, but at about half past nine that night Carol came to my house. She told me that Jimmy had picked her up from the hospital that morning in a van he had borrowed, but it had broken down and she had had to get on a bus. She said that Jim and Pat had been out for a drink at dinner time and when he came back he said he and Pat were going to stop in with her, but after he had had a sleep with her, him and Pat had gone out. She didn't say what time they had come in or gone out again, but she was a little upset about it.

Mrs Bennett couldn't remember exact times, but her memory of that day fitted Carol's story. Moreover, it left little time in the day when Jimmy Robinson could have gone to Yew Tree Farm and murdered Carl Bridgewater.

The early statement was just a sketch. On 19 January 1979, Susan Bennett was taken to Wombourne where she had a long interview with Detective Sergeant Leo Eccleshall. In as much detail as she could, she went over the events of the days before the murder, and of the 19th itself. Once again she told of Tracey's panic about the sick child, and of Carol's visit to her flat that evening:

> She told me that she had only come down to my place because Jimmy had gone out and left her and she had tried to make him jealous by saying to him that she was going to her sister's at Moseley.
>
> Carol told me while she was at my flat that evening that Jimmy had got her two bunches of flowers that day – one before he went to the pub on the lunchtime and one when he came back. I know that Jimmy went out for a paper early in the morning and he could have got a bunch of flowers then.

The next day (Wednesday, the 20th) Susan Bennett said she went to Carol's flat, at about half past nine. 'I saw that there were two bunches of flowers each one in a coffee pot on the sideboard,' she said. 'The flowers were rust and lemon-coloured chrysanthemums and pink, white and yellow gladioli.'

Even before Jimmy Robinson was charged with the murder (on 9 February), therefore, police inquiries had discovered the following:

1) Carol Bradbury had told them (without seeing Jimmy) that Jimmy and Pat had brought her home from hospital, gone to the Cali, and come home with a bunch of flowers. Her certainty about the date she got the flowers faded when police suggested her story conflicted with what they had learned from the flower shop.

2) A similar story about the flowers was told by Susan Bennett, who remembered Carol telling her she had had two bunches of flowers from Jimmy that day, one on getting back from the hospital (in the morning) and the other when he came back from the pub in the afternoon.

Could Carol and Susan have been thinking about the flowers he'd brought in the morning? No because:

3) Vi Collins said she had seen Jimmy with some flowers for Carol *in the afternoon* – at 3.30. But Mrs Collins wasn't sure about the date. It could have been the day Carol came out of hospital, she said, or the next day.

Could the whole flowers episode have taken place on the Wednesday then, not the Tuesday? Most probably not, because:

4) Susan Bennett remembered seeing two bunches of flowers in Carol's flat at 9.30 in the morning on the Wednesday, and

5) Yvonne Hards had seen other flowers in Carol's flat when she herself brought flowers later on the Wednesday morning.

A great deal hinged on the flowers. If Jimmy Robinson and Pat Molloy had played a part in the robbery of Yew Tree Farm, they must have busied themselves as soon as they left the California pub with meeting their fellow conspirators and getting to the scene of the crime. They did not have time to buy a bunch of flowers and return, at about half past three as Mrs Collins suggested, to Carol's flat. Moreover, if the flowers had been bought by Robinson that Tuesday afternoon, the whole of the rest of his and Carol's story about his movements that afternoon – their sleep together in bed and getting up for *Star Trek* – was likely to be true too.

There was one obvious place where immediate checks could have been made to establish the truth about the flowers. R.A. Lock's greengrocers stands immediately opposite the California pub, in a row of shops. In 1978, Mr Lock tended another shop close to the centre of the city. His shop in Weoley Castle was staffed by two women.

It was, surely, routine for the police to make inquiries at Lock's to establish whether either of their suspects could be recalled by the people serving in the shop; or if they had any way of remembering the dates at which the two men did (or did not) buy flowers.

The police, however, *did not make any inquiries at the shop*. Neither of the two women who were serving in the shop at the time were interviewed until the late summer of 1979. Mrs Yvonne Hall-Annieson was in charge of the shop. She was interviewed for the defence on 9 July 1979. In her statement then, she said that she could not, of course, remember, over a period of ten months, who had come to the shop on a day the previous September. Surprisingly, however, she said she had *never been seen by the police* at any time until then. When I interviewed her in her spacious house in Barnts Green in January 1986, she was adamant that no police had made inquiries at the shop at any time before the defence solicitor came to see her. 'It would have caused a stir,' she said. 'People would have talked about it.' Nothing of the kind happened.

Not many days later, in January 1986, Ann Whelan, Michael Hickey's mother, tracked down the other woman serving in the shop – Mrs Adrienne Whitehouse, who still lives in Weoley Castle. Mrs Whitehouse too said that she had not been seen by the police after the murder. Like Mrs Hall-Annieson, she was not interviewed until July 1979, eight months after Robinson was taken into custody. Indeed, she didn't know until seven years later that the shop had had any relevance to the Carl Bridgewater murder. Exasperatingly she added: 'What a pity! I'm sure I would have remembered what happened on 19 September. It's my wedding anniversary.'

When Staffordshire police charged Jimmy Robinson for the murder of Carl Bridgewater, then, they had in their possession strong evidence that Robinson had spent the afternoon of 19 September 1978 exactly where he said he was – at the California public house, and in Carol Bradbury's house and bed. Four women backed that story in official statements: Carol Bradbury, Vi Collins, Yvonne Hards, and Susan Bennett. The statements of two of these – Vi Collins and Yvonne Hards – were 'starred'; the defence were not allowed to see them.

What about the inquiries for the defence? The burden of the work of confirming the alibis of Jimmy Robinson and Pat Molloy fell on an enthusiastic and hard-working solicitor called Tony Fryer.

Tony Fryer came into the case because he represented John Burkett. He went to see Burkett in the cells of Bromsgrove police station on 9 December 1978, the day after Burkett had been arrested for the Tesco robbery, and was being interrogated about the Bridgewater murder. Burkett mentioned to Tony Fryer that his friend Jimmy Robinson, who had been arrested for the same offences, badly needed a lawyer. Tony Fryer didn't see Jimmy Robinson until 12 December – six days after Robinson was first arrested. At once, in some relief, Jimmy asked Tony Fryer to represent him, and told him of his harrowing experiences the previous week.

Tony Fryer was from the outset entirely convinced that his new client had nothing to do with the Carl Bridgewater murder. He had dealt with many guilty criminals, and was well-accustomed to the devious ways in which they sought to hide the facts from their lawyers. Robinson behaved quite differently. From the first interview he was completely frank. He admitted the Chapel Farm and Tesco robberies without a tremor. But he denied the Yew Tree Farm murder with consistent and passionate intensity.

Mr Fryer's early certainty about Jimmy's innocence was reinforced when he met Carol Bradbury. She told him she was quite convinced that Jimmy had nothing to do with the newspaper boy's murder. At once, both in informal conversation and in formal statements, she told Fryer what she had originally told the police: that Jimmy Robinson had collected her from the hospital, had taken her home, gone to the pub, and, exhausted from the previous night's robbing, had spent most of the afternoon asleep in her house. Pat Molloy had been with him. Of this she was certain. How and why Molloy could have made his confession was a mystery to her – and to Tony Fryer.

Gradually, over the following months, Tony Fryer pieced together the details of his client's alibi. He took a long statement from Carol Bradbury which was almost identical with the statements she had given the police. To Fryer, however, she said she was certain that Jimmy had bought her the flowers on the afternoon she came out from hospital – the Tuesday.

Tony Fryer talked at length to Tracey, Carol's eldest daughter, who was then twelve years old. He was struck by her self-assurance and by the clarity of her memory. On 25 May 1979 he took a full witness statement from Tracey, the crucial part of which went like this:

I remember Mum coming in and sitting down in the chair next to the fire. Jim went upstairs and got a blanket and came down with it and put it over her. He more or less put her to bed in the chair by the gas fire. I don't remember much about that morning, except that I do recall Jim and Pat going out again.

I remember that I went to the Post Office for Mum. I took Michelle in the pram and I went to the Post Office to get the family allowance. I would think this would be just before 12 o'clock because the Post Office closes then. I think I also got some stamps for Mum.

When Michelle and I came back, Jim and Pat were still not there then. They'd gone out before I'd gone to the Post Office and hadn't come back by the time I'd returned.

Mum cooked the lunch. In fact, she was up and about when I got back from the Post Office. I think she'd been up and had a bath. I had my lunch and Michelle had a bit. I don't think Mum had any lunch. At this stage Pat and Jimmy were still out.

I remember Pat and Jimmy coming back at about three o'clock. This was quite usual because I think the pub closes about three, and then they'd just come home and have lunch. They'd always have lunch after we'd had ours.

I remember that Mum had gone up to bed for a rest after lunch and that Jim's and Pat's lunches were in the oven. I was sat in the living room watching the TV and Michelle [Carol and Jim's baby daughter] was having a sleep. I think she'd gone upstairs with Mum.

I do remember Mum coming down before Jim and Pat had their lunch because Jim asked me where Mum was and I told him 'up in bed'. I saw he'd got some flowers, and he went up to her. I remember Jimmy had some flowers in his hand, and Pat had got some spring onions that he was carrying. Mum came down after Jim had gone up and put their lunches out for them. She stayed down for a bit, and then went back to bed. After lunch Jim and Pat sat in the living room and I think Jim went to sleep first.

I stayed in that afternoon watching TV. Pat and Jim didn't go out again as far as I remember. I remember Mum calling me upstairs and asking whether Jimmy was coming up. I went back down and Jim was still asleep. I woke him up and told him what Mum had said and he then got out of the chair and went upstairs. He was at that time sat in the chair nearest the fire the one in the corner, and Pat was in the chair next to him.

After Jim had gone upstairs, I came back to the living room and sat on the sofa watching TV again. Pat was sat in a chair. He had been awake for a bit, and then fallen asleep in the chair. I don't remember whether Pat stayed asleep in the chair all afternoon, or whether he went up to sleep in his room.

I can remember Mum and Jim getting up at about 7 o'clock in the evening. I recall Michelle crying upstairs about twenty minutes before that but I think Sonia [Carol's second daughter] may have gone up and brought down the baby.

I remember Mum getting up and also Jim getting up. I would say this was about 7 o'clock because I was watching *Star Trek*. Jim came down and watched the programme till the end, and Pat came down about fifteen minutes after him and Mum. I think he came in the lounge and watched the TV.

This statement confirmed in almost every detail what Carol and Jimmy had told Tony Fryer. The solicitor warned everyone concerned not to put too much on Tracey's statement. The prosecution would make out that she had been instructed by her mother and by Jimmy Robinson to corroborate the story, and the evidence of a twelve-year-old girl would be treated by the court with caution. But Tony Fryer himself was impressed by Tracey's statement. He knew she had *not* been browbeaten into saying anything.

Spring onions, for instance, had not been mentioned by either adult – but Tracey remembered them. On a visit to Jimmy in prison shortly before she made the statement, Tracey Humphreys found herself leading the conversation about the day her mother came out of hospital. On 27 May, after the visit, Jimmy wrote to Carol: 'Cal, I've thought hard about what Tracey said regarding that day, and she is dead right. Pat did get a bundle of spring onions and was eating them going down the road. He got them while I was paying for your flowers – fancy Tracey remembering that. I remember laughing at him as he ate them.'

When Tracey made her statement, it was sent to Robinson in Winson Green. At once (on 31 May) he wrote back: 'I read Tracey's statement and it's marvellous. She had put it all so plainly and verified all of what we know to be true.'

Nor was Tracey's the only statement which had been sent that week to Jimmy Robinson. Violet Collins had also come forward. She insisted that her story should also be made available to the defence.

Mrs Collins' statement to Tony Fryer, dated 21 May 1979, said she was twenty-seven and lived at Weoley Castle with her six-year-old daughter Samantha. It went on:

> The police have been to see me on numerous occasions at my flat, particularly over the Christmas period of 1978. They are in fact saying that I sold the silverware [from Yew Tree Farm] because Pat Molloy had told them it had been given to me to get rid of. According to them, Pat had also told them that if they searched my flat they would find the silverware in the wardrobe.
>
> In fact the police never searched my flat, that was the stupid thing about it. I never even had a wardrobe.

Mrs Collins said the police had been to her about a month previously and had said that if she would lead them to the silver from Yew Tree Farm they would get her out of all the trouble she was in. She didn't know of any trouble she was in, and took the remark as a threat. However, as she didn't know of any silver, there was nothing she could do to help the police.

She went on to say that some time during the summer her daughter Samantha had stayed with Carol, Jimmy and Pat at 35 Wolston Croft:

> They looked after her very well. For this reason I can't believe that

either Pat or Jimmy would be involved in the murder of this young boy. I know Jimmy loved kids. I've seen him with his own little girl, Michelle; also Carol's two girls, and later on the boys when they came back to live with Carol, having been living with their father in Ireland. I have also seen him with my little girl Samantha and in fact she used to run to him for him to pick her up when she saw him in the street.

One day sometime last September I was hanging out some clothes on the balcony soon after Carol came out of hospital but I don't really know when she did come out of hospital.

I had spoken to Pat and Jimmy on the Sunday and they had told me that Carol was in hospital again.

I did not see Jimmy or Pat or even Carol the next day, which was the Monday, but the day after that, which must have been the Tuesday, I was hanging the washing out when I saw Jimmy on his own walking down the road towards his flat from the direction of the shops on the main road at Barnes Hill. I called down to him jokingly: 'You needn't have brought me any flowers'. He looked up and laughed and said they were for Carol. I asked how she was, and he said she was all right, and carried on walking to his flat. If I remember right, the bunch of flowers in his hand were red and yellow. Jimmy didn't stop and have a chat. He just carried on walking round to his flat and shouted up to me in answer as he went by.

I would say this was about between 3.30 p.m. and 3.45 p.m. that afternoon, just before my little girl got home from school with another little girl from nearby, the school finishing at 3.30 p.m.

When I spoke to the police I wasn't sure whether it was the Tuesday or the Wednesday when I had seen Jimmy with the flowers, and I think this is what I said to the police.

If I recall correctly in fact, I told the police it was the Tuesday, but they said that in fact it wasn't and that it must have been the Wednesday, and not the Tuesday. For this reason because of them talking to me in that way and keeping on about it being the Wednesday and not the Tuesday, I can't remember what I said in my statement to them.

Mrs Collins was ready to go to court to give evidence in line with this statement. In Winson Green prison, Jimmy Robinson was delighted. He wrote to Carol on 27 May: 'Also I read Vi's statement and she *does* admit to the episode of the flowers when she was on the balcony. She also admits that the police continually tried to drum it in to her that it was Wednesday and *not* Tuesday that I had the flowers.'

Tony Fryer did not know it, but there was one small discrepancy between Mrs Collins' statement to Tony Fryer and her statement to the police. To the police she had described the flowers as 'red and white'; to Fryer as 'red and yellow'. Moreover, in her statement to Fryer she said that Jimmy was walking on his own, while Robinson said he had come back with Pat Molloy. Robinson has said since that Molloy was walking on ahead of him – had turned the corner, and was out of sight of the balcony.

Worse, however, was Mrs Collins' vagueness about the date. As far as Mr Fryer knew, it was quite possible that Jimmy Robinson had bought Carol the flowers on the day *after* she came out of hospital – 20 September. Violet Collins' statement on its own, though it appeared to support the alibi, was open to the charge that she had seen Jimmy with the flowers on a different day.

A few days later, Tony Fryer saw Susan Bennett, Carol's friend and neighbour. She gave him a long statement which was very similar to the statement she had given the police. She described how Carol had come to her flat on the evening of the 19th, but her statement did not include the conversation she had had with Carol about Jimmy bringing flowers back from the pub. However, the statement said, she had gone to Carol's house 'first thing' on Wednesday the 20th, the day after the murder. The statement continued: 'That morning when I was in the flat, I saw some flowers. There were some orange-goldy and some yellow chrysanthemums and also white, yellow and pink gladioli. They were mixed up together, but were in two vases. One vase was by the window and one was on the sideboard as you came in by the door.'

This confirmed what she had told the police, that Carol mentioned two sets of flowers which Jimmy had brought her on the day she came out of hospital, the day of the murder, one in the morning and one when he came back from the pub. They were still in the house early the next morning. Obviously, these flowers could not have been bought on the Wednesday afternoon. So Susan Bennett's statement strongly suggested that the flowers which Vi Collins had seen in Jimmy Robinson's hand in the afternoon were bought on the Tuesday and were being carried home at a time which made it impossible for Jimmy to have gone to Yew Tree Farm in time to murder Carl Bridgewater.

Tony Fryer took one more statement about the bunch of flowers. On 9 July 1979, as we have seen, he interviewed Mrs Yvonne Hall-Annieson. She agreed that she had been serving in the shop on 19 September the previous year. Not surprisingly, though, she could not remember anything at all about a sale of flowers (or of spring onions) ten months previously.

Tony Fryer had almost covered the same ground as the police in following up the 'flowers' alibi. He had statements, as the police did, from Carol Bradbury, and Vi Collins and Susan Bennett. These were supported by Carol's daughter, Tracey. Tony Fryer never saw Yvonne Hards, because he never knew she had anything to say about the flowers, nor was there any reason why he should. Her statement to the police, which offered such crucial confirmation that the flowers were in the flat on the morning after the murder, was 'starred', and therefore not available.

As the trial drew close and Mr Fryer consulted more frequently with James Pyke, the junior barrister representing Robinson, what was the position about the alibi? Robinson's story, outlined in his alibi notice which was submitted in June, was that he had been out robbing a Birmingham butcher all night on the 18th/19th. This was not challenged. After selling the stolen goods in the early morning market, he and Molloy had collected Carol from the hospital. They had brought her back, and gone to the pub at lunchtime. On the way back from the pub they had bought some flowers. When they got back, they had had their lunch and gone to sleep, Pat in his chair in the living room, Jimmy in bed beside Carol upstairs. They had got up at about seven, watched the end of Star Trek, and gone out to the pub again.

This was well supported, and accepted by the prosecution, until the point when the two men left the pub at about 3 p.m. After that, it was supported for the defence by Carol Bradbury, her daughter Tracey, Susan Bennett and Violet Collins. Carol Bradbury and Tracey fully expected to be called to the witness box. Though Jimmy Robinson and Tony Fryer warned them that they would get a rough ride, mother and daughter were not too worried. 'We were telling the truth,' Carol says now. 'We knew we couldn't really be shaken from that.' (Interview with me, 27 May 1984.) Tracey nodded in agreement.

The lawyers were not so sure about Mrs Collins – but she too was warned that she might be called, and she too, as she said in her statement to Tony Fryer, was ready and willing to give evidence. Susan Bennett was a prosecution witness because Jimmy Robinson's gun had been hidden in her flat. So she was certain to be called.

Meanwhile, what was Pat Molloy saying? On 10 December he made his fateful confession. For the next eight days, as we have seen, the police tried unsuccessfully to get him to support it with facts which only a culprit could have known. Throughout all this period, the wretched Molloy begged for a lawyer. He knew no lawyers, and had no access to any of his friends who might get him one. Finally, on 17 December, nine days after his arrest, the police themselves contacted Argyle's – a solicitors' practice in Tamworth. On 18 December John Wiggall, a partner in the firm, went to Wombourne to interview his new client. Mr Wiggall knew the position was bad. His client had made a statement only eight days earlier in which he had confessed to his involvement in one of the worst crimes in the area's history. He had provided details in his statement and signed it.

Yet as soon as Pat Molloy was introduced to his solicitor, and as soon as the preliminaries were completed, the Irishman declared roundly that he had had nothing to do with the Yew Tree Farm robbery or the murder, and had made up the confession to get the police off his back and in indignation at being named by Vincent Hickey.

Patrick Molloy was utterly consistent about this from that moment. He never wavered, and no one who met him or heard from him got a different story from him. The statement he made to his lawyers before the trial reflected exactly what he said on that first meeting with Mr Wiggall on 18 December, and continued to say ever afterwards.

It started with an unequivocal denial: 'I have been charged with the murder of Carl Bridgewater on the 19th September 1978, and also with a burglary at Yew Tree Farm on that date. I deny any involvement whatsoever in either of these alleged offences.'

It ended, equally certain: 'I was not responsible for the murder of Carl Bridgewater and was not involved in any burglary at Yew Tree Farm on 19th September 1978. I do not know who was responsible.'

In between were twenty pages of detail of Molloy's life and experience in the period leading up to and following 19 September 1978. On that day, he had, he said, got up early to sell stolen meat with Jimmy Robinson. He had gone with Jimmy to pick Carol up at the hospital, returning home partly by stolen car, partly by bus, at about 11.30:

> At about 11.30 a.m. or shortly thereafter Jim Robinson and I left to go to the California public house. Robinson was going to meet John Burkett to give him part of the proceeds of the meat job. I think we would have got to the California at about 12.00 and I remember we saw John Burkett and the missus.
>
> I remained in the pub until about 2.50 p.m. Then I left with Jimmy Robinson to go back to Wolston Croft. We were walking, and visited a florist's shop on the way home to get some flowers for Carol. We got back to Wolston Croft at about 3.00 and Carol was in bed. The eldest daughter Tracey had put the dinner out for us. We had this, and then Jim went up to bed also.
>
> After I had had my dinner, I stopped in an armchair watching TV and probably dozing until I went out with Carol Bradbury's daughter Tracey at about 4.20 to 4.30 p.m. At this time I think Jimmy Robinson was still in bed. I do not think that he could leave the house without my knowing it. I was out with Tracey for about half an hour or so visiting local shops and I think that I bought some comics for her. We returned to Wolston Croft at about 5.15-5.30 p.m. I remained there until I went back to the California public house at about 7.00 p.m.

Pat Molloy's story fitted Jimmy Robinson's and Carol Bradbury's.

With the small exception of the half-hour visit to the shops, it was also supported by Tracey Humphreys. As we have seen, there was at least one witness in the California public house who supported it.

Why then, on 9 December, had he told a quite different story to the police in which he implicated himself, his friend and two others in a horrible murder?

To this question his statement addressed itself again and again, at length:

> The statement that I made to the police on the 10th December 1978 is not a true statement although I admit I made it. I am not saying this because I am frightened. I made the statement because of the pressure put on me and in particular because I was shown a statement by Vincent Hickey implicating me in something that I was not involved in. . . It stated that he [Vincent Hickey] was at the farmhouse and was the driver. It said that Jimmy Robinson and myself were with him. The statement did not mention the shooting as far as I can remember. It was that Vince drove the vehicle and that me and Jimmy Robinson were there.
>
> As far as I am aware, the blue Cortina does not exist, and I repeat that the statement is not true. It is one that I made up, and there is nothing in there that is the truth. I think that there may have been a van at the Dog and Partridge at some time. The details in the statement are invented out of my own head together with things that the police have told me. I have not been threatened by anyone.

To his great relief, Pat Molloy was able to make the same points to someone else. Soon after he was charged (on 28 December), he was moved to Leicester prison, where he was kept away from the other three defendants for the entire ten months to the trial. On 16 January 1979, a few days after he settled in at Leicester, he got a friendly letter from Carol Bradbury. Carol wanted to know why he had made a statement implicating Jimmy Robinson in a murder she knew they could not have committed. She had not written to him or communicated with him before that, so Molloy's reply was his first chance to explain his behaviour:

> Dear Carol,
> I have received your most welcome letter of the 15th January. What I am about to write here to you is the truth.
> Now the reasons why I made the statement to the police were because, first, the police showed me a statement made by Vince Hickey stating that me and Jim were at that farm where the lad was shot, I knew that was not right, because we were not there. As you

know we were in the house with you all the time, and were seen there by other people in your house. I was very upset about that statement mentally.

I made that statement to the police to try and get the *truth out of Vince Hickey*. I know now it was a mad thing to do. I am deeply sorry for involving Jim like that. God forgive me, I did not expect this to happen. I was very upset from days and nights of continual questioning, and made that untrue statement. My solicitor knows all about what I have done. (Molloy's emphasis.)

In the rest of the letter, Molloy (whose memory seems to have been sharper than anyone else's) asked Carol if she remembered coming out of hospital, going home on the bus, and his visit to the shops with Tracey – all just as he had outlined it to his solicitor. Carol wrote again, at once, reminding him of the flowers, and Pat wrote back recalling the visit to the flower shop. 'I believe I gave Jim £1 towards the cost,' he wrote.

On 10 February, Molloy wrote again to Carol Bradbury:

I realise how serious this has got to now, especially for me and Jim. But tell him not to despair as all of us will be proven innocent of this. . . You know where we were all that day, also your daughters. I am very relieved that you will stick up for us, and not fall into the trap that I did. Tell the truth, and nobody can counteract it.

Tell James I will take him for that walk and I will walk the legs off him; also that I will run him down the green hill if he gives me twenty yards start. Give my love to all the kids, especially Michelle.

The correspondence abruptly stopped. Molloy's contact with his other defendants was limited to their brief appearances in court on remand, when strict silence was enforced. Despite his pleas, Carol Bradbury was not allowed to visit Molloy. She showed his letters to Jimmy Robinson, who was not impressed. He wrote to her on 25 May: 'As you say, darling, he can apologise and vow his repentance till he's blue in the face for the terrible stupid lies he's told, but doesn't mean a thing. It's the jury he's got to convince.'

When the four men were committed for trial at Wombourne Magistrates Court on 15 May, there was more time to talk. Robinson reported to Carol in a letter dated 26 May: 'When they were reading the bullshit in court, P.M. was muttering "dirty, rotten liars"; as though he was a paragon of virtue. Maybe he'd forgot it was his own fucking lies that put me in in the first place. I'd love to know what sort of a brain pattern (if any) he'd showed during his psychoanalysis as his upper story is definitely lacking something.'

Despite these very understandable reactions, Pat Molloy continued to try to repair the damage done by his confession. In June, his lawyers formally submitted a notice of alibi, declaring that Molloy had been in Carol Bradbury's house at the time of the murder. The purpose of such alibi notices is to alert the prosecution to any alibi the defendants may be claiming, so that it can be properly checked. A notice in almost exactly similar terms was lodged in the name of James Robinson.

Mr Wiggall was by now working closely with Mr Fryer. Both men had good reason to be reasonably optimistic about their clients' alibi. Carol Bradbury remembers that Mr Wiggall was 'really chuffed' after she gave him a statement in Tony Fryer's office. The two men's alibi *was* supported by Carol, Tracey and Vi Collins. It was not cast iron, but the witnesses were ready and willing to go to court.

Vincent and Michael Hickey

By curious coincidence, the same sort of events led to the same sort of alibi claimed by the other pair of defendants, Vincent and Michael Hickey. They claimed they had been together for most of the crucial afternoon; that they could remember the date because of events proved by documents; and that there were witnesses who would support their story in court.

When the Hickeys were first arrested, neither could say where they were on 19 September. Vincent Hickey had started by saying he had done the murder with Robinson and Molloy. When he switched stories, suddenly denying any involvement, he refused to help any of his interrogators with any information about where he'd been on the 19th.

Michael Hickey, as we have seen, was arrested later and had had time to think about the Bridgewater affair, and about his alibi. The first question he was asked – by Detective Sergeant Brian Harrison – was where he had been on the 19th. 'That's a long time ago,' replied the teenager, cautiously.

Sergeant Harrison then told his suspect that Dave Waller's baby had been born on the 19th. At once, Michael replied: 'I know, I was in the Dog and Partridge till 4 o'clock. . . I stopped and had some afters. I got a taxi to my mother's house. I had a cup of tea with the taxi driver and got changed. I then went to Karen's. We had an argument. I got the same taxi back to the Dog and Partridge. We got there about 6.30.'

Unhappily for Michael, this had all happened – but not on the 19th.

Two days later, the police proved it. Sergeant Leek, in another interview, told Michael he didn't believe the taxi story and was able to prove it was false. At once Michael replied: 'It must have been another day

116

then. . . I wish I could remember, because I was not at the farm. It is nothing to do with me.'

In the cramped cells of Brockhill Remand Centre all through the bitterly cold January of 1979, Michael racked his brains, trying to sort one day from another. It was a miracle that Dave Waller's party had been on that day. But the police were telling him he had left the pub at about 3.0 p.m. What had he done then?

In February, he was charged with the Carl Bridgewater murder. He joined his cousin Vincent and Jimmy Robinson in Winson Green prison. All three were banged up in their cells for twenty-three hours out of twenty-four. The only occasion for talk was in the hour set aside for exercise (often abandoned because of the cruel weather). On the few occasions the cousins were allowed to exercise together, they could not help each other with their whereabouts on the day of the murder.

They were rescued by Vincent's girlfriend, Linda Galvin. Linda visited Vincent in Winson Green as often as she could. One day in late February she reminded him that 19 September was the day her new furniture suite had been delivered. She had, she said, told the police who now held the records from Hardy's, a Birmingham furniture store. Sure enough, as though by another miracle, the suite *had* been delivered on the afternoon of the 19th.

The cousins were delighted. Both at once remembered that they had been in Linda's flat on the afternoon the suite had been delivered. Michael remembered spilling his egg, chips and beans all over it.

At some stage before the committal proceedings in May, the cousins reminded each other of an incident which had happened on the afternoon the new suite was delivered. Stephanie Galvin, Linda's thirteen-year-old daughter, came home from school and took the household's washing to the launderette. When she returned she remarked that there was a pair of stand-up ashtrays in the ironmonger's shop round the corner, which would go nicely with the new suite. Vincent told her to go and find out how much they were. When she came back with the news that they cost just under £5 each, Vincent fished out a fiver and sent Stephanie off to buy one. She returned with it, and proudly set it in place beside the settee.

It was not every day that Vincent Hickey had fivers to throw around. The incident with the fiver set both the cousins on another track, reminding them of more that had happened on the murder afternoon.

They had been looking for cars. That morning, they recalled, they had borrowed a red car belonging to Alan Murray who was staying at Linda's, to go to Bromsgrove where they were paid £400 for a roofing job. They divided the money and drove back to Birmingham to look for a secondhand car. At Terry's Garage, Selly Park, Michael fancied a Cortina and filled in the hire purchase forms in the name of Higgins. He was told that an application would be made to the hire purchase company. The couple left for the Dog and Partridge.

Vincent was looking for Joe Hickey, who wasn't at the Dog, so he went on to Joe's home. Michael stayed in the pub to join in the celebrations for Dave Waller's newborn child. At about three o'clock Vincent returned, still driving Alan Murray's car, and he and Michael left the pub.

They left the party early because they still wanted to buy a car before the money ran out. They stopped at a couple of garages on the way back to Linda's, and had a long look at a row of cars at Bristol Road Garage, just down the road from Linda's. They went back to Linda's to check whether they could trade her car for one of the ones they fancied at Bristol Road. After admiring the new suite and buying the new ashtray, they set off again, in Linda's car, to Bristol Road Garage, Northfield, not five minutes' drive away.

They were met there by the proprietor, a Greek called Andrew Zannetos. He test-drove Linda's car, and was not satisfied it would make a fair exchange for the Rover they wanted. He was prepared, he said, to take the 1100 in part exchange for a pink Marina, which was the cousins' second choice. The proprietor promised to apply to his finance company for the hire purchase loan.

Vincent Hickey handed over £50 cash as a deposit and filled in the forms, using the name James Galvin. If the finance company agreed, said Mr Zannetos, the couple could come back, fill in the remaining forms, take on the hire purchase commitment, and swap the cars. The couple drove back to Linda's, arriving after five. After egg and chips (spilled on the new suite), Michael and Vincent separated. Michael got a lift from Alan Murray to the Dog and Partridge. As they passed the Bristol Road Garage, Michael pointed out the pink saloon that Vince was going to buy.

This was the story which, without much difficulty, and without much deviation, the cousins independently told their lawyers. If true, of course, it was a complete alibi to the Carl Bridgewater murder. The purchase of the ashtray and the payment of a deposit for the car were incidents which involved other people. Could they be corroborated?

The most important witness was Linda Galvin. She had been interviewed almost weekly by the police since her arrest for the Chapel Farm deception in December.

It was her evidence, and that of Alan Murray, which had incriminated Vincent Hickey over Chapel Farm. On 30 January she was convicted of deceiving the old people at Chapel Farm with the lies about the coal, put on probation and ordered to pay £200 compensation. She told the police, as she told Vincent in prison, that her new suite had been delivered on 19 September. They questioned her closely about Vincent's

118

movements on that day, and she could not remember. But as the interviews progressed, she seemed to become more and more certain that
neither Vincent nor Michael had come home during the afternoon.
Alan Murray, she remembered, had gone to hospital for a chest X-ray.

'I was at home when Alan returned,' she said, 'because I remember
making him a cup of tea and he then went to bed. I don't remember what
time it was that he returned but I don't think he was away for long.
Neither Vinny nor Michael returned to my flat during the morning or
afternoon of Tuesday 19th September, 1978.' She could not remember
what time Vinny did return, or whether Michael was with him. Nor
could Alan Murray, who was in bed in a back room. Murray, however,
said in a statement that he could remember Vincent coming back to the
flat about 6.00 p.m.

Linda's statements were amalgamated into a main one, which she
signed on 22 February. The police saw her as a useful prosecution witness. She was living with Vincent Hickey and she could testify that he
had not come back to the flat all afternoon. They warned her, and her
daughter Stephanie, that they might have to give evidence for the prosecution at the committal proceedings against the four men – at
Wombourne on 15 May.

Linda and Stephanie *were* called to Wombourne for the committal
hearing. George Brown, Vincent's solicitor, insisted on it. In court he
asked both of them, under oath, about something the prosecution had
never heard of. The clerk's record of Linda's answers read like this:

> I have a stand-up ashtray. It was bought to go with the suite. I
> didn't buy it. Vinny bought it. It was bought either that day or the
> day after. The ashtray was delivered after my daughter came home
> from school. My daughter went to fetch it.
>
> He paid Stephanie the money to go out and fetch it. She went
> just round the corner to a hardware shop to buy it. There was an
> accident on the settee with some egg and chips. When the accident
> took place, Vincent and Michael was there. Just the two of them
> and Stephanie; she remembers that. I can't remember if that was
> the day the suite was delivered. It could have been.

When Stephanie was asked about the ashtray, she thought at first that
her mother had bought it. Then she remembered, 'I had a five pound
note to buy the ashtray with,' she told the court. 'I went to buy it with a
five pound note. I can't remember if it was the day the suite was
delivered.'

The defence lawyers were pleased with this evidence since it seemed
to support what the Hickey cousins had told them. An ashtray had been

119

bought. But was it bought on the right day? Linda had told the court: '*It was bought either that day or the day after.*'

The defence lawyers took their time before checking out this vital piece of information. The police did not. After a hurried conference, senior officers sped straight from the court at Wombourne to Northfield to test the 'ashtray' alibi.

That same day, 15 May 1979, Staffordshire police took three statements about the ashtray. None of them were shown to the defence, or saw the light of day for five years.

The police went to Linda Galvin's house, borrowed the ashtray, and took it to the hardware shop round the corner in Westcote Avenue. The proprietress, Pauline Moore, was there. She confirmed at once that an ashtray such as the one shown her by Sergeant Harrison *had* been sold. Two had been delivered to the shop the previous August, and one was still there. She couldn't remember when or how the ashtray had been sold, but she did very little selling anyway. Mrs Valerie Fulford, who had served in the shop the previous September and worked in the afternoons, said she couldn't remember who had bought the ashtray or when.

As for Stephanie Galvin, both women knew her well. Mrs Moore confirmed the girl had started paying money on a Christmas card savings account in the shop on 22 September the previous year, 1978.

Armed with this information, Sergeant Harrison went back to Lower Beeches Road to return the ashtray and to take yet another statement from the twelve-year-old. Stephanie still insisted that she had got the £5 from her mother. She could not remember the day or date she bought the ashtray but felt it might have had something to do with opening her Christmas card account – three days after the 19th. She could not remember coming home from school and seeing the new suite, and ended her statement: 'To the best of my knowledge it was not the same day that I purchased the ashtray.'

On the face of it, these statements did considerable damage to the 'ashtray' alibi which had emerged in Wombourne Magistrates Court. But there was one further, crucial, fact.

Mrs Moore said: 'Both shops are open for business at 9 a.m. till 6 p.m. Monday to Saturday inclusive, *except for Wednesday when we trade from 9.00 a.m. till 1 p.m.*'

Mrs Fulford said: 'The shop closes on a Wednesday afternoon.'

Linda Galvin had confirmed that her daughter had bought the ashtray in the afternoon, after coming home from school. '*It was either that day or the day after*' she had said, on oath at Wombourne. But the shop was closed on Wednesday. Did that not point to the sale of the ashtray on the Tuesday, 19 September 1978, at almost exactly the same time as Carl Bridgewater was being shot at Yew Tree Farm, more than twenty miles away? Perhaps it did, perhaps it didn't. Certainly the police and prosecution did not think it necessary to pass on this information to the defence. Instead they 'starred' the statements of Mrs Moore and Mrs Fulford (and Mr Moore, whom they interviewed the next day), ensuring that they did not fall into the hands of the defence.

It was on 26 June – six weeks later – that Richard Gilkes, Michael's solicitor, went to the shop at Westcote Avenue. He took handwritten statements from Mrs Fulford and Mr Moore. Both told him that opening hours the previous September were from 9 a.m. to 6 p.m. Neither mentioned the early-closing day on Wednesday. Perhaps they were not asked. So the Hickeys' lawyers were never aware of the crucial fact that the ashtray could not have been bought on the Wednesday afternoon.

By the end of March 1979, both Hickeys had told their lawyers that they had visited the showrooms at Bristol Road Garage, Northfield, in the late afternoon of 19 September.

On 31 March, Richard Gilkes for Michael Hickey went down there himself, and spoke to the proprietor, Andrew Zannetos. Mr Gilkes asked if there was any record of a transaction the previous September with a man calling himself James Galvin, and giving an address in Lower Beeches Road. Mr Zannetos returned with a document which proved that a man who had given Linda Galvin's address *had* called the previous September and paid a £50 deposit on a Morris Marina; £40 of the deposit had been paid back a few days later.

Infuriatingly, the document had no date on it. Mr Zannetos went on to explain, however, that he would certainly have passed Mr Galvin's request for hire purchase facilities for the Marina to the General Guarantee Corporation in central Birmingham, with whom he dealt.

At General Guarantee, Mr Gilkes found further proof that his client's story might be true. The clerk who dealt with proposals for finance on the telephone, Pamela Massey, showed him the 'day book' in which all these proposals are recorded. Under 19 September there were no proposals recorded from Bristol Road Garage. But on 20 September, there were two proposals. The first name was J. Galvin, the second W.T. Nee. J. Galvin had been interviewed for credit-worthiness on 21 September, and his proposal had been accepted on the 26th – though the deal had never been completed. Mr Nee's application had been accepted within hours of its coming through – on the same day, the 20th.

Mr Gilkes asked Pamela Massey, and her boss, Michael Hurley, about these entries. Both confirmed that the date they appeared in the book need not always be the date they had been received. If a phone call had come the previous day, late in the afternoon, it might have been jotted down on a piece of paper, and not entered in the day book until the next morning. Similarly, Mr Zannetos said that if an application was made late in the afternoon, he would postpone the telephone call about the finance till the following morning. Mr Zannetos had said he closed his showroom at 6.00 p.m. – while the General Guarantee office closed for business at 5.00 p.m. It followed that anyone who tried to buy a car at Bristol Road Garage after five, or near to five, had to wait till the next morning before the proposal could be put to the hire purchase company.

These early enquiries were all good for the Hickeys. In prison, in letters to his grandmother during April, Michael rejoiced at 'good news from Mr Gilkes'. But they were not conclusive. Mr Zannetos had been shown a photograph of Michael Hickey and had not recognised it. He could remember nothing about the transaction the previous September, and had to rely entirely on the documents to prove it happened. At General Guarantee, all the documents about credit-worthiness and others which might help with the precise date and time of the visit to Bristol Road Garage had been destroyed. It was beyond doubt that Vincent Hickey, using a false name, had gone to Bristol Road Garage and tried to buy a car. But there was still the possibility that he'd done so on the day the proposal for the finance was entered in the day book – 20 September, the day after the murder of Carl Bridgewater.

Fortunately for the Hickeys, there was someone else who could help. By a stroke of remarkable luck the Galvin application was accompanied by another. Indeed these two applications, which were recorded together, were the only ones from Bristol Road Garage to the General Guarantee Corporation all that week (and, for that matter, all the week before or the week after). This was the 'W.T. Nee' recorded in the day book, who, Mr Gilkes quickly discovered, was Mr William Mee, who lived in Ivy House Road, Kings Norton.

Gilkes took an (undated) statement from Mr Mee at his home. The young man confirmed he had bought a Ford Consul estate car from Bristol Road Garage the previous September. He collected the car, he said, on Monday, 25 September. He had been to the garage the previous week 'either on a Tuesday or a Wednesday'. He couldn't be sure of the date or time, but *was* sure that he had been at the garage 'definitely later in the afternoon'. He had gone, he said, with his brother Robert.

Once again, the news was good for the Hickeys. For if the Mee brothers had been at the garage late in the afternoon, they must have been there on the Tuesday. They could not have gone on the late afternoon on the Wednesday, as their proposal could not then have been accepted by the credit agency on the Wednesday – as it was. So if the Mees went to the garage on the Tuesday afternoon, and their transaction was recorded on the Wednesday, the same probably happened to the Hickeys – especially as the name Galvin featured *before* that of Mee in the day book.

Was there any clue in the day book at General Guarantee which-pointed to the time of day that the entries were recorded? The first three entries, all in the same handwriting, came from a company called Stirling. These had come in the morning post, which was opened immediately the office was opened at nine o'clock. The next – from Hadley Garage, the single name Singh – was entered in different handwriting to the first three. Then came 'Galvin' and 'Nee' from Bristol Road and A.C. Smith from another garage, which was illegible. Galvin, Nee and Smith were all entered in the same handwriting. The next three names were in three different handwritings.

Clearly, different people were putting entries in the book at different times in the day, and logically they would do so in the order in which the phone calls were received. Certainly, they were not all put in at the end of the day, in one hand, higgledy piggledy, regardless of the order they had been phoned in.

Since Galvin and Nee were the second and third entries after the ones which came in the morning post, and since it was the habit of garage proprietors and dealers to ring through their names from the previous late afternoon and evening as early as possible, everything pointed to the probability that Mr Zannetos had done just that with his two.

If so, it was *most likely* that Vincent Hickey had visited the Bristol Road Garage at almost exactly the same time as Carl Bridgewater was being shot at Yew Tree Farm near Wordsley.

Mr Gilkes passed on the names of Zannetos, Massey, Hurley and Mee to the prosecution. The police acted at once. On 3 April (three days after Mr Gilkes' first visit to Bristol Road Garage) they went to the General Guarantee Corporation. Pamela Massey confirmed to them that she couldn't remember what time of day she got the applications from Galvin and from Mee. 'I would say,' she concluded, 'that these two applications were received by me during the morning of Wednesday, 20 September 1978, rather than during the afternoon.'

On 10 April police interviewed William Mee who gave them a much longer and more detailed statement. He said he had travelled with his brother to look for a car, which he wanted by that weekend (23/24 September). They had called at the garage, he estimated, at 4.15 p.m. and had stayed for about an hour. He was not certain of the day, though he felt it was the Tuesday.

On 14 May police went to see Robert Mee, who filled in a few more details. He told police that he and his brother were not the only people in the car. Paul and Gayle Wyton, a young married couple who lived in the same road, had travelled with them in William's orange Mini. 'My brother was looking for a larger car,' he explained. He too said in his statement that the four had travelled from home to the garage, as though they had gone there directly. Since William left work at 3.30, Robert estimated the time of their arrival at Bristol Road Garage vaguely at '4 p.m. to 5 p.m.'. They stayed there about half an hour, and left in a hurry, he said, because Gayle Wyton wanted to get to the shops before they closed at six.

The defence never knew that there were two other important witnesses – Paul and Gayle Wyton – who were at the Bristol Road Garage on the afternoon of the murder. The police interviewed the couple at length on 9 July (Paul) and 10 July (Gayle). Both these statements were 'starred' – and kept away from the defence.

Paul Wyton estimated the time of the visit in the afternoon at 'around 5 p.m.'

Gayle Wyton, however, remembered the event in greater detail. She said: 'We went to several garages during the afternoon. I recall one in particular being on the Stratford Road.' Stratford Road, Small Heath, is several miles away from Kings Norton where the Mees and Wytons lived.

Despite these visits to several garages, the Mees and the Wytons couldn't find the car they wanted, and set off home. Their route back to Kings Norton took them past Bristol Road Garage. As they went past, Robert Mee noticed a white car of the type they were looking for. They turned at a roundabout and went back to the garage – as a last resort. While William did the paperwork, the other three walked up the road to the insurance office, where they asked about insurance costs. Gayle estimated they were at the garage between 4.30 and 5.00 p.m.

Neither the Wytons nor the Mees saw any other customers at the garage. The Mees, coincidentally, had been at school with Vincent Hickey and were certain he was not at the garage when they were there.

One further witness was not found. From the moment he remembered the visit to Bristol Road Garage, Michael Hickey had spoken of another Greek in the garage with Zannetos. He was 'very large', said Michael, and was related to Zannetos. 'I think it was his father or his grandfather,' he told police and his lawyers.

Neither the police nor his lawyers, however, made any inquiries to follow up this lead. It was not until May 1984 – five years later – when Ann Whelan and I visited the Bristol Road Garage and spoke to Mr Zannetos that anyone interested in the case knew that Mr Zannetos' father, Mr Georgiou, and his father-in-law Mr Tsokalides, had been in Birmingham in September 1978. Both men, Mr Zannetos told me, were accustomed to visit him at the garage, and to sit in the office talking to him. His father, he said, was a short, stocky man, but his father-in-law was large, 'a very big man indeed'. It was, he agreed, highly likely that one of these two men were with him in the office during September

1978. Yet neither Mr Georgiou nor Mr Tsokalides was interviewed by the police or by the defence. No one tested their memories with photographs of Michael and Vincent. By the time we knew that they were possible witnesses to the alibi, it was far too late to test anything.

Indeed, the inquiries of both police and defence lawyers had fallen well short of establishing the truth of what the important witnesses had to say about the Hickeys' alibi. In January 1986, I interviewed William Mee at his home in Tamworth. He told me he had been desperate to change his car that week in September 1978, because he had promised to take his sister Ann and her entire family (husband plus three small children) to their holiday in Weymouth. He wanted a bigger car by Friday, the 22nd, so he was most anxious to clinch the deal as quickly as possible. In the event, he remembered, he had not got the Consul in time for the weekend and had had to cram his sister's family into the Mini for the journey to Weymouth. He'd got the Consul the following Monday, and remembered collecting his sister's family with it. Josiah Parkes, the Birmingham engineering firm where William Mee's brother-in-law works, confirmed to me that their autumn holiday in 1978 started on 22 September.

Robert Mee remembers going to the garage late to buy the car. He remembers the old Greek in the office. He remembers – as did Paul and Gayle Wyton – being asked by Zannetos to move the Mini from the forecourt so that the cars on show could be put away for the night. So the atmosphere of a rush to buy a car was confirmed by all the witnesses. This *proved* only that the Mees and the Wytons were definitely at the garage that Tuesday. It *suggested* that Mr Zannetos was in no doubt that William Mee wanted his car quickly, and that the application to the hire purchase company should be made *first thing next morning*. It suggested, though it does not prove, that Zannetos phoned General Guarantee with Mee's application on the 20th *before doing anything else*. Since he obviously phoned the two names in the order they appeared in the day book – Galvin, Mee – the most likely explanation was that Galvin (Hickey) had visited the garage on the Tuesday afternoon before the Mees got there – a precious alibi for the Carl Bridgewater murder. It was still *possible* that the Hickeys went to the garage and bought their car at the earliest possible moment on the Wednesday morning, but this was, by a long way, the less likely alternative.

As with the 'ashtray alibi', the Hickeys' defence lawyers approached the trial with only half the story. The statements of Zannetos, Hurley, Massey and William Mee all helped substantially to support their clients' alibi at Bristol Road Garage. The support was even greater once the whole picture of the Mees' journey had been painted – by Robert Mee and the Wytons. But this evidence, like that of the hardware shop's early closing, although known to the police, was withheld from the defence. Nevertheless, before the trial started, Mr Gilkes and Mr Brown, the Hickeys' solicitors, could be reasonably happy with their clients' alibi. The documents, and at least four witnesses tended to support the Hickeys' assertions that they were buying a car in a Northfield garage only minutes after the gun went off at Yew Tree Farm.

Both sets of defendants had registered alibis. Both alibis were supported by witnesses. There seemed every reason to hope that the witnesses would convince the jury. As the trial approached, the hopes of all four men were high.

CHAPTER FOUR
Trial

'I am quite satisfied that the trial can be properly and fairly conducted here in Stafford which is accustomed to dealing with trials of importance.' Mr Justice Stephen Brown had this short answer to the pleas of all four defendants to move the Carl Bridgewater murder trial out of the county. Their pleas were heard on 6 July, at Stafford. All four barristers referred to the saturation coverage of the case in newspapers like the Wolverhampton-based *Express and Star* and the *Stafford Chronicle*. They pointed to the local functions to raise money for the Carl Bridgewater kidney fund appeal (a charity which had been patronised by Staffordshire and West Midlands police). Local people felt very strongly about the murder, it was argued, and the defendants stood a better chance of a fair trial elsewhere. The judge disagreed. The trial should go on at Stafford.

Mr Justice Stephen Brown was not a rigid man. Two years later he dealt with a similar application from four Birmingham prison officers accused of beating a prisoner, Barry Prosser, to death. The judge on that occasion made great play of the need of a trial free from local prejudice, and allotted the case to Leicester.

The Bridgewater trial started on 8 October 1979. There was glittering legal talent on display. In the judge's seat was Mr Justice Drake, the presiding judge on the Midlands circuit. As Maurice Drake QC he had made a name for himself at the commercial and criminal bar. He led the highly publicised prosecution of building worker pickets at Shrewsbury in the early 1970s.

The chief prosecutor in the Bridgewater case was one of the country's most senior barristers, Philip Cox QC. He was assisted by another Queen's Counsel, Igor Judge, and W. Coker. Pat Molloy was represented by John Gorman QC and Malcolm Lee; Vincent Hickey by Desmond Hollis QC and Norman Jolly; Michael Hickey by Richard Tucker QC and Richard Wakerley, and Jimmy Robinson by Douglas Draycott QC and James Pyke.

The case started with two days of crucial legal argument; could the robbery at Chapel Farm be used in evidence? The prosecution argued that the fact that three of the defendants had robbed another farmhouse not far from Yew Tree Farm, and had used a sawn-off shotgun there, was one of the reasons (indeed, the central reason) why they had been arrested in the first place. To delete all reference to Chapel Farm, as the defence insisted, would be to remove one of the central planks of the case against the three.

Mr Justice Drake came out clearly against the use of such evidence. Any reference to the Romsley robbery, he said, would prejudice the accused far beyond any advantage to the cause of justice. The prosecution were ordered to alter all the documents (of which there were more than 1,000 pages) so that all references to Chapel Farm were deleted. The defence had won the first round.

It was not until the third day – 10 October – that the jury took their seats, and the prosecution case opened.

The Case for the Prosecution

The Blue Car

The first batch of witnesses were those who had seen a car at or around Yew Tree Farm on the afternoon of the murder.

There were, as we have seen in Chapter 1, many of these, but most of them did not give evidence at the trial. Police inquiries had established that the four defendants were in pubs in Birmingham until three o'clock in the afternoon. So the prosecution did not call on the witnesses who said they had seen a car at or near the farm before 3.25 p.m. – the earliest the four men could possibly have got there.

The jury, therefore, never heard from Robert and Janet Light who had seen a blue car reversing from the farm at 12.25; or from Alfred Bishop who saw what he thought was a blue Vauxhall Viva going down the drive at 1.30; or from Roger Edwards who had seen a man in uniform driving a blue Vauxhall Viva into the farm drive at about 2.50; or from Peter and Joseph Hadley who had seen a blue car parked in the driveway of the farm at shortly before three o'clock; or even from Frank Cogsell who saw a blue car in the drive at 'between 3.30 and 4.30'.

Kathleen Moyle and Nicholas Holden who had seen blue cars near the farm, and had both gone to identification parades to see if they could pick out Jimmy Robinson and Molloy, were not called to give evidence. They had seen the cars too early (Mrs Moyle at 'about 2.40', Holden at 'about 3.00') for Robinson and Molloy to have been in them. Mr Leonard Bick, who had seen a man in the farmyard at 3.15, wasn't called either. *Anyone* who suggested that there was a suspicious car or suspicious person at the farm before 3.25 was not called.

Other witnesses who had seen cars at or around Yew Tree at the very time of the murder were not called either. All these were either sure that the car they saw was *not* an estate car, or were uncertain about it. Margaret Heary had seen the back of a blue car in the farm drive just after passing the newspaper boy in the road – but she couldn't say whether it was an estate or a saloon, and she was not called. Edward Dickens said he'd seen a medium-ranged car – not an estate – in the drive at 4.45 – and he wasn't called. Mrs Geraldine Waldron and her aunt Monica Ellison said they'd seen a dark blue car – not an estate – at the bottom of the farm track at about 4.45 – and they weren't called.

In Chapter 1, we met twenty-four 'sighting witnesses' of cars or people at the farm. Fourteen of these – sixty per cent – did not fit the police case and were not called to give evidence.

Who *did* give 'sighting' evidence? Three witnesses told the court they had seen a blue car parked in the drive of the farm between 3.45 and 4.15. Mrs Gladys Jones, the neighbour who had seen a car backed up against the door of the farmhouse with its boot up, and who noticed it had gone by 4.30, had dropped her early certainty that the car was a Ford Cortina estate. She described it more vaguely as a 'Ford estate'. Fred Edwards said he'd seen a blue car in the farm drive soon after passing the paper boy in the road. Highways inspector Anthony Cross said he'd seen a Ford estate with a roof rack parked in the farmyard at 3.50 as he inspected a footpath notice.

Wendy Stagg said she saw a blue estate at 4.45 with two people in it reversing from the farm; it had stopped in the mouth of the drive while the driver engaged in conversation with another driver. And Terence Phelps said he saw a blue car which he was 'pretty sure' was an estate coming frontwards out of the drive with two or three people in it at about five past five.

Terence Madeley said he saw a *dark green* estate coming out of the drive, but couldn't remember whether it was the day of the murder, or the day before, or four days before. Mario Sabetta said he'd seen a blue estate car parked in Lawnswood Road at about half past three, about 100 yards from the farm. He had also seen two men, one of them carrying what he thought was a shotgun, crossing the road from the back of the car towards the hedge on the farm side. John Mills from Wall Heath said he'd seen a light blue estate car with two men in it driving down the A449 main road near the farm at about the right time. To these, whom we have met before, the prosecution added two other witnesses whom we have not. Both had seen vans in the road some way from the farm. Neither had been considered more than marginal when first interviewed.

So eight witnesses gave evidence to say they had seen a car at the farm at or around the time of the murder. In his summing-up to the jury Mr

Justice Drake invited them 'without hesitation' to conclude that the car was a 'light blue Cortina estate'. Seven of the eight said it was light blue. Seven of the eight said it was an estate. Only two of the eight mentioned the word Cortina, and one of them, Mr Cross, merely said the car was a 'Cortina-type'. So the prosecution hardly proved that the car *was* a Cortina.

Why were they so anxious to do so? Because Vincent Hickey had once owned a blue Ford Cortina estate. That was why he had been taken to Cannock police station a few weeks after the murder.

On that occasion the police let him go. When they arrested him again for the Chapel Farm robbery, the coincidence seemed too strong. Not only had this man robbed a farm in circumstances similar to those at Yew Tree. He also owned a blue Cortina estate.

Or did he? This was an important question at the trial. The prosecution produced two witnesses, both neighbours of Vincent Hickey in the days he'd lived at Badger Close, Redditch.

Mrs Pauline Colverson, the first of the two, was asked by Mr Judge, for the prosecution: 'In the period before he left Badger Close at the end of August, what sort of car did you see him driving?'

Mrs Colverson answered: 'There was a blue Ford Cortina saloon and a Ford Cortina estate.' (*Trial transcript, vol.6, p.14.*)*

Obviously, if Vincent Hickey had been driving a blue Cortina estate at the end of August, it might have been the blue Cortina estate which the prosecution couldn't prove had been at Yew Tree Farm. But when she was cross-examined, Mrs Colverson's story was qualified by doubt:

> Q. 'The suggestion I want to put to you for you to deal with is that the blue car was superceded by a red car. What do you say about that?'
> A. 'There was a red Cortina and a blue Cortina saloon. I cannot remember which way round they were though. . .'
> Q. 'Do you think I may be right in suggesting the red one came after the blue one?'
> A. 'I honestly cannot remember which way round they did come.' (*6.14*)

Mrs Eileen Birch, the other neighbour, was firmer. She told Mr Judge that she and her husband had bought a blue estate in March, and four months after that she had seen another one outside Vincent Hickey's house. She had also seen Vincent driving it. Under cross-examination, she stuck to the story. But when Mr Hollis asked if the car which she'd

---

* Hereafter the volume and page references only are given, e.g. *6.14*.

said she'd seen Vincent driving was 'some visiting vehicle' she said: 'I can't remember now.' (*6.18*)

Mrs Birch's memory was flatly contradicted by Vincent Hickey, and by the other evidence. In December 1977, he said, he had bought a royal blue Ford Cortina estate. A few weeks later, he had parked it on top of a hill so that it would start easily. One frosty morning, a policewoman drove into the back of it, almost writing it off. Vincent had not bothered to claim on the insurance and had sold the car to a Christopher Barron for the price of the engine.

All this was perfectly true, as the police knew well enough. They had taken a statement from their colleague who had had the unfortunate accident. She confirmed everything. Mr Barron agreed that in March or April, at least five months before the murder, he had bought a blue Ford Cortina estate from Vincent Hickey, cut up the body, and retrieved the engine. Mr Barron provided all the documents. There was no doubt about it. The Ford Cortina estate which had led to Vincent's first interview at Cannock had been disposed of long before the murder.

Had Vincent got *another* blue Cortina estate after March? His answer was no. He said he had immediately started to drive a red Cortina, which belonged to his uncle.

This was supported on every side. Linda Galvin, a prosecution witness at the committal proceedings, had said in a statement to police in December 1978: 'When I first met Vinny in August 1978 he had a red-coloured Cortina car, but a short time later, possibly a week, the car disappeared. Vinny told me one of his mates had got the car. After the red Cortina went missing, Vinny used my car which was a beige 1100 car with a black bonnet.'

In another statement (30 December), she said: 'I can't recall seeing Vinny with any Cortina motor car apart from the red Cortina saloon he had when we first met.'

Alan Murray, who was living in the same flat as Linda and Vincent at the time of the murder, said in a statement in February 1979: 'I have never seen Vince or any of his mates with a blue Ford Cortina estate, or any other blue estate vehicle.'

Was there another estate which Vincent could have been driving before he left Badger Close, and which could have been seen by Mrs Birch and Mrs Colverson? Yes, there was. Les Godridge, uncle to the Hickey cousins, had a blue Toyota estate in the early months of 1978. This was often borrowed by Vincent. For some reason, however, Les Godridge was never called at the trial and the truth about the Toyota – which could not possibly have been the murder car – was never told.

The Three Vans
What about the van? Even if he hadn't got a blue Cortina estate at the

time of the murder, perhaps Vincent had a van?

Was there a van at the farm at all? Before Vincent Hickey was arrested on 4 December 1978, none of the prolific police statements or press conferences had mentioned a van. The position was accurately summed up by Detective Sergeant Bob Lessemun when he was interviewing Vincent on 8 December 1978, four days after Vincent's arrest.

This was the key interview when Vincent started to suggest to Sergeant Lessemun and Detective Constable Ivor Millington that he knew what happened at Yew Tree Farm. After about an hour's questioning by the police officers, the conversation went like this:

> Lessemun: 'Just tell us one thing that will show you've got something.'
> Vincent: 'All right, then, there were two motors on it.'
> Lessemun: 'Two?'
> Vincent: 'Yeah, the police didn't know that, did they?'
> Lessemun: 'No, we didn't.'
> Vincent: 'The one was a Ford Cortina – and a blue van.'
> Lessemun: 'We've always known about the blue Cortina estate, but to the best of my knowledge I've never heard of a blue van.'
> Vincent: 'Well, there was, and it had a white roof rack.' [Vincent always insisted that he had said 'white roof' not 'white roof rack'.]
> Lessemun: 'I wonder why that hasn't been clocked then.'
> Vincent: 'It only visited the farm once. It was parked well away.'

Sergeant Lessemun was almost right when he said he'd 'never heard of a blue van'. Certainly, no one had seen two vehicles at the farm. Almost all of those who had seen one vehicle at the farm or coming out of the drive had seen a car, not a van.

After Vincent Hickey's extraordinary revelations, the detectives trawled the 'sighting' statements for any information of a van. They could find *only four people* who had seen a van near the farm on the afternoon of the murder.

As we have seen, two people said they saw a van at the farm.

Mrs Dorothy Southall, some 300 yards up the hill, and looking for what she said was only 'a moment', said she saw a mid-blue vehicle behind the hedge of the driveway of Yew Tree Farm. 'I am certain that it was a van,' she said. 'It was mid-blue in colour, but it looked like a Transit van or something smaller. . .' Mrs Southall said she knew a bit about cars since her husband and her son ran a haulage business. She did not see any other vehicles at the farm. The time, she reckoned, was 4.10 p.m. – when the murderer must still have been at the farm.

On the other hand, the murderer had almost certainly left the farm long before Brian Clarke drove past – at about five past five – in his Range Rover. He reported seeing a medium blue van in the drive, and a man standing beside it. He identified the vehicle at once as an Austin/Morris J4. He too knew about vehicles – and was quite specific about the make.

The police found two other witnesses who said they saw vans outside the farm. Stephen Bridgewater (no relation to the murdered boy) could not remember the date. It might have been the Tuesday of the murder, he said, but it could just as well have been the day before. He remembered a Transit van parked in Lawnswood Drive just five yards away from the entrance to the farm. It was dark blue all over. If he'd seen the car on the Tuesday, the time would have been 4.50 p.m., probably after the murderer had left.

Finally, there was John Wakelam, a steel worker. He had come forward to tell the police in some detail about two cars he'd seen parked in Cot Lane, the road which runs from Kingswinford into Wordsley. After passing these cars, he said, he went on to the junction between Cot Lane and Lawnswood Road, arriving there at about 4.35 or shortly afterwards. As an addendum to his main point, he said:

'As I looked to the right, I seem to remember a vehicle coming from the direction of Yew Tree Farm towards Wordsley. This, I think, was a tatty-looking and dirty light blue van, possibly a Bedford of the type that may have passenger and driver's sliding side doors, the type of Bedford that is sometimes made into a Dormobile. . . The Bedford van that I have mentioned I would describe as ice blue in character.'

The evidence that a van was involved at all, then, was not formidable. Each of the four saw a different make of van: Bridgewater definitely a Ford Transit; Mrs Southall 'like a Transit or something smaller'; Clarke an Austin/Morris; and Wakelam 'possibly a Bedford'. Stephen Bridgewater wasn't at all sure that the Transit he saw was there on the afternoon of the murder (it might have been the afternoon before), and Clarke saw his J4 almost certainly after the murderer left the farm. Mrs Southall's 'certainty' that she saw a van was based on a glimpse of a roof at about 300 yards.

It was not a lot to go on. Perhaps that was why Sergeant Lessemun had never heard that a van *had* been at the farm on the fatal afternoon. But it did leave a few tiny openings. If Vincent Hickey or any of the others *had* any of these vans, could such a van be traced to the murder?

Vincent's statement was followed by a furious and meticulous van-hunt, which enveloped the world of small builders and 'bodgers' in which the Hickey cousins lived.

Fairly soon, the police discovered that Vincent Hickey *had* owned a light blue Transit van, with a white roof. They found this out from Vincent's uncle, Les Godridge, who took them to an address in Perry Barr and pointed out the house where Vincent had bought the van. They established that the van was bought in January or February 1978.

It had not been a happy purchase. Almost as soon as it was bought, the van was stolen. When it was finally recovered and returned to Vincent, it was a write-off. The engine had seized up. Joe Hickey organised the sale of the van – for £10 – as scrap to Kenny Jordan, the brother of Joe's girlfriend. Kenny Jordan collected it from Joe's house one day in August 1978 and towed it to a friend's house, where it stayed a week or two. Then Kenny sold it on to his brother, Philip. In evidence at the trial Philip agreed he had bought the van – which was completely seized up – from his brother in September 1978. He could not be sure whether he had bought it before or after the murder, but was quite clear that the vehicle had not moved for weeks before the purchase.

After plundering the van of any spare parts which could be sold, Philip arranged for it to be towed to a scrapyard, where it was dumped and later cut up.

This light blue van with the white top plainly had not carried anyone to Yew Tree Farm in September 1978.

Was there perhaps *another* blue Transit van with a white roof which could fit the bill? Police interviewed a friend of the Hickey family, John Smith, who lived at the Maypole, South Birmingham. The police found a light blue Transit van outside his house. They made him drive it to Redditch where they inspected it. The car had a black roof, but the roof had originally been white and had been painted over. Was this a case of disguising the guilty car? Was John Smith a guilty man? He was arrested, and held at Wombourne for three days.

At once, John Smith told the police who had sold him the van – several months previously. The seller quickly confirmed that the van roof had been black for months if not years before the murder.

Then John Smith produced documents to show that his van had been out of action in September. He had the receipt for a new cylinder head, and evidence from a scrapyard to show that his van was off the road at the time of the Carl Bridgewater murder. Another van which had looked promising had to be ruled out.

There remained an old blue Bedford van (with a blue roof) which belonged to Joe Hickey, and which was on the road (just) at the time of the murder. Police discovered that this van had been in the charge of a man called Edwin Burke. Burke had gone on holiday for the week 18-25 September, and had left the van at the Dog and Partridge. Joe Hickey had the keys.

It *was* true, then, that Vincent and Michael had access to an old blue Bedford van.

Could the Bedford van have made the journey to Yew Tree Farm on 19 September? Yes, theoretically it could – but there was a problem.

Only one person in all the scores who had seen the vehicles at the farm or near it on the day of the murder had mentioned a Bedford. This was Mr Wakelam, who thought he had seen a 'tatty-looking' Bedford driving along Lawnswood Road at about 4.35 on the afternoon of the murder. Apart from its hesitancy and vagueness, Mr Wakelam's statement presented a further difficulty. It described the colour of the Bedford as 'ice blue'. Joe Hickey's Bedford was not ice blue. It was dark blue, impossible to mistake for ice or anything like it.

The prosecution did not anywhere assert that the Bedford van had gone to Yew Tree Farm. Perhaps they reflected that if the Bedford *had* been the van at Yew Tree Farm it was certainly not seen by three out of the four witnesses who said they saw vans. It could not have been the van seen and described by Mrs Southall or Mr Bridgewater or Mr Clarke. Nor, obviously, was it the van Vincent had mentioned in his 'confession': a blue Transit with a white roof – or roof rack. The most the prosecution would say was summarised by Mr Justice Drake when he said that the Hickeys 'had access' to the Bedford van that day. They *might* have gone to the farm in it, but (with the single extremely slender exception of Mr Wakelam) there was absolutely no evidence that they did.

What were the jury to make of the prosecution evidence about the vehicles seen at Yew Tree Farm?

Mr Justice Drake, in his summing up, concluded: 'From all this you may have no hesitation, although it is a matter always entirely for you, Members of the Jury, in concluding that the farm was raided that day by a number of men, possibly four, and that they went there in two vehicles: one a light blue Cortina Estate, and probably also a Transit or Bedford type of van, and that they arrived at the farmhouse itself shortly before a quarter to four and left by about 4.40 or 4.45.'

If any member of the jury had 'no hesitation' in concluding that, he or she had clearly not been listening to the evidence. Only one trial witness, Brian Clarke, had said he'd seen anyone at the farm itself that afternoon. He'd seen one man only, and that was at least twenty minutes after 4.45, when the judge reckoned that the murderers had gone. None of the other four people (Jones, Cross, Southall, Edwards) who saw a vehicle *parked* at the farm *saw anyone at all*, or could offer any evidence whatever as to the number of people who raided the farm. Mr Sabetta saw two men, one with a gun, in Lawnswood Road at 3.25/3.30; Mr Phelps saw two or three in a car coming out of the drive long after the judge's deadline for the killer(s) leaving. Mr Mills saw two in an estate in the main road. Wendy Stagg, who emerged as a key witness, had seen two cars together at the mouth of the drive – but one of these was a 'plum-coloured' saloon car which no one ever suggested had anything to do with the murder. She thought at the trial that there might have been three men in the blue car (though her original statements were quite definite that there were two). Apart from her evidence, which referred to the mouth of the drive of the farm at the very end of the judge's deadline, *no one saw two vehicles at or near the farm. And no one saw four men there or in the vicinity, either together or separately.*

No one could conclude what the judge invited the jury to conclude 'without hesitation', that the motley, contradictory and unsatisfactory evidence about the sighting of vehicles proved anything at all about the number of people who took part in the raid, or at what time they arrived or left. All that could be concluded was that a blue car, perhaps an estate, was at the farm between 3.45 and 4.30 and that the car almost certainly had something to do with the murder.

Identification

There was no identification evidence against Vincent Hickey. From the moment he was charged, he was advised by his solicitor, George Brown, not to stand on an identification parade, and he did not do so. In a caustic comment to police on the day he was charged, Vincent said: 'My solicitor has told me not to stand in an ID parade. I think he thinks I'm guilty.'

Michael Hickey, on the other hand, was very happy to stand on an ID parade and instructed his solicitor, Richard Gilkes, to co-operate with all arrangements. A parade was organised for Michael Hickey on 23 February 1979 at Cannock police station.

When Mr Gilkes saw the line-up of young men who were to stand with Michael, he was horrified. None of them had beards – yet Michael had a thick beard, both at the time and the previous September. Moreover, Michael was by far the tallest person on the parade. With his height and beard he stood out at once. Mr Gilkes complained to the police officer in charge, DI Wordley, who grumbled that this was 'the best we can do', and had no proposals for finding anyone with a beard. He suggested to Mr Gilkes that Michael shave his beard off. Mr Gilkes strongly recommended him not to do so. His client, he insisted to DI Wordley, looked very much as he had done the previous September, and that was how he should appear on the parade. There was no breaking the deadlock. On his solicitor's advice, Michael refused to take part, and was taken back to Winson Green prison.

Pat Molloy had also agreed immediately to co-operate with any identification parade. In the afternoon of Tuesday, 16 January, a parade was organised in Redditch police station. Eight witnesses were brought to inspect the parade. They were Catherine Moyle, Nicholas Holden, Terence Phelps, Mario Sabetta, Wendy Stagg, John Wakelam, John Mills – all of whom had seen people in or near cars on roads outside Yew Tree Farm.

The parade was conducted quite properly.

Not one of the witnesses picked out Pat Molloy. Nor did any of them say anything to anyone which suggested that Molloy had been in any of the cars they had seen.

Jimmy Robinson, too, immediately agreed to stand on a parade, and urged his solicitor Tony Fryer to do everything possible to co-operate.

The parade was held at Cannock on 23 February, the same day as Michael Hickey's.

The same eight witnesses that had failed to identify Pat Molloy a month earlier walked down a line of twelve men, as Jimmy Robinson shifted his position among them. No one picked him out. Most of the witnesses walked down the line, said 'no', and walked out of the room. One or two of the witnesses asked the parade to turn sideways. Mrs Moyle became greatly interested in one of the men on the parade who was not Jimmy Robinson, but she did not pick anyone out.

Robinson was jubilant. In a letter to Carol dated 27 February, he said: 'None of them picked me out. It gives you a pretty sunny feeling, a feeling of satisfaction that the truth will come out.'

And on 16 March he wrote: 'I've been cleared on ID. I offered myself to any test or ID they ask.'

On 28 March, Tony Fryer brought bad news. Jimmy wrote again on that day to Carol: 'Apparently one of the ID witnesses (a woman) is supposed to have told the police that she recognised me on the parade but was too scared to touch me. . .'

This was true. When the trial came, several months later, the truth was even worse. No less than three of the witnesses who had not picked him out said in court that he did resemble the man they saw near Yew Tree Farm.

The first – the woman mentioned in Jimmy's letter – was the Wordsley teacher, Wendy Stagg.

Immediately after leaving the parade, Wendy Stagg made a statement to the Staffordshire police. 'I was unable,' she said, 'to make a positive identification but the person standing in the line-up third from the right held a great resemblance to the person I saw standing on the pavement outside Yew Tree Farm on Tuesday 19th September 1978. His height, build and general features were similar.'

On 27 February, four days later, Wendy Stagg was visited at her home by senior policemen who took another, more detailed, statement about her experiences in the ID parade. She said:

I then commenced to walk down the line from the left to the right, looking at each man individually. As I did so, I looked further down the line towards the right and my attention was caught by the man standing third from the right, who immediately struck me as being the same man I saw standing outside Yew Tree Farm on Tuesday 19th September. On seeing him, I felt alarmed. . . I felt sure in my own mind that the man I was looking at was the one I saw outside Yew Tree Farm. The reason I didn't touch him was that I felt the weight of responsibility so great that I couldn't bring myself to do it. Consequently, when I was asked by the Chief Inspector if I could identify the man, I answered 'No'. I immediately regretted the decision and realised I couldn't leave without saying something.

As I reached the door . . . I stopped and said: 'I want to say something.' The solicitor who was standing near me said: 'Don't tell me, I'm not a policeman.' The Chief Inspector said: 'Don't say anything, follow me.' I was then taken by him and a solicitor back to the office where I had originally came from. The Chief Inspector asked me in the presence of the solicitor what I wanted to say. I said: 'You told me that I was to be one hundred per cent positive, but how can I be? I think it was the man standing third from the right.'

Miss Stagg repeated this story when she gave evidence at the trial. It was contradicted by Jimmy Robinson's solicitor, Tony Fryer, who gave sworn evidence from the witness box. He described in some detail, from notes made at the time, what happened:

She was reminded she had seen a car parked by the side of the road and that she had seen persons either in the car or around it. She was then asked by the inspector if she would inspect the line-up, to tell him by touching the person or persons if she recognised anybody there that she had seen on the day. We were nearest the doorway when that was said to her and she was led up to the top of the line by the inspector and then commenced to walk slowly down the line back towards me. When she had gone about two or three persons down she asked the inspector if the men could turn half sideways. The inspector asked all the persons there to do so, and they did. She then continued to walk down the line to the end nearest the door where I was stood. She looked back up the line from where she stopped, then she went back up fairly quickly to the top end, again looked down the line and then started coming slowly back down the line towards the door. She got to the end of the line nearest the door, turned to the chief inspector and said: 'No'. He led her to the door, opened it for her, and she went out. The chief inspector rejoined me some two or three yards from the door, and called for the next witness to be called in. There was then some delay before that second witness came in. The chief inspector left the room. (*18.53*)

138

Cross-examined by Mr Cox, Tony Fryer stuck firmly to his story.

'She did not pause in the doorway at all,' he said. 'She went out and the door was closed. She did not say anything at all other than "No".' (*18.55*)

Asked by Mr Judge for the prosecution what her state of mind was when she saw the man third from the right (who was Robinson) Miss Stagg replied: 'One of immediate recognition and familiarity.' (*3.29*)

To Mr Draycott for Robinson she suggested that she had a 'photographic image' of the man at Yew Tree Farm. (*3.29*)

Her certainty had grown with time. In the statement on the day after the murder she said of the man she'd seen by the blue estate car: 'I did not see him too well.' In the statement she made immediately after the parade, she said: 'I think it is the man third from the right.' In the statement she made four days later, she said she was 'quite sure' that the man on the parade was the man at the farm. At the trial this had turned into 'immediate recognition and familiarity', and a 'photographic image'.

One important feature which Miss Stagg had noticed so photographically in her glimpse of the man was his hair, as Mr Draycott found out in cross-examination:

Q. 'Did you see his hair?'
A. 'I did see his hair, yes. He didn't wear a hat.'
Q. 'What colour was it?'
A. 'It appeared to be almost, I would say, a mousy colour, but the sun was shining very brightly that afternoon. There was a glare in the cars, a glare over the hair-style.'
Q. 'What are you saying? Are you saying that because of the conditions I can't say anything about the hair?'
A. 'I am saying that to say it was black or brown or blond would be too definite a colour. It is merely a choice of the words for colour. It appeared to be dark, but there was sunlight gleaming off it, in which case it could have been grey.'
Q. 'Dark or grey?'
A. 'A blend of the two. Dark with sunlight on it.'
Q. 'How much hair was there?'
A. 'A reasonable amount.' (*3.30*)

The two other witnesses who identified Jimmy Robinson after failing to pick him out from the parade also recalled his hair.

An hour or so before the murder, Mario Sabetta, the restaurant manager, had seen two men, one carrying what he thought was a shotgun, come out from behind an estate car parked in Lawnswood Road some distance from the farm, cross the road and look over the hedge. Mr Sabetta·went to the identity parade where Robinson was standing. He walked crisply up and down the line without pausing, said 'No' to the police officers, and left. He made no statement then, or for eight months later. On the very morning he attended Stafford Crown Court on 10 October, a few minutes before he went into the witness box, he made another statement to DI Wordley. The statement is timed '10.15 a.m. to 11.20 a.m.' Sabetta said:

> I walked along the line of men and did not stop to look at any particular man. I particularly noticed the man who was standing fifth in the line from my left as I faced the parade. I strongly suspected that this was one of the men who I had seen near Yew Tree Farm on the afternoon of Tuesday 19th September. I felt that this was the taller of the two men who I had described in my statement to the police. He was not the one who I had described as carrying the gun. I felt in my own mind that this man fifth from the left was in fact the man I had seen near to Yew Tree Farm, but was not absolutely certain enough to make a positive identification.
>
> I have had time to think this matter out since the time of the parade. I am still of the same frame of mind in as much as I feel fairly certain but not absolutely certain that the man I saw on the parade was the same man I saw near to Yew Tree Farm.
>
> Following the parade, and whilst on my way to my home, I did mention what I have just described to a plain clothes police officer.

Hardly had this statement been typed and handed to the defence as formal evidence than Mr Sabetta was in the witness box, answering questions. He told prosecution counsel that one of the men 'seemed familiar'. 'He was standing fifth from the left into the parade, and at the time I believe he was wearing a three-quarter raincoat, pale blue, but of course I wasn't sure. . . He was not the one who was carrying the weapon.' (*3.20*)

Mr Draycott, for Jimmy Robinson, was quite unprepared for this entirely unexpected piece of evidence. Until that morning, the position about Mario Sabetta, agreed by both sides, was that he had not identified anyone on the parade and had made no formal statement about it to anyone. The plain-clothes officer to whom he said he spoke on the way back from the parade was not identified or produced. Suddenly, after nearly nine months to 'think it over', Sabetta was saying that Jimmy Robinson (for it was he wearing the raincoat) had 'seemed' like the taller of the two men whom Sabetta had glimpsed walking across a road eleven months earlier.

Mr Draycott did not ask how Mr Sabetta had decided on the 'familiarity' of the suspect after all this time. But he did ask about the hair.

Q. 'The second man, do you remember his hair?'

A. 'His hair? I can't remember very clear about the hair, but I can remember, shall we say, the person concerned as tall, perhaps 6 feet, well-built, weather-beaten face.'

Q. 'Do you mean like someone who worked outdoors?'

A. 'Yes.'

Q. 'What was the hair like of the person you think might be the man – you say he seemed familiar – if he was on the identity parade?'

A. 'Well, difficult, shall we say, perhaps to remember, but it was a rather darkish colour.'

Q. 'What about length?'

A. 'Length of hair? Ordinary collar length.' (*3.23*)

The last of three witnesses to 'identify' Jimmy Robinson without picking him out on the parade was Terence Madeley, the Wordsley painter and decorator. Mr Madeley's problem throughout his evidence was that he hadn't a clue what day he had seen a Cortina (which he described as 'racing green') coming out of the Yew Tree Farm drive. It might have been the day of the murder. It might equally have been the day before, or the Friday, four days before.

On the day of the parade, Mr Madeley looked carefully down the line of men on which Robinson was standing. He seemed to look specially hard at Robinson and the man next to him. He did not touch anyone, as he had been instructed to do on recognition, said 'No' and walked out of the parade room.

Like Miss Stagg, he had second thoughts. In the office upstairs he gave a statement to Detective Sergeant Leek.

I could not identify anyone with a hundred per cent certainty as any of the men I had previously seen leaving the driveway of Yew Tree Farm on or near the day of the murder of Carl Bridgewater. However, whilst looking at the parade of men, the one standing fifth from the left in the line seemed very familiar and looked very like the man I saw in the passenger seat of the car leaving the farm driveway, but I could not be one hundred per cent sure, but he was definitely the same age, build, and type of hair colour as the man I had seen.

Mr Draycott was ready for this one, and Mr Madeley had a difficult time. His cross-examination would have been comic farce, had the implications not been so appalling.

In his statement, Madeley had described the passenger in the car as in his early thirties, 'with fairish curly hair, and he gave me the impression of being stoutish'. Jimmy Robinson was in his mid-forties, he had light brown, straight hair, and was not noticeably stout. In evidence, Mr Madeley abruptly changed the colour of the passenger's hair:

Q. 'What did you notice about the passenger?'
A. 'Exactly what I have just said: he was a rough-looking character with curly hair.'
Q. 'What colour curly hair?'
A. 'Dark.'
Q. 'Dark curly hair?'
A. Darkish. (*3.12*)

A few questions later, Madeley changed back to the colour he had first mentioned.

'The passenger was an older man. [In his statement after the murder he said he was the same age as the driver.] I'm pretty sure he was an older man, but he'd got fairish hair, if you like, lightish, fairish hair.'
Q. 'It was darkish a minute ago.'
A. 'But it has been 12 months since this happened. . .'
Q. 'Whoever you picked out at the identification parade did not have fairish curly hair, did he?'
A. 'How would you define curly? I would define "curly" with a few kinks in it, or something like that.' (*3.15*)

This went on for some time, with Mr Madeley concluding with the interesting information that he had had blond hair when he was at school. He complained at one stage that Mr Draycott was 'tying me up in a way'.

If the jury were confused about the colour of Jimmy Robinson's hair at the time of the murder, the reality was simple. On 19 September 1978, Jimmy Robinson had no hair at all. On 25 August, after a row with Carol about other girlfriends, Jimmy Robinson, partly in penance, partly in fun, had persuaded his friend Patrick Tierney to shave his head bald. Susan Bennett, Carol's neighbour, who gave evidence for the prosecution, said she'd seen Jimmy's head being shaved. At the time of the murder, Jimmy's head was still almost bald, with only a few bristles sticking out of it. He had, as he put it, 'had a Kojak'. As he wrote to Carol: 'I stuck out like a white sheep in a crowd of black ones' (or, perhaps more accurately, *vice versa*).

This was very embarrassing to the prosecution's identification witnesses Wendy Stagg, Mario Sabetta and Terence Madeley. All had in one way or another singled out Robinson after the identification parade, when Robinson had a full head of hair. All had described their man near Yew Tree Farm as having a full head of hair (though of sharply-conflicting colours and lengths). No one mentioned a hat (except Wendy Stagg who said her man definitely wasn't wearing one). Indeed, not one of the witnesses who saw anyone near Yew Tree Farm on the fatal afternoon had seen anyone in a hat or mask, or anyone whose head looked like that of Kojak.

The Staffordshire police had stumbled on the 'Kojak problem' quite early and had moved heaven and earth to solve it. Regulars at the California and friends of Robinson were questioned and cross-questioned about wigs. One or two were found who said they had once seen Pat Molloy with a wig, but when and where they could not remember. In the event, no evidence was produced about wigs. It was left, rather remarkably, to the judge in his summing up of evidence, which had included no mention of wigs, to raise the matter for the first time:

You must of course bear in mind the evidence that on August 25 Robinson for some reason or other had his head shaved, his hair shaved off altogether, and by September 19 it follows that he would not have had very much hair still, and no one suggests that the person they identified or saw outside Yew Tree Farm that day had a shaved head or very little hair indeed. They suggest quite the contrary, and so it follows that if that person was Robinson he must have been wearing some form of wig. You will bear in mind that those who saw him in the California at about the same time did not speak of him going in there with a completely bald head. So it may be you will conclude that he did somehow conceal the shaving by wearing some sort of wig.

How did this reflect the evidence? Six witnesses told the court that they had met or seen Jimmy Robinson in the California pub: Timothy Roberts, Carol Wilson, Peter Orton, Sean Tierney, Jimmy Dundas-Ure and Patricia Copus. None of them were there to give evidence about what Jimmy Robinson looked like. They were asked about what time Jimmy came into the pub, and about what he said there.

Witnesses do not, in general, volunteer information. They answer questions. *No questions were asked of any of them about Jimmy Robinson's appearance or his hairstyle.* To conclude from their silence on this matter that Robinson wore a wig or had access to a wig was nothing but presumption.

As Carol Wilson, a barmaid at the California, put it in an interview with Ann Whelan in February 1986: 'Of course I knew Jimmy hadn't got any hair at the time. I would have said so in court if anyone had asked me.' Moreover, in the trial itself evidence was given that Robinson was well known for his bald head. Anwar 'Spider' Mohammad, a prosecution witness, volunteered in his evidence that he had called Robinson 'Baldy' at the time – for obvious reasons. (*4.48*) Somehow Mr Justice Drake left this observation out of his summing-up.

Mr Justice Drake warned the jury about the identification evidence against Jimmy Robinson. He concluded: 'I would say to you in this case that if that were the sole evidence against Robinson, it would be unsafe to convict on that evidence and on that alone.'

But he quickly countered: 'The evidence is evidence which it is right that you should consider coupled with all the warnings that I have given, and if you think it assists you then it can slot into place as one of the pieces of evidence which make up the case for the prosecution.'

The judge did not explain in detail to the jury the purpose of identification parades and the regulations which govern them. In July 1978, only two months before the Carl Bridgewater murder, the Home Office issued a new set of regulations governing identification parade procedure. Rule 20 stated: 'It is generally considered desirable to touch the person identified; but if the witness is nervous, for instance if it is a woman or a child, or there has been a sexual assault or violent attack, it was permitted to point out the suspect, *provided that the identification is made clearly and in the view of the suspect and in the presence of his solicitor or a friend.*' (Author's emphasis.)

In all three cases in which Jimmy Robinson was 'identified', this rule was flagrantly breached. As soon as the witness had said 'No', that should have been the end of the matter. The witness should not be allowed, as Robinson put it in his defence at the trial, a 'second bite at the cherry' in circumstances in which the police officers to whom they made statements knew where their suspect was standing on the parade.

In spite of the unusual manner in which the three identifications were made, in spite of the short glimpses each witness had, in spite of their remembering full heads of hair on a man who was at the time almost entirely bald, in spite of Mr Madeley's not knowing even what day it was he saw his suspect, the fact that there were three identifications *did* tell against Jimmy Robinson. In his cross-examination of Robinson, Mr Judge came back to the 'coincidence' of the three identifications again and again.

But at least the judge had said that if there was no other evidence the identifications could not convict. *Was* there any other evidence against Robinson, or indeed against any of the others?

The Gun and the Cartridge Case

'It is the prosecution case that this single-barrel shotgun was the one which killed Carl Bridgewater.' With these words, Mr Philip Cox QC introduced the jury to Exhibit 25, a sawn-off single-barrelled shotgun with its stock cut down to make it easy to carry and disguise.

The gun had been bought by Jimmy Robinson about three weeks before the murder. He had bought it from a Birmingham racketeer called Anwar 'Spider' Mohammad. Spider told the court that he had sold it to Robinson with its barrel still intact. This was denied by Jimmy Robinson in his evidence. He said he'd bought the gun with its barrel sawn off.

It was a point of small consequence. No doubt the jury preferred the word of the witness to that of the accused. They did not know the full facts about Spider Mohammad. Four years later, in 1983, a man called Dennis Nott complained of systematic damage which, he alleged, Spider Mohammad had done to his property and his car. He also alleged that the police would not take action because of their close relationship with Spider Mohammad. In the course of the proceedings Mr Nott received a letter from a Birmingham solicitor, Christopher Carney-Smith. The letter, dated 24 October 1983, told Mr Nott that Detective Chief Superintendent Holder of the West Midlands Regional Crime Squad 'has confirmed that it is accepted that Spider works for [Detective Sergeant] Hornby'. Hornby was one of the interviewing officers in the Carl Bridgewater inquiry.

The informer was preceded in the witness box by David Kane, who said he was a friend of Jimmy Robinson. Kane said Jimmy Robinson had wanted to buy a gun and Kane led him to Spider Mohammad. David Kane was asked twice if the gun in court was the same gun which Spider sold Jimmy. He agreed it was, but he told the court: 'It looked longer at the time' and 'it looked bigger when it was bought'. (*4.46,47*) David Kane's evidence suggested, as did Spider Mohammad's, that the gun had been full-barrelled when sold, and that Jimmy Robinson had sawn the barrel off.

Some years later, David Kane told me that he had *not* intended to convey anything of the kind. 'The gun definitely *was* sawn-off when Jimmy bought it from Spider. I know, because I saw it plainly. Jimmy was quite right about that, and Spider was lying.' (Interview with me, 14 April 1986.)

Whatever the state of its barrel, however, Jimmy Robinson bought the gun in September 1978, and Burkett used it at the Tesco supermarket and at Chapel Farm, Romsley. As soon as he was arrested on 6 December 1978 he confessed to both armed robberies. The following evening he took his interrogators to a patch of waste ground behind the California pub where he had hidden his gun and eleven cartridges. He did this, he told the court, because he wanted to prove to the police that he had nothing to do with the Carl Bridgewater murder. He believed, he said, that it would be possible to prove at once that his gun had not been used at Yew Tree Farm.

If, as Mr Cox asserted, Jimmy Robinson's sawn-off gun *had* been the murder weapon, it was surely extraordinary that he led police to where it was hidden, and where it was most unlikely to be found. To add to their valuable catch, moreover, police found another cartridge at Carol Bradbury's house, which they added to the eleven they had retrieved by courtesy of their suspect.

The gun was taken to the Home Office Central Ballistics Centre at Nottingham where it was examined by Thomas Warlow, one of the country's top ballistics experts.

Mr Warlow knew, as Jimmy Robinson did not know, that it is *not* possible to tell whether a particular shot has been fired by a particular shotgun. In court, he explained to Mr Cox that a rifle or a pistol is normally identifiable by the impressions which its borings make from the single bullet it fires, but because a shotgun has no rifling, and shoots up to 250 pellets at a time, there is no way it can be identified by shot or wadding of the type found at Yew Tree Farm. All he could say was that Robinson's was a 12-bore shotgun, along with thousands of others in regular use throughout the country, and that Carl had been killed by a single shot. Mr Warlow was not even able to say whether the shotgun which killed Carl had been sawn-off or not. 'For all intents and purposes, at very close ranges such as that involved in this offence, the effects of a full-length double-barrelled gun are very similar to that of sawn-off weapons such as the one I am holding in my hands now (Exhibit 25).' (4.34)

So Carl could have been shot with any other 12-bore gun, whatever the state of its barrel. There was nothing which enabled Mr Warlow to connect the shot and cartridge wadding he had picked out of Carl Bridgewater's head and around the sofa on which the boy died with the gun which was shown to the court as though it were unquestionably the murder weapon.

In cross-examination, Mr Warlow confirmed that the cartridges which had been found with Robinson's gun were not of the type which killed Carl Bridgewater. Nor was the single cartridge found at Carol Bradbury's. It carried 3 size shot, compared with the 5 size used to kill Carl. So while no one could say whether Robinson's gun had been used at Yew Tree Farm, Robinson's cartridges certainly had not.

Mr Cox's assertion had taken a few knocks, but worse was to come. Cross-examining Mr Warlow, Mr Draycott asked a series of technical questions about the peculiar markings which Jimmy's gun seemed to leave on cartridges which had been loaded in it. The point of these questions was not clear. But their effect was dramatic. Mr Cox, as he listened to the answers, recalled another piece of evidence which had been available to the prosecution.

This was the empty cartridge case which, as we have seen, had been found on a main road about a mile away from Yew Tree Farm, on the day after the murder.

Previous forensic tests had eliminated this cartridge case from the inquiry. But Mr Cox thought perhaps it should be looked at again in the light of what the court had heard from Mr Warlow about Jimmy's gun leaving nicks on the rim of the cartridge cases. Might there be such nicks on the cartridge case found in the road? If so, might that not prove that Robinson's gun killed Carl?

He asked for the cartridge case to be retrieved for further examination. As the court rose for lunch on the day after Mr Warlow gave evidence – 12 October, the fifth day of the trial – Mr Cox mentioned the matter to Mr Draycott, counsel for Robinson.

When the court convened again after lunch, Mr Draycott rose. In ponderous tones he said he had just heard of 'what seems to be the murder cartridge'. 'None of the defence counsel,' he complained, 'knew anything about this.'

At the time, however, the discovery of the cartridge case on the day after the murder had been announced with great excitement by the police in the media, local and national. The front page of the *Express and Star*, for instance, on the Saturday after the murder, proclaimed in a headline: 'CARTRIDGE CLUE', and reported: 'A shotgun cartridge may have been thrown from the car of the fleeing killers of Carl Bridgewater, it was revealed today. It had been fired recently, and could be from the murder weapon.'

The *Birmingham Evening Mail* of the same day (23 September 1978) parroted: 'Detectives may have found the cartridge which killed Carl. Panicking killers may have thrown it out of the car.'

Chief Superintendent Robert Stewart and his detectives made no secret of their delight at the discovery of this cartridge case. It had been fired in the previous forty-eight hours. It was an Eley 5, exactly the same type as that used in the murder. It had been found by a bread-roundsman in Doctors Lane, where it joined the A449 only just over a mile away (and straight up the main road) from the farm. The case was found in the middle of the road, among some gravel. The roundsman was astonished. He had been supplying the area and travelling down Doctors Lane for many years, but he had never before seen a cartridge case. He connected it at once with the Bridgewater killing, picked it up and drove straight to Yew Tree, where he handed it in to the police at the caravan. He made the point that this was the first time he had been in Doctors Lane since the murder.

There was no doubting the importance of the clue. But Mr Warlow reported almost at once that Jimmy Robinson's gun could not have fired the cartridge from that case. As Mr Cox told the court, it was 'eliminated from the inquiry altogether'.

Now, however, the cartridge case was reintroduced. The jury on their return were told by the judge that 'a further point has cropped up which had been somewhat unexpected'.

147

The following day, Mr Warlow was in the witness box once more. He had known about this cartridge case since he had inspected it way back in September the previous year. On the main point, which he had decided then, he remained firm. Prosecution and defence agreed that without doubt the cartridge from the case at Doctors Lane could not have been fired from Jimmy Robinson's gun.

But then there was a further question. Could the cartridge case have been fired from the gun which killed Carl Bridgewater? The case was manufactured by Eley in 1977. After 1976, most Eley cartridges of this type were packed in a wadding made of waxed Thames board. Before 1976, the wadding was made of leatherboard.

The wadding found at Yew Tree Farm was leatherboard. It seemed at first sight that the two did not match. But then Eley revealed that there *were* substantial batches of cartridge cases made after 1977 which were packed in leatherboard wadding. The more they searched the records, the more batches they found. They finally came up with a figure of 2,800,000 cartridge cases with leatherboard wadding produced in 1977. That was only 2.8 per cent of the total of 100,000,000, but nevertheless a substantial figure. It was, therefore, entirely possible that the Doctors Lane cartridge case had contained the shot which killed the newspaper boy.

As Mr Draycott pointed out in his closing speech to the jury, Jimmy Robinson's sawn-off shotgun started the trial in the front of the stage. It was paraded in front of the court and fondled by witnesses as though it were the murder weapon. After the cartridge case episode, however, 'it slipped quietly into the background'. There was no proof whatever that Jimmy's gun killed Carl Bridgewater. The evidence about his cartridges suggested otherwise. The murder weapon was never produced. If, as was possible, the mysterious cartridge case found at Doctors Lane *had* been connected with the murder, it had nothing at all to do with Jimmy Robinson's gun.

Knowledge of the Area
Throughout the trial, all the defendants insisted they had never been to the Wordsley area, and had no idea where Yew Tree Farm was. Two witnesses were brought by the prosecution to disprove this. The most impressive was a relation of the Hickeys, Reginald Hickey, who came to the court from Gloucester prison. He told the court that in the months immediately before his arrest in February 1978 he had done roofing work with his cousins in the area around Yew Tree Farm. On 8 January that year (1979), following the arrest of his cousins, he was taken from prison on a tour of the area he said he had worked, and had pointed out various pubs and addresses in the area around Kingswinford, Wordsley and Sedgely where he said he had gone roofing with Vinny and Michael.

Reg's evidence was a little vague. He did not mention the one specific address – 34 Queens Road, Sedgely – which he had pointed out to the police officers on the drive. The pub he named had not, he stressed, been visited. But he was absolutely certain, and he was unshaken by Mr Tucker or Mr Hollis on this main point, that Michael and Vinny had been 'knocking up' in the area around Yew Tree Farm less than a year before the murder.

This was strong evidence. As the judge pointed out in his summing up, it suggested not just that the Hickeys knew the area, but that they had lied about their knowledge of it. The only conceivable reason why they should have lied was to cover up about the murder. Reg Hickey added real substance to the prosecution case.

Neither Mr Cox nor Mr Hollis (for Vincent) nor Mr Tucker (for Michael) asked Reg Hickey why he was in prison. As we have seen in Chapter 2, Reg had a substantial score to settle with Vincent. It was Vincent who had named him as the prime mover in the Hertfordshire robbery which had earned Reg four years in prison while Vincent, charged only with deception even though he had had his share of money from the robbery, walked free from St Albans Crown Court.

There was another point about 34 Queens Road – the only actual address which Reg Hickey pointed out as the one where roofing work had been done in December 1977 and January 1978. This belonged to a Mrs Phoebe Lloyd. On 12 January, four days after Reg Hickey's tour with the Staffordshire police officers, the police went back to 34 Queens Road, Sedgely, and took a statement from the old lady.

She said: 'I can say that about 4/5 years ago three men called at my home. They told me the roof was in need of repair and that it would leak if it was not done. I was not aware of any repair that required doing; the roof certainly did not leak. I agreed to have the repair done, which was carried out the same day. I think the men replaced some tiles on the roof.'

This happened 'four to five years ago' – long before the time Reg Hickey had given. Mrs Lloyd stressed: 'I am quite sure that the work was carried out about five years ago.' Five years before January 1979, Michael Hickey was twelve years old. Reg had stressed that Michael had joined the roofing team in December 1977, nearly four years after the job had been done at Sedgely. Once again, the supporting evidence did not back the prosecution evidence. Mrs Lloyd was not produced at the trial.

Reg Hickey had claimed that Tommy Forbes had been with the gang on the 'bodgings' at Wordsley and the area around it. Tommy Forbes, however, contradicted this. He said in evidence that he had never been out working or stealing with the Hickeys except in the London area. Asked if he had ever been with Vincent or Michael in the area round

Yew Tree Farm he replied: 'No.' (*16.11*)

There was one more small piece of evidence that Vincent Hickey had been somewhere near the farm. Mrs Daphne White said in a statement read out in court that she had employed Vincent's mother Ann at a public house in Kingswinford – the Cottage Inn. The Whites and Mrs Hickey had moved into the pub on 22 August 1978. Mrs White said that Vincent and his wife had visited his mother there soon afterwards. They had arrived in the evening about 8 p.m. and left about 11 p.m.

Mr Cox made a lot of this visit, and tried to argue that Vincent may well have passed Yew Tree Farm on the journey to Kingswinford. Vincent replied that he had gone along main roads from Redditch, through Stourbridge, Old Swinford and Amblecote, which took him straight to the Cottage Inn. This meant that he passed on the other side of Wordsley from the farm, and was never at any stage less than three miles from it. Apart from the evidence of Reg Hickey, that single car journey at night was the only occasion the prosecution could find when any one of the four defendants could be placed in all their lifetimes within a twenty-mile radius of Yew Tree Farm.

Did the Four Know Each Other?

One major difficulty for the prosecution was the fact that the four men had, apparently, hardly met each other before September 1978. Vincent and Michael, of course, were constantly together. Robinson and Molloy were inseparable. In November 1978, the Hickeys got to know the other pair, especially Robinson, and Michael carried out the two robberies with him. But in September, all the evidence suggested that the two couples had hardly met, and were only on nodding acquaintance in the Dog and Partridge.

It was important for the prosecution to produce at least *some* evidence that the Hickeys were close to Robinson and Molloy. One witness only could help them. Mrs Catherine Guy lived on the same walkway as Carol Bradbury. Mrs Guy knew both Jimmy and Pat quite well. While the four men were on remand, police visited her home. They had with them photographs of Vincent and Michael Hickey. They showed these to Mrs Guy and asked her if she had ever seen such a man in or near Carol Bradbury's flat. Mrs Guy immediately said she had never seen anyone like Michael. She thought, however, that she might have seen Vincent going along the walkway and made a statement that she had seen him there twice.

Vincent Hickey denied at once that he had ever been in Carol Bradbury's flat, or any other house occupied by Robinson or Molloy. He said he had never been on the landing. His counsel, Mr Hollis, pointed out that Mrs Guy had not been asked to pick out Vincent from an identification parade, or even from a large number of pictures. When Mr Hollis asked *when* she had seen the man, she replied: 'I don't know. I just seen him walk up and down the landing, that's all.'

But alone among all the witnesses, Mrs Guy could provide a tenuous link between the Hickeys and Jimmy Robinson's flat.

Verbals
The evidence about the murder vehicle or vehicles, which were never found or traced to the accused; about identification which, as the judge insisted, could not convict on its own, and anyway referred only to Robinson; and about the gun and cartridge cases which did not link Robinson's gun with the murder; the evidence of Reginald Hickey about knowledge of the area and of Catherine Guy linking the two accused couples was the sum total of what can be called the 'tangible' evidence against the four men.

There was no evidence of fingerprints; no evidence of tyre marks; no forensic evidence of any kind to link any one of the four with Yew Tree Farm. There was no evidence about any of the stolen property, none of which was ever found. All the rest of the evidence in the trial sprung from what was alleged to have been *said* by or about the accused *after* the murder.

First, a group of civilian witnesses said they had heard the accused speak about the murder.

Helen Johnston By far the most damaging to the defendants was Helen Johnston, the barmaid at the Dog and Partridge. Together with all the other regulars at the Dog, Mrs Johnston was interviewed over and over again by police officers in the murder hunt.

Indeed, she had been interviewed *before* the four men were arrested. On 9 November Staffordshire police came to her home in Selly Oak. They wanted to know about another Dog and Partridge client called Tommy Vallance, whom they had some reason to suspect of involvement in the Bridgewater murder. Mrs Johnston told them Tommy Vallance had been in the Dog and Partridge on the afternoon of the murder. *She said nothing about anyone else.* It was only *after* the Hickey cousins and Molloy and Robinson were arrested that she started to incriminate them in a series of statements which were brought together in February 1979:

About the end of September, beginning of October 1978, it could have been a Wednesday because I finished at nine o'clock and the gaffer of the pub had gone to the dogs at Hall Green. The night was quiet, there was only about four in the pub. This was after seven o'clock. Jim and Pat were in the pub. They were standing by the

151

juke box but it wasn't on. I was standing to the end of the bar and was close to them. Pat was saying to Jim: 'If we are ever caught and seen by the police, you must say that the gun went off accidentally.' I heard that as plain as anything. They both had their heads bowed forward. I know they were on about the murder of the newspaper boy because Pat had also said something about the boy. They both looked very sick, not normal and very worried. Pat kept repeating: 'Whatever you do, whatever you say, keep your word, the gun went off accidentally.' He said this about five or six times. I went and served a customer and when I went back to the end of the bar, Pat was still on about saying the gun went of accidentally.

I wanted to tell the police then, but I was very frightened. I didn't sleep for weeks over this. I think they may have known I was listening but they trusted me. After this, I was off work sick for a week. This was because of the worry over this. I just didn't know what to do or who to see. I was really scared. I still am scared to tell you the truth.

This story, without some of the histrionics (no one ever checked when and why Mrs Johnston was off sick for a week) was told in hushed tones to the court at Stafford. Mrs Johnston cut a sympathetic figure. She was allowed to sit down because she had just had a baby.

There was, however, one grave problem about her story – the date. She said the incriminating conversation took place 'about the end of September, beginning of October'.

She stuck to this at the trial. Mr Cox asked her:

Q. 'Can you help us about when this was, Mrs Johnston? We know that Carl the newspaper boy was killed in the middle of September. Can you help us about the date, the approximate time when you overheard this?'

A. 'It was about two or three weeks after.' (*6.35*)

Apart from her saying it all happened on a Wednesday, this was the only date offered by Mrs Johnston for the conversation between Molloy and Robinson. It cannot have been right. Jimmy Robinson was in prison from 21 September – two days after the murder – to 23 October, five weeks later. It was not difficult to grasp that if Robinson was in Winson Green prison he could not have been discussing the Carl Bridgewater murder with his mate in the Dog and Partridge.

Prosecution and judge dealt with this problem in different ways. In his opening speech to the jury, Mr Cox put the date soon after the murder: 'Helen Johnston puts the date in late September/early October, but it must have been no later than the evening of September 21st.'

Mr Cox assumed, perhaps naturally, that if the conversation could not have taken place when Mrs Johnston said it did, it must have happened earlier – nearer to the murder. It was not quite right of him to say that it could have happened 'no later than the evening of September 21st' – since the evening of 21 September was also spent by Robinson in custody – he had been arrested at 3 a.m. on the 21st. This left only one evening after the murder when the conversation could have taken place: the 20th September, which was, by coincidence, a Wednesday.

What were Robinson and Molloy doing that day? They went, as usual, to the California pub at lunchtime and had several drinks. The best description of what happened next comes from James Robinson who wrote a long account of his experiences in his own distinctive style.

On the spur of the moment, after a heavy lunchtime drinking bout, Molloy and I decided to go to Tamworth. I was maudlin drunk and wanted to see my kids, while Molloy told me he wanted to look up some old pals.

I'm not sure what time we got to Tamworth, but we both decided we needed further liquid courage to face Doreen [Mrs Robinson], and hung about for some time until the pubs re-opened for the evening trade. Eventually we ended up in a pub called the Globe (I think) where Molloy played for the pub team at dominoes (incidentally the mode of transport to Tamworth was a stolen Ford car; we had a lot of trouble as the gearstick kept lifting completely out of the selector box).

As the night progressed all thoughts of Doreen and kids disappeared, being replaced by thoughts of burglary, and after closing time we set off to find a likely place, ending up in us getting into Tamworth Co-Op abattoir. We hacked and sawed at whole sides of beef into carryable portions loading it into a Co-Op box van. After it was loaded, and I got into it, I couldn't start it, and after trying for ten minutes or so, we decided to return to Birmingham and come back in a Dormobile we knew was available.

They got back to Birmingham at three in the morning, where they were intercepted by a police car. Molloy ran off, and Robinson was arrested. He was not released until 23 October.

The police already had detailed accounts of this escapade. It had been checked with many witnesses in the Tamworth pub where Molloy was the domino king. They knew perfectly well that Molloy and Robinson were out of Birmingham from the afternoon of the 20th until three o'clock in the morning on the 21st.

It followed that the conversation which Mrs Johnston said she'd heard could not have taken place on 20 September, as Mr Cox asserted.

No doubt, as the trial continued, the extent of Mr Cox's gaffe was made clear to him and his colleagues. By the time Mr Igor Judge, Mr Cox's relief Queen's Counsel, came to cross-examine Jimmy Robinson on 31 October, the prosecution had changed its tune. Mr Judge asserted:

> Whether she says it is two or three weeks after the death of Carl Bridgewater and whether you were in custody until the 23rd October may not matter very much: the date of it may not matter very much. (*18.8*)

In his summing up, Mr Justice Drake was inclined to push the date *back* from the date given in evidence.

> She said she thought, without being able to fix any date, that it was about two or three weeks after Carl's death. We know that that cannot be the accurate date, if you find those events happened, because Robinson was in custody until the 23rd October, which would be more like 4 or 5 weeks after Carl died.

Could Molloy have had this incriminating conversation with Robinson in the Dog *after* Robinson was released from prison, perhaps on the first Wednesday after that, 25 October, five whole weeks after the murder? It was at least possible. But the conversation itself, as reported by Helen Johnston, suggests something which had happened recently. Molloy is supposed to have mentioned the gun going off accidentally again and again, five or six times. The conversation reeks of urgency, of the likelihood of imminent capture and interrogation by the police. It does not suggest that they are discussing something which happened five weeks previously.

Finally, there was the discrepancy between Mrs Johnston's assurance that she wanted to tell police about the conversation at the time it took place, and her failure to utter a word of it when the Bridgewater case detectives came to see her on 9 November. Here was a perfect opportunity for Mrs Johnston to put an end to all those sleepless nights – an opportunity, however, which she failed to grasp.

Jimmy Robinson in court and Pat Molloy in his statement to his lawyers vehemently denied that the conversation which Mrs Johnston said she'd heard ever took place, or could have taken place. It certainly could not have taken place at or anywhere near the time that Helen Johnston said it did. Prosecution lawyers tried to find a possible date either before or after the date given in evidence, without much success. One alternative they could not tolerate was the one which seemed most likely – that Helen Johnston's story was invented, made up to satisfy relentless police questioning which was based, as was the interrogation of suspects, on police *certainty* that the four men had committed the crime.

Mrs Johnston went on to tell another damaging story about her former friend, Jimmy Robinson, at the Dog and Partridge.

She said she was sitting one evening at a table with Jimmy, Carol and some of their friends. Jimmy and Carol had had a row. He threatened to go back to his wife in Tamworth.

Carol had retorted (according to Helen Johnston's first statement to police): 'I'll shop the pair of you for this murder if you go back to Tamworth. I'm not having Pat back at my house, he's the murderer.'

At the trial, this had changed to the slightly more incriminating: 'She said to him she was going to shop him for the paper boy.' (*6.36*)

Was there anyone else who heard this extremely damaging conversation? The prosecution brought one witness to court who, they had every reason to hope, would back up Helen Johnston and testify to the conversation.

Sean Tierney was a close friend of Jimmy Robinson. His brother Paddy had shaved Jimmy's head in August 1978, and indeed Sean himself was part of the original bet to have *his* head shaved as well. Soon after Robinson and Molloy were arrested in December, Sean Tierney was visited again and again by Staffordshire police officers. In his first statement to them, he said he had been in the Dog and Partridge on the night of the alleged conversation between Jimmy and Carol. He had been selling trousers around the pubs, and had come to the Dog and Partridge with a small group of people including his girlfriend Angela Handcox. He offered Robinson a pair of trousers. Impulsively, Robinson stripped his off and tried on a pair. There was some raucous comment about the table to the effect that Robinson was 'well blessed'. Robinson replied with a vulgar boast. Carol's temper snapped and a row ensued.

In his first statement, Sean Tierney's account ended there. But in his second statement, a few weeks later, he added that he had heard Carol warn that she would 'shop him over the newspaper boy'.

This was powerful corroboration of Helen Johnston's story, and the prosecution naturally expected that Sean Tierney would repeat his second statement in court.

He didn't.

Mr Cox questioned him closely about the incident with the trousers, and then went on:

> Q. 'I just want you to tell the jury what you heard said between Jimmy and his missus.'
> A. 'They started arguing about going back to his missus, or

something like that, and when they started arguing I just got up and walked over to the bar and started drinking.'

Q. 'Did you hear Carol say anything?'

A. 'No, they were just arguing in a roundabout way – a general husband and wife tiff, like.'

Q. 'I want you to think carefully. Did you hear Carol say something to Jimmy Robinson?'

A. 'Just general arguing.'

Q. 'You say general arguing, what did you hear her say, if anything?'

A. 'Stop flashing yourself off in public, and he should have bought a pair of trousers because they suited him, and about going back to his wife.' (*6.48*)

Mr Cox came back to the subject again and again, but Sean Tierney stopped there. According to his account in court, there had been no mention of the murder at Yew Tree Farm or a newspaper boy. When he was asked about Helen Johnston, Sean Tierney said that she was not sitting with Jimmy and Carol, but with Tierney's girlfriend and another woman, Maureen Murphy.

Many years later, on 21 February 1986, I asked Sean Tierney about the difference between what he said in his statement and what he said in court. He told me:

'I told the truth in my first statement. But then the police kept coming back. I would be going to work or at home or in the pub, and they would be there. They would ask me to go and sit in the back of a car and talk again about what happened in the Dog that day with Jimmy and Carol.

'They kept saying I would have nothing to worry about if I just went with them to the station and made another statement that Carol had mentioned the newspaper boy. Eventually I told them I would make the statement if that would get them off my back, but if I went to court, I'd tell the truth, so I made the statement as they wanted me to, and they let me alone.

'When I got to the court, I did what I'd said I'd do. I told the truth.

'Jimmy and Carol were just bickering that night. I was embarrassed, so I stepped on the cat's tail to try to stop the bickering. I thought it was all my fault for bringing the trousers in, and I wanted everyone to be in a good mood again. There was nothing said about a newspaper boy or anything like it – and if there had been, Helen Johnston couldn't have heard it.'

No one else in the pub that evening heard the conversation – or any mention of a newspaper boy.

Sean Tierney's girlfriend Angela Handcox had said in a statement on 19 December 1978: 'He [Robinson] tried on a pair of trousers in the

Dog. Carol was annoyed by it, and so was I. We discussed what a bastard he was for doing that in the bar. There was not a row about it, although Carol was annoyed.'

In a later statement, Angela recorded hearing that Helen Johnston was reporting a conversation in which Carol had mentioned Carl Bridgewater that night. 'I certainly was not present when Carol was supposed to have said this,' she said.

Maureen Murphy, Helen Johnston's friend, confirmed she was there too, and saw the row. She went on: 'I have not heard anything said about Carl Bridgewater.'

Angela Marshall, Martin Tierney's girlfriend, was more specific. In a statement on 9 December 1978, she said: 'I remember Jimmy took his trousers off in the bar and tried some of these trousers on. I do not remember any other incidents or disputes between Jimmy and the woman he was with occurring whilst we were in the Dog and Partridge.'

No one else in the Dog that night recalled any remark about the Carl Bridgewater case from Carol. Carol herself and Jimmy Robinson furiously denied that anything like that was said, or could have been said. The police had many statements to contradict the extraordinary allegation of Helen Johnston. Only Sean Tierney's was brought to court. All the others – Angela Marshall's, Angela Handcox's, Maureen Murphy's, Carol Bradbury's – were not.

James Dundas-Ure The next person produced by the Crown to give evidence against the accused was a pimp of considerable notoriety in South Birmingham. He was James Dundas-Ure, a young man who had spent a remarkable proportion of his life in prison. In 1974 he had been given a routine sentence of three years for dishonest handling and living off the earnings of prostitution. He came out towards the end of 1976, but was soon peddling in prostitution once again. By the time he met Jimmy Robinson and Pat Molloy in the California pub on the day after the Carl Bridgewater murder, the police were looking for him, and he was on the run. He knew if he was arrested he would be liable for a stiff sentence.

The police caught up with Dundas-Ure in November, and he was arrested on the 25th. He faced a nasty clutch of vice and handling charges. Jimmy Robinson and Pat Molloy were arrested the following week, and Molloy was charged on 28 December. Almost as soon as Dundas-Ure heard that Jimmy Robinson was in prison (though not yet charged) for the Carl Bridgewater murder, he decided to make a statement about him. On 23 January he volunteered to talk to the Staffordshire police. Mr Draycott, representing Robinson, came straight to the point when he asked Dundas-Ure at the trial:

Q. 'Did you want to do something or to say something that you thought might stand you in good stead when it came to mitigating or reducing your sentence?'
A. 'Did I?'
Q. 'Yes.'
A. 'Oh, yes.' (*5.53*)

In his statement, Dundas-Ure alleged that in a conversation with Jimmy Robinson and Pat Molloy in the California the previous September, the subject of the Carl Bridgewater murder came up, and Jimmy Robinson suddenly said the killing had been an accident. Dundas-Ure alleged he then asked if Robinson had done the murder, and Robinson spread his arms in a noncommittal gesture. Dundas-Ure had then protested that Robinson would get thirty years for that.

Dundas-Ure admitted: 'I was seeing the police every day, and I was more or less relating to them what Jimmy Robinson said. They were just saying: "What's he said?" and I was just telling them, like.'

He was not telling them very much because Robinson was not saying very much. But on one occasion Dundas-Ure alleged that Robinson had told him that 'Paddy was upstairs'. Asked by the judge: 'Did he say where he was?' Ure replied: 'I think he said he was outside.'

Jimmy Robinson utterly denied any such crude confession. He said he had never spoken about Carl Bridgewater to the pimp in the California or in prison.

There was an eye-and-ear witness to the conversation in the Cali – James Dundas-Ure's girlfriend, Patricia Copus. Somehow, though she was sitting at the same table and in the same group, and no one else was talking, Patricia Copus hadn't noticed the dramatic confession which Jimmy Robinson had made. 'I didn't hear any of the conversation,' she told the court. 'All I heard was my Jimmy say something to Jimmy Robinson.'

'What did you hear him say?' asked Mr Judge.

'Jimmy, you could get thirty years for that,' she replied. (*5.57*)

That was all. She had been sitting there for half an hour and never heard a word about Carl Bridgewater or Yew Tree Farm.

Whether or not Dundas-Ure was telling the truth, he was richly rewarded for his assistance. On 2 February, 1979 he was convicted and sentenced at Birmingham Crown Court to two years in prison. Not satisfied with the surprisingly light sentence, he appealed. His formal grounds for appeal were that he had assisted the police in the Bridgewater case, and wanted to be home with his family by the time the trial started. The normally stern Court of Appeal were moved to mercy. It sliced six months off the sentence. Lord Justice Bridge said: 'Although the sentence of two years was proper, sufficient credit should be given to Dundas-Ure for the assistance he had given.' A judicial miracle had been worked. By the time the pimp climbed into the witness box at Stafford Crown Court to give evidence against his mate, he was a free man.

Michael Lee In the first four days of the trial there was no evidence produced against Michael Hickey. All the 'tangible' evidence (identification, gun, cars and so on) was directed to the other three defendants.

On the fifth day, Michael Lee went into the witness box. He was a regular at the Dog and Partridge. Unlike most of the others, he had a salaried job – as a service engineer.

In late November 1978, shortly before the arrests of the four men, Mickey Lee and his brother were playing cards in the Dog when a furious family fight broke out between the Lees and the Hickeys. It started with an argument between Mickey Lee and Joe Hickey, but Lee's brother and Michael Hickey quickly joined in.

On 3 December, as the police were hunting the Hickey family for the Chapel Farm robbery, Michael Lee gave police a detailed statement about the movements of the Hickeys on the day of the robbery. On 16 December, when Robinson, Molloy and Vincent were being held and questioned about Carl Bridgewater, and Michael Hickey was on the run, Michael Lee made another statement. In this he said that although he had been in the Dog and Partridge for most of the afternoon of 19 September, Michael Hickey and Vincent Hickey were never there.

'I have been asked about my connection with these men,' he said. 'I know they can be violent because on one occasion my brother and I had an argument in there over a game of cards, and we both finished up being thumped although I couldn't identify which one hit me.'

He then 'made it clear' that he had never bought any property off the Hickeys or their friends, thus suggesting that the Hickeys were often selling property.

It was a statement which did damage to the Hickeys, but there was nothing in it to connect them with the murder at Yew Tree Farm.

On 20 December Michael was arrested, and vigorously denied any connection with the murder. After Molloy was charged on 28 December, the police surveyed their evidence. Molloy and Vincent Hickey had incriminated themselves. Robinson had had a gun. But against Michael there was nothing except the word of Molloy, which would technically be of no value in court, unless Molloy went into the witness box.

On 4 January, Mickey Lee was pulled in again for another statement. This time, *for the first time*, he included a story about a conversation with Michael Hickey on the way back from a snooker game in a club. Lee says he asked casually where Joe and Vinny Hickey were. Michael had replied: 'They are getting rid of some stuff.' He then mentioned 'that farmhouse'. Lee said that at the time he thought Michael was bragging, and took no notice.

Lee could not date this conversation. He could not remember even which club they had played snooker in. But he was warned as a witness. After making two more statements in February and in September, he became the first of two civilian witnesses against Michael Hickey. His trial evidence was even more vague than his statements. Mr Judge pressed him for more information about 'the farmhouse job' which Michael had allegedly mentioned. The judge intervened:

> *Mr Justice Drake:* 'The farmhouse job?'
> A. 'Yes, I think that's what he said, and he said, you know, I think he said, you know "that kid".'
> Q. 'And what kid did you understand he was referring to?'
> A. 'Automatically thinking about it, sir, I thought that it was that Carl Bridgewater because that was the thing that was in the paper at the time. I do remember thinking that. (5.35)

This was the first time, in spite of five previous statements, that Michael Lee had mentioned anything being said about 'that kid'. It was thrown in, suddenly remembered, some thirteen months after the conversation supposedly took place.

That was all. Michael Hickey, of course, said that no such conversation did or could have taken place.

His counsel made the point that even if such a conversation had taken place, it did not in any way implicate Michael himself in the murder. At most, it suggested that Michael knew that his cousin and his father had some stuff from the farm.

Prodigious police inquiries were made to follow up this suggestion. Albert Chatterly and Joe Hickey told me on 2 January 1986 that they were in and out of police stations 'like yo-yos' for several weeks after the murder and were both questioned again and again about allegations that they had been selling antiques at Bromsgrove. Not a scrap of proof was found to prove any such thing. The houses of both men were searched again and again. Their contacts in Bromsgrove were all interrogated. No one could produce any proof that either man had sold anything, let alone antiques, in the entire period between the murder and the arrests.

One statement which was not available to the jury when they were assessing Michael Lee's testimony was one given on 22 January 1979 by John Greensmith, a detective constable in the West Midlands police. He said:

Particularly well known to me is Mickey Lee, who I see regularly at the British Legion where he is a member and I have been a member since about 1969. I have regularly spoken to Mickey Lee about the murder of Carl Bridgewater. In conversation he has told me he understood there was a blue car involved. I asked him if he had any knowledge where the blue car had gone. He told me he understands a blue car, I am sure he said a Ford Escort, had been over in the garage at Redditch belonging to Hickey's sister, and I presumed he meant Vincent Junior.

The only other statement that Mickey has made in relation to the murder is that he considers that it was Michael Hickey who used the gun in the murder, but he was unable to give any reason for this.

Mickey Lee, in my experience, is an exhibitionist and can tend to exaggerate, but he is very frightened about this murder, and I believe in the right conditions could be most helpful to your enquiries. He undoubtedly has been rather close to the Hickey crowd. It is to my knowledge that he is closely associated with the Hickeys and Billy Griffiths for at least nine years. I believe he has more information than he has already told me, but I have not questioned him about the murder as I do not know the full details relating to the offence.

Mickey Lee has given me information relating to certain crimes in the past. He has never given me information that has directly cleared up a crime, but what he has told me has on occasions been instrumental in clearing up crime. He does not like giving information, but in the right conditions he does. The right conditions are that he is sober at the time and that he trusts the person he is talking to. Over the years, Mickey Lee has developed a trust in me.

Dennis Eaton The only other civilian witness to give evidence against Michael Hickey was a Northfield taxi driver called Dennis Eaton.

He had regularly driven Michael round Birmingham. When Michael was first questioned about the murder, he said he had been in Eaton's taxi on the afternoon of the murder. The police quickly checked this, and told Michael his story didn't stand up. Michael admitted at once that he could have been wrong and that the journey he described could have taken place on another day.

All this happened before Christmas 1978. Michael was remanded pending further inquiries at the Remand Centre at Brockhill, near Redditch. One afternoon, Dennis Eaton was himself visiting a prisoner (whom he never identified). As he walked into the visiting room, he came across Michael talking to his mother and his girlfriend. Michael hailed him.

At the trial, Eaton then described what happened next: 'He asked me if I had made a statement, and I replied "No" because I didn't want to tell him that I had, and he said: "Well, I was with you. Remember I was with you in the taxi, remember."'

Mr Judge asked him: 'What did you think he was referring to?'

Dennis Eaton replied: 'He wanted me to give him an alibi for that date.' (*7.8*)

Michael Hickey had a different version of this conversation, and he was supported in court by his mother, Ann Whelan:

> Q. 'What did you hear of the conversation between the man and your son?'
>
> A. 'Dennis Eaton walked into the room to visit someone else. He stopped and spoke to Michael. Michael said: "Hello." He said: "Hello." Michael asked him what he was doing there. He said he had come to visit someone. Michael then said: "Have the police been to see you yet?" and he said "No" and with that he passed on to his visit.'
>
> Q. 'Was there anything said by Michael to Dennis Eaton to this effect: "Well, I was with you, remember? I was with you in the taxi, remember"?'
>
> A. 'Nothing at all.' (*17.50*)

Mickey Lee and Dennis Eaton were the only civilian witnesses to give evidence against Michael Hickey. Neither, of course, provided any proof that Michael had been at Yew Tree Farm. Even if their hotly contested accounts of the conversations were true, Lee's only suggested that Michael knew others were selling stuff from the farm; Eaton's that Michael wanted an alibi, which could have been because he could not remember where he was on the 19th. Both conversations were suspect. Lee was a police informer. Eaton was contradicted directly by Michael's mother. Clearly, if this were the only evidence against Michael Hickey there was not the slightest chance he would be convicted. What else had the prosecution to offer?

The Prison Evidence

'Prison evidence' is the testimony of prisoners or prison officers about what accused people are alleged to say about their crimes while in prison on remand. As Mr Justice Drake told the jury: 'I have reminded you more than once and warned you more than once already of the dangers of acting on the uncorroborated evidence of people such as prisoners unless there is other evidence from an independent source which supports such evidence.'

'Tex' Ritter The first prison witness to give evidence in the Carl-Bridgewater trial surprised and delayed the court by insisting that he take the oath according to the Old Testament. Mr 'Tex' Ritter was, he explained in a hurried and whispered conversation with the prosecution, a religious fundamentalist who would not subscribe to the watered-down version of the Scriptures represented by the words of the standard oath.

The fundamentalist, forty-one years old, had been stealing, assaulting, forging and deceiving since he was twenty-three. He'd got three and a half years at the Inner London Sessions in 1973 on twenty charges of theft and assault, with thirty-eight others taken into consideration. In September 1977 he was back again in court, this time at Leicester, where he got five and a half years for fourteen charges, with no less than 101 offences taken into consideration. This was a remarkable, not to say fundamentalist, record of crime for the few months in which Ritter had been on the loose.

Ritter was locked up in Leicester prison. Soon after Michael Hickey joined Vincent and Jimmy Robinson in Winson Green, Ritter was transferred there. He was not a 'Category A' top security prisoner, and so spent most of his time on the main wing. On 31 March, because of what he described as 'internal problems', he was suddenly and mysteriously moved onto landing D3, the landing confined exclusively to top security prisoners. This new posting meant that he exercised with the defendants in the Carl Bridgewater murder case.

He was in the same yard as Robinson and the two Hickeys for the first four days in April. On each day, he said, he managed to get into conversation with Robinson (at least twice, he said, Michael Hickey was there too). Robinson, he said, was prepared to discuss the case with him because, as he modestly explained, 'I am more intelligent than the majority of the inmates.'

The Old Testament fundamentalist complained that Robinson and Michael Hickey were always 'laughing their heads off' in a 'cynical and hysterical manner', which shocked him. Most of the conversation which he reported with Robinson fits what Robinson remembered: namely that he was completely innocent of the murder and was being 'fitted up' by the police and by Pat Molloy. But towards the end of the fourth day, Robinson is alleged to have said: 'A dead kid can't speak, can he, particularly when he's got his head blown off?' At this, according to Ritter, Robinson laughed.

On the afternoon of 5 April, Ritter approached the authorities with the news that he had information which could damage Robinson. Staffordshire police rushed to the prison and looked at the careful notes which the fundamentalist had made in his cells each day after exercise. They cannot have been completely satisfied. That evening, Ritter met

Robinson 'slopping out'. He said he was being transferred the next day to Walton prison and expected to get parole soon. He offered to do anything to help. Jimmy asked him to take a message to Carol. Ritter agreed. What happened next Ritter described to the court like this:

Q. 'What else did you say?'
A. 'And that if he needed any help I would try and give it to him, but I cannot give him any help unless I know the truth of what happened.'
Q. 'Having told him that, did you ask him anything?'
A. 'Yes, I asked him who murdered the child.'
Q. 'What did he say?'
A. 'He said: "It was an accident, Tex." I asked him again "Who killed Bridgewater?" and he said, "I did, but it was an accident."'
(*12.20*)

Robinson denied this completely. He said that he'd asked Ritter to get in touch with Carol for exactly the opposite reason: to confirm to her that they were all being fitted up and to comfort her.

The crude confession at the last possible moment conflicts grotesquely with Ritter's own account of what Robinson said in the four days before it.

Mr Justice Drake seemed to be rather touched by Ritter:

'I don't know how Ritter struck you,' he told the jury. 'Various comments have been made about his evidence from counsel addressing you. You may recall him as a person who went into the witness box and then we had to wait for some time because he would not take the oath save on the Old Testament. I say that to bring him to your recollection. It is, as I say, a matter entirely for you. He is of course a prisoner. Perhaps you found his evidence unusually convincing for a man of his background. I know not.'

Brian Sinton   Michael Hickey too had consistently upheld his innocence of the Bridgewater murder. Michael's clean record of denial was sullied by another prisoner, Brian Sinton. Sinton was a much younger man than Ritter. He was only twenty-two. His short life had been devoted almost exclusively to crime. He had started stealing, and being caught for it, from the age of nine when he first came to Pontefract juvenile court. He was convicted at Grimsby Crown Court once in 1975 for burglary, twice in 1976 for theft and deception, at Barnsley Magistrates Court once in 1977 and once in 1978. He was finally given a prison sentence suspended for two years. He didn't last that long, and in February

1979 he came up on six more charges, including a breach of his suspended sentence, and was sent to prison for eighteen months.

This was Sinton's first prison sentence and since his crimes were petty (he made a speciality of defrauding the Department of Health and Social Security out of Giro cheques) he was obviously not a Category A prisoner. Yet he too, oddly, found himself very close to one of the highest security prisoners in Winson Green prison – Michael Hickey.

Sinton had been involved in a fight with another prisoner, and had acquired a substantial black eye. He had been moved, apparently for his own protection, to the hospital wing. From there, most surprisingly, in the early morning of 9 June 1979 he was taken to have a shower at exactly the same time as was Michael Hickey.

Strict prison rules insist on the permanent separation of remand prisoners (like Hickey). They also separate Category A prisoners (like Hickey) from ordinary prisoners (like Sinton). On both grounds the two prisoners should have been kept apart. It was even more extraordinary that they were taken for a shower at the same time. Michael Hickey was kept in his cell for twenty-three hours a day. He was allowed one shower a week. He would normally be taken to shower with another prisoner from his wing – usually Robinson, occasionally another prisoner of Category A status. He had asked if Vincent could accompany him, but had been refused.

He had never had a shower with a non-Category A prisoner before, and never did so again. The two men had been in the shower hardly a minute before the conversation turned to the reason Michael was in prison. After it was established that he was to stand trial for the Bridgewater murder, the conversation according to Sinton, went like this:

Q. 'What did you say to him?'
A. 'Well, there was a few questions asked actually. It is like cons ask each other questions. It is difficult to explain, but I asked why it was necessary, and if he did it, and I said it out of curiosity more than anything else.'
Q. 'What did he say?'
A. 'Between you and me and the four walls, yes. I had to. The kid was crying.'
Q. 'When he said to you. "I had to, the kid was crying" did he say anything else about why he had to?'
A. '"He was howling and crying" were the exact words, and he had seen him.'
Q. 'Did he say anything else?'
A. 'He said something about a witness being against him, and they only caught him because. . .'
Q. 'Did he tell you anything else about what had happened

when this Carl Bridgewater was killed?'

A. 'About the child crying, do you mean?'

Q. 'Yes?'

A. 'Yes, he said that as the police were questioning him a police officer apparently said: "I bet Carl Bridgewater wasn't smiling" and Michael Hickey said to me: "No, he wasn't smiling, he was crying his eyes out and howling, and that is why I had to pull the trigger."'

Q. 'When Michael Hickey told you these things, how was he behaving?'

A. 'Well, sir, there was no question about it, he was more bragging than anything else. He had a grin on his face, and I can still see that grin now.' (*12.3*)

Michael Hickey's version of this conversation was entirely different:

Q. 'Did one of you mention the Carl Bridgewater murder?'

A. 'Sinton mentioned it.'

Q. 'He mentioned it?'

A. 'Yes.'

Q. 'What did he say about it?'

A. 'He said to me: "Are you one of the ones in for the Carl Bridgewater murder?" I said: "You already know that", and then he just went quiet when I said that and started to talk about his brother. He said: "My brother's in for murder."'

Q. 'Did he mention what he would do or what he would say to anyone about having met you?'

A. 'He told me, he said: "I'm going out in two or three days' time. I'll have to tell my missus I had a shower with one of the ones that done the Carl Bridgewater murder."'

Q. 'What did you say to that?'

A. 'I said: "You had better tell your missus you had a shower with one of the four who are pleading not guilty to the Carl Bridgewater murder", and I said: "I am one of the innocent ones as well."' (*16.42,43*)

The court heard two other matters which bore on this conflict of evidence. Prison Officer Westley told the court that he had escorted Michael Hickey to his shower that morning. He could give no explanation at all as to how his charge came in contact with a prisoner from whom the rules barred him. 'I think it is a case of circumstances,' he said, unhelpfully.

Mr Westley was asked to look at the prison records book in which the movements of prisoner Michael Hickey all through his stay at Winson

Green were noted. The record of Michael's trip to the shower on 9 June was signed by another officer, not by Mr Westley. There was some embarrassment in court as Mr Westley explained that there were *two* officers escorting Hickey, one for each end of the shower. The signature in the book, which he could not read for certain, must have belonged to the other officer.

Michael Hickey said that one of the officers who escorted him to the shower that day was Officer Kelly, who had shown a great interest in the case, and appeared as a prosecution witness against Michael. Mr Westley said that Mr Kelly was not there.

Strong doubt was thrown on Sinton's account by another witness, the pathologist Dr Benjamin Davis. Dr Davis concluded that the newspaper boy was not crying at the time he was shot. The evidence pointed to the conclusion that he had not cried at all, though the pathologist could not discount the possibility of a few tears.

Immediately after his shower with Michael, Brian Sinton was despatched to another prison – at Preston. He was released after serving just under eleven months of his eighteen-month sentence, despite breaching the original suspended sentence.

Peter Bryant   The third prisoner to give evidence in court came into the frame late in the preparations for the trial, when the weakness of the evidence for the prosecution must have seemed very clear to the lawyers and police who were preparing it. The identity of the person supposed to be carrying the gun across Lawnswood Road, seen by Mario Sabetta, had not been established and the nature of the vehicles used was unclear. Then there was the curious failure of Pat Molloy to recognise the farm when he had been driven to it, and the alibis for both couples of men, which, by early July 1979, were looking good. In addition nothing had been said by anyone about the property from the farm. The accused had never stolen antiques in the past, nor was there the slightest indication in any of the men's records that they knew anything about antiques. Another big problem was that there had been nothing said by Robinson or Michael Hickey about the details of the robbery on the farm. Even the crude 'confessions' to Ritter and Sinton had not dealt with those.

It was not until 9 July that Peter Bryant agreed to make a statement and was interviewed by Sergeant Tooth of the Staffordshire CID. Bryant was twenty-two. His youth in petty crime had culminated in January 1979 when he was sent down for three months for stealing whisky. While in prison he came up on another charge of robbing £1,580 in cash. He got two years for that and was sent to Winson Green prison. In November 1978 he tried to escape from a prison bus, and was placed on prison punishment, with incriminatory 'patches' on his clothes. 'Patches' prisoners had to exercise with top security prisoners, and so Bryant found himself, in Vincent's phrase, 'tagging along' on exercise with Vincent, Michael and Jimmy Robinson in the early months of 1979.

In these conversations, Bryant alleged, all three men had incriminated themselves over the Carl Bridgewater murder. He said that Jimmy Robinson had talked about the antiques taken from the farm, and had, with others, taken them to a fence, who would not handle them when he recognised them as goods from Yew Tree Farm. Bryant said Jimmy mentioned a carriage clock which had been stolen.

This was denied by Jimmy Robinson. His barrister, Mr Draycott, pointed out that no carriage clocks were stolen from Yew Tree Farm. Michael Hickey, in his notes to his lawyer on Bryant's statement, pointed out that Jimmy *had* mentioned a carriage clock during these conversations. It had been stolen on quite a separate occasion, in Weoley Castle.

Robinson was also alleged to have told Bryant some of the details of what happened when the farm was raided. He said, according to Bryant, that he had given Molloy 'a bollocking' for not 'coming downstairs when the car came into the drive'. Carl Bridgewater, of course, had not gone up to Yew Tree Farm in a car.

Bryant said that Vincent had commented on Mr Sabetta's evidence about the man in the road with the shotgun. According to Bryant, Vincent had all but admitted being the man with the shotgun, and had demonstrated how he had carried the gun, so that Sabetta could not have seen it.

Vincent did not deny talking to Bryant about Sabetta, but said, convincingly, that he was trying to show how Sabetta could not have seen as much of the gun as he said he had because the gun could be hidden under a man's coat.

Peter Bryant's evidence had come very late, and was full of contradictions.

Michael Kelly Perhaps the most damaging of the 'prison evidence' came from an experienced prison officer at Winson Green prison, Michael Kelly. He was not of course someone whose evidence had to be 'viewed with caution', as did the prisoners' evidence. Kelly told Mr Hollis, for Vincent, that he had considerable experience of listening to remand prisoners' conversations and reporting on them to his superiors.

Q. 'Have you done it on other occasions?'
A. 'Not to this degree on a trial, but on minor matters, yes.'
Q. 'Giving eavesdropping evidence?'

A. 'No, factual evidence.'

Q. 'There is no distinction to draw, is there?'

A. 'I don't know what you mean by eavesdropping. I am there to listen. That is my job.'

Q. 'That is how you see your job?'

A. 'With Category A men, that is why I was there. That is why I am in the wing every day of the year.' (*13.30*)

Mr Kelly reported a number of conversations which he overheard between the Hickeys, and which he alleged he had had with Michael Hickey. In April, he said, and again in June, Michael had told him that Robinson had shot the boy, and was mad. Michael denied ever saying such a thing. He also denied being on close terms with the prison officer, who was twice his age. Mr Kelly said Michael had called him 'Ned'. Michael replied contemptuously that the only name any inmate was allowed to give prison officers was 'boss'.

The judge gave a rather wide interpretation to these quotations. 'You must ask yourselves,' he told the jury, 'what effect it has on Michael if he did say that it was Robinson who shot Carl. Does that mean he was saying he was present at any rate at Yew Tree Farm and present in a room where it happened?'

The answer to that question was no. Even if Michael did tell a uniformed prison officer what he steadfastly didn't tell the police or anyone else – that Robinson shot Carl – it by no means meant that Michael himself had been at Yew Tree Farm.

It could have meant simply that Robinson had told him that he had shot the boy, or that he had got the information from someone else.

Mr Kelly's quotations did not end there. At one stage, while listening to Vincent Hickey talking to his family during a visit to the prison, he said he heard Vincent say: 'I am having bad dreams. I keep seeing the kid's face.'

Mr Kelly admitted that he often heard things wrongly. One conversation about a football match was cast in some doubt when it was shown that no football match of the kind had taken place at the alleged time. On another occasion he heard 'Edna' for 'Linda'. Mr Hollis for Vincent suggested that Vincent was trying to convince his family he had had nothing to do with the boy's murder, and had said that if he *had* killed him, "*I'd* be having bad dreams. *I'd* keep seeing the kid's face.' The difference between the two versions was a single consonant, and Mr Kelly admitted he was a good distance away. Vincent's version was just as, if not more, convincing.

Evidence From the Accused

The evidence from the prisons concluded the verbal evidence against the four men. The rest of the verbals came from the accused themselves. This consisted in the main of interminable evidence from twenty-eight police officers over four and a half days of the trial. The officers recounted the interviews they had with the defendants immediately after their arrest and during the time the four accused were denied access to their solicitors and their families. All these interviews, outlined in Chapter 2, were recorded in court. Hardly a sentence from the policemen's notebooks was left out. The interviews were taken in indiscriminate order. Each officer rattled through interviews which took place at different times, different dates and different police stations. Even in transcripts and typewritten statements, the interviews are extremely difficult to follow. At the trial, they must have been almost incomprehensible.

One or two features stood out, however. The first in date order was the most powerful evidence which the prosecution levelled against Vincent Hickey. It was that he himself had first mentioned the Carl Bridgewater murder to detectives; that he himself had implicated the other three and, eventually, himself. What other explanation could there be for such behaviour, unless it was that Vincent Hickey had himself taken part in the murder?

Mr Cox went back to this theme again and again in the course of his long cross-examination of Vincent. The young man went into the witness box shortly after the lunch adjournment on Wednesday, 24 October. His barrister, Mr Hollis, had finished with him by the end of the afternoon. For the whole of the next day, the 25th, and most of the 26th, Vincent muttered his replies to Mr Cox's carefully constructed line of questioning. Again and again, the judge asked Vincent to speak up in his own interest.

On the main question, Vincent could not answer directly. He was hampered by the judge's direction that the robbery at Chapel Farm must not be mentioned. He was allowed only to refer to the much lesser crime of deception which he and Linda had committed the previous September. The only answer he could give to the question 'Why did you shop Robinson and incriminate yourself for this horrible murder?' was 'To get the deception charge dropped, and to get bail.' The answer was pathetic. The deception charge seemed a trivial matter against the towering monstrosity of the Carl Bridgewater murder. The *fact* was, however (though the jury never knew about it), that Vincent was facing a serious armed robbery charge which was likely to land him in prison for eight years at least. *That* was a charge worth trying to escape by giving information on other offences, even if the information was entirely false.

The ban on any mention of the Chapel Farm robbery handicapped Vincent in another set of questions and answers. Vincent had attempted to describe to his interrogators the features of Jimmy Robinson's gun.

170

He had made a poor show of it, referring to some nonexistent silver engraving on the gun's side. But his rough and ready description did fit Robinson's gun. This was incriminating if he had never seen it before its alleged use at Yew Tree Farm. As far as the jury were concerned, he had never seen it. But of course he *had* seen it, only a few days before he described it, when he and Robinson had gone to rob Chapel Farm. Because the jury could not know about Chapel Farm, they could not know about Vincent's seeing Robinson's gun there.

In spite of these difficulties, and the dreadful mess he had got himself in with his own verbals, Vincent put up a reasonable show in the witness box. He had, he insisted, never been to Robinson's house; he had never been to the area around Yew Tree Farm and had no idea where it was; he had made up everything he'd told the officers about the robbery. He had told them two cars were involved, and described two cars – a Cortina estate and a van with a white top – which he knew he had disposed of well before the murder. He had shopped Robinson because he was the only criminal he knew who had a gun, and Molloy because he was Robinson's mate. He had attempted to shop Burkett for the same reason. The more 'information' he had made up to satisfy the officers so that he could get bail, the more they pressed him. 'They kept egging me on,' he explained. In the end he said far more than he ever intended to say, and, as the trap opened wide in front of him, shied away from it and denied everything.

His story hung together – except in two crucial areas. The first was his story to the officers that he had rung Bournville police station and talked about the Bridgewater murder long before his arrest. The police produced a policewoman who had indeed received an anonymous call at the end of October or the beginning of November from someone who had talked about the Bridgewater murder. At the trial, Vincent denied that he made any such phone call, he had simply told the officers that he had rung his local police station with such a call in order to satisfy their insatiable desire for more facts. The coincidence that such a call *was* made to Bournville police station was not explained.

In his second, more serious difficulty, Vincent acquitted himself much better. In his interviews he had apparently described the inside view of Yew Tree Farm looking in from the door through which Carl Bridgewater went before meeting his death. When Mr Cox asked him how he had been able to do that, Vincent said he had seen it on television. This revelation was greeted with impatient incredulity by the Queen's Counsel:

Q. 'When had you seen something on the television?'
A. 'When?'
Q. 'Yes.'

A. 'I can't remember the exact date.'

Q. 'Just do your best, would you? Just help us.'

A. 'It is impossible to remember the exact date.'

Q. 'I am not asking you for the exact date. I am asking you to do your best to tell the court when you saw something on the television that told you there was no hallway?'

A. 'Between when Carl Bridgewater was killed and when I was put in custody.'

Q. 'Yes, I know that it must have been that. Well?'

A. 'It was on the television a lot of times wasn't it? Nearly every news there was something about it.'

Q. 'You saw it on the telly. I am not asking you to even give us possibly the month, all I am asking you is was it weeks or months after Carl had been shot?'

A. 'I haven't a clue if it was just weeks or months. I know I seen it on the telly. I saw a lot of programmes concerning Carl Bridgewater on the television.'

Q. 'Tell the jury what you saw on the television.'

A. 'I can't remember. I can't tell you. I saw a lot of programmes.'

The wretched Vincent was floundering badly. Mr Cox went on:

Q. 'I don't want you to go through all the programmes. I just want you to tell us what you saw in relation to the layout of Yew Tree Farm.'

Vincent answered in sharp detail:

A. 'On the one occasion there was a young lad who was riding a bike along the road and he got off the bike and he walked to the doorway of the farm, and the camera was as if it was your eyes following him, and they were asking anybody if they remembered seeing this lad walking up to this door, and you had a glimpse inside and I think the door shut. I don't remember exactly. That is what was in my mind.' (*15.15,16*)

The more Mr Cox probed, the more precise were Vincent's answers. It took only a little bit of research to discover that Vincent was describing in remarkable detail the 'reconstruction' ordered by Staffordshire police on 3 October 1978, two weeks after the murder. A schoolfriend of Carl Bridgewater had taken the part of his dead friend, and the episode had been televised on both commercial television and on the BBC. No programme on the case had wider coverage.

As a result of his clear answers, the jury asked to see the programme. It was shown to the court as the very last piece of evidence. The sequence of events was exactly as Vincent had described it. As the camera came up to the house after the disappearing boy, the viewer had a clear look inside. There was, as Vincent had said, no hallway. The camera faced straight into the room where the boy was shot and then cut. The point was made. The 'fact' offered by Vincent to back his confession, which the police thought could only have come from someone who had personally visited Yew Tree Farm, had been shown throughout the nation on television.

Although Vincent had incriminated himself by his interviews with police in the days after he gave himself up, his evidence, as the judge pointed out, was *not* evidence against any of the others he named. All four men were charged as accomplices. It is an iron rule in English law that one accomplice cannot give evidence against another, except in the witness box. So Vincent's interviews could not tell against Robinson or Molloy. Nor could they tell against his cousin Michael, though in truth Vincent had hardly incriminated Michael in the first place.

Michael, moreover, did not incriminate himself. In all the interviews he endured without friends, family or lawyers, there was only one brief occasion when the interrogating officers suggested that was a hint of a confession. This was when Michael was having his fingerprints taken in the middle of the day on 22 December. Detective Sergeant Clive Williams gave evidence of this short burst of conversation:

> Williams: 'Was the paper boy smiling when the gun went off?'
> Michael: 'No, he wasn't.'
> Williams: 'Do you realise what you've just said?'
> Michael: *No reply.*
> Williams: 'You must have been there to know that.'
> Michael: 'I wasn't there, I know nothing about it.'
> Williams: 'Now come off it, you know what you've just said. I think you pulled the trigger.'
> Michael: *No reply.*
> Williams: 'Are you going to answer me?'
> Michael: 'I've got nothing to say.'

Michael denied the conversation. He remembered police officers asking if the boy was smiling, and he remembered answering as he had answered all other questions on the subject: 'I don't know; I wasn't there.' As Constable Clive Massey admitted to Mr Tucker in cross-examination: 'He denied it throughout, yes.' (*10.3*)

He denied it throughout his long cross-examination on 29 and 30 October, too. There was not a single moment in all his time in the wit-

173

ness box when he wavered or seemed in doubt. At one moment truculent and defiant, at another almost silent in apparent boredom at the constant repetition, the teenager kept repeating that he had never been anywhere near Yew Tree Farm, and had no idea what happened there on 19 September.

The same was true of Jimmy Robinson. The prosecution made considerable efforts, through recounting the long police interviews, to prove that Robinson, in the judge's words, 'went to the very brink of admitting he had been at Yew Tree Farm'. When he had been reduced to his knees, begging the officers to believe his denials, he had said (according to the police): 'God help me and if I have done this terrible thing, help me to remember.'

On another occasion, confronted with Molloy's statement. Robinson is alleged to have said: 'If I admit it's me, it's thirty years. I'd tell you if I done it. I'd get it behind me. Would you admit it if you'd done it and due for thirty?' Asked if *he* would, Robinson then said: 'No, for Christ's sake.' On another occasion, again in great distress, Robinson shouted at the officers: 'Leave me alone. If I have done this thing and had a mental block, leave me alone for a bit and I'll see if I can remember the day.'

These were the only three passages which the judge cited to justify the prosecution's argument that Jimmy had gone 'to the brink' of confessing. Against them, ranged over nearly a week of the harshest interrogation, were the hundreds of times Robinson said he had never been anywhere near Yew Tree Farm, would never shoot a child and certainly had not shot Carl Bridgewater. These denials became stronger in the courtroom. At the end of his first day in the witness box, Robinson broke down as Mr Draycott asked him about the other prisoners. The memory of the hatred and contempt which had been heaped on him during his year on remand exploded. He burst into tears, pointing his finger at Vincent Hickey and denouncing him for his denunciation. The following day, in cross-examination, Robinson cooled down. Not without the occasional flash of anger and humour, he continued his consistent denials. Whatever the evidence against him, he, like Michael Hickey, gave the clear impression that he had from the first moment protested his complete innocence of the crime.

In sum then, what was the admissable evidence against the three men?

Against Robinson were the three identifications from people who had failed to pick him out on an identification parade; the fact that he had a gun which could have been used at Yew Tree Farm; the evidence of Catherine Guy that Vincent Hickey had gone to his house; and the verbal admissions he was alleged to have made (and denied making) to

174

Helen Johnston, Dundas-Ure, Ritter and Bryant.

Against Vincent were his own admissions, never signed and then denied, that he had been involved; the evidence of his two neighbours that he had a Ford Cortina; the evidence of Reg Hickey and Mrs White that he had been in the area of the farm; the evidence of Catherine Guy that he had visited Jimmy Robinson's house; the story that Bryant told about him pretending to hold the gun; and Prison Officer Kelly's version of his remark about bad dreams and seeing the kid's face.

Against Michael there was the verbal confession allegedly made to the prisoner Sinton; the denunciation of Robinson to Prison Officer Kelly (strongly denied by Michael); the evidence of Reg Hickey that Michael had worked in the area; and the chance remarks to Michael Lee that Joe and Vincent Hickey were getting rid of 'stuff' from 'that farmhouse' and to the taxi driver Eaton that he was with him on the day of the murder, when he wasn't.

It was at the very best a threadbare case, unsupported by forensic evidence, and put together almost entirely by interrogating police officers, informers, and criminals who stood to gain from what they said. What could the three men say in reply?

The Case for the Defence

The case for Jimmy Robinson and the Hickey cousins was very simple. It was that they were elsewhere at the time of the murder. We left all three men at the start of the trial with strong alibis, supported in each case by independent witnesses.

The Hickeys' alibi stood on two legs. There was the 'ashtray alibi' supported by Linda Galvin, her daughter Stephanie, who bought the ashtray, and the shopkeepers Mr Moore and Mrs Fulford. The alibi was stronger than the defence knew. Linda Galvin had said at the committal that the ashtray had been bought on the afternoon her new suite had arrived, 19 September or the day after, 20 September. But the shop from which it was bought was shut on the 20th. So, if Linda was right, the ashtray was bought with Vincent Hickey's money at about the time Carl Bridgewater was being shot.

Linda Galvin and her daughter Stephanie were crucial, of course, to this part of the alibi. Apart from the officer in charge of the inquiry, they were the only prosecution witnesses to give evidence at committal at Wombourne. In his opening address to the jury at the trial, Philip Cox QC outlined the importance of Linda Galvin as a witness.

In September 1978, Vincent Hickey had separated from his wife and was living with Linda Galvin at her flat 35/4 Lower Beeches Road, Northfield. This is a three bedroomed flat and on the 19th September a man called Alan Murray was also staying at the flat as he had nowhere else to live. Young Michael Hickey frequently stayed overnight at Galvin's flat at this time and on the morning of 19th September Alan Murray had to go for an X-ray. Linda Galvin recalls this day that Vincent and Michael went off in her beige 1100 car in the morning, and that she remained home for the rest of the day, during the afternoon of which a new three-piece suite was delivered. She is unable to recall the time that Vincent Hickey arrived home. Alan Murray recalls that Vincent arrived home between 5 and 6 p.m.

The purpose of opening speeches to the jury is to give an account of the evidence of *the witnesses whom the prosecution intend to call*. Any name connected with any evidence mentioned in such a speech is certain to become either a living person in the witness box, or a signed statement which is read out.

The fact that Mr Cox referred to Linda Galvin did not surprise anyone. She had been a witness at committal at Wombourne. She was on the list of witnesses. Obviously, she would be called in due course to say she couldn't remember what time Vincent came back to her on that evening, and the defence lawyers would be able to put to her the story of the ashtray, as they had done at Wombourne.

The trial started on 8 October, when Mr Cox made his opening speech. On the fifth day – 12 October – prosecution lawyers announced that they would not be calling Linda Galvin, Stephanie Galvin or Alan Murray as witnesses.

Mr Hollis and Mr Tucker for the Hickeys were dumbfounded. Their defence rested on the alibi with which they believed Linda Galvin could help. She and Alan Murray had also important things to say about the cars. Both had been quite certain that Vincent was not driving a blue Ford Cortina estate in August or September 1978.

The Galvins had both given evidence at Wombourne. They were prosecution witnesses. Linda had been banned by the prosecution from seeing Vincent in prison after the committal. The defence had not interviewed her. They assumed she would be coming to trial at the behest of the prosecution.

On Tuesday, 16 October, the jury was cleared from the court while the lawyers fought the matter out. Mr Hollis and Mr Tucker argued that the prosecution, having mentioned Linda and Stephanie Galvin in their opening statement and having called them at Wombourne, were obliged by law to call them at the trial. If they refused to do so, the lawyers suggested, the judge himself should call the witnesses and submit them to cross-examination.

It was an awkward time for both the judge and Mr Cox. The judge insisted that the issue was whether or not the prosecution believed Linda Galvin to be a 'witness of truth' or a 'credible witness'. If they had reason to believe she was not, they were not obliged to call her.

Mr Cox replied that Linda Galvin, on the issue of the alibi, was not a credible witness. In a remarkable passage, he explained:

> It is right in my submission that the prosecution should take the view, having regard to the nature of the alibi notice, having regard to what she has said in her statement already that, if she is called by the prosecution, in relation to what time Vincent Hickey arrived home that afternoon, she may say: 'I didn't see him until seven or eight o'clock that night. I simply cannot remember what time he came back' – but on the other hand in my submission there is a grave risk that she might say: 'Oh yes I remember him coming back at half past three' and give chapter and verse as to why she did remember it.

There was a 'grave risk' that Linda might provide the Hickeys with a cast-iron alibi! She had not done so previously, so she was clearly not a credible witness.

This was too much for Mr Tucker, Michael's barrister. For once the natural courtesy between barristers seemed to crack, as Mr Tucker exposed the prosecution's position:

> I am surprised, I am bound to say, to hear what my learned friend Mr Cox has said because we were not told until last Friday of that decision and, indeed, we were given a list of witnesses who were to be called last Friday and Linda Galvin's name was on it. She was listed as a witness. Presumably the decision was taken on Thursday afternoon that she should be one of the witnesses called on Friday, and her name appeared on the list. Something therefore had occurred prior to last Friday morning, 12th October, to make the prosecution reverse that decision. I do not know what it was but, whatever it was, it is a far cry from saying Linda Galvin is no longer to be regarded as reliable or credible on an important issue.

What could have occurred to make the prosecution reverse that decision? As the prosecution lawyers sat down that Thursday evening to discuss the witnesses for the Friday, they must have noticed a glaring discrepancy. Linda had said in evidence at Wombourne that the ashtray must have been bought on the Tuesday or the Wednesday. But the ashtray shop was closed on the Wednesday afternoon. If Linda was called to the witness box, to be followed there inevitably by the witnesses from the ashtray shop, this discrepancy would certainly be exposed, with the 'grave risk' that Linda would provide the Hickeys with a firm alibi.

After what he called a lot of 'anxious consideration' the judge agreed with the prosecution. There was, he said, a 'wide discretion' for the prosecution to call what witnesses they liked, and he did not want to interfere with that.

The defence was now in an intolerable position. The obvious option was to interview Linda Galvin themselves, and call her as a defence witness. As Mr Tucker told the Judge: 'I would be hostage to fortune, am I not? Either I call her, knowing and risking that she would then be cross-examined by the prosecution who have declined to call her, or I do not call her and risk the comment: "Where is your principal alibi witness?"'

Mr Tucker was reluctant to call Linda Galvin. She would be liable to cross-examination on the basis of her original statement that Vincent did not come back all afternoon. Mr Tucker would then be risking the charge that his client was faking an alibi. On the other hand, *not* to call her, as he said, denied his client his principal alibi witness.

In the event, the defence lawyers decided not to interview Linda, nor to call her to the witness box. As a result they could not call Mr Moore or Mrs Fulford either.

The jury heard the story of the ashtray from only two witnesses – Vincent and Michael Hickey themselves. Their alibi for the earlier part of the afternoon was not supported by anyone else, and was of course incomparably weaker as a result.

The second limb of the alibi was the visit to Bristol Road Garage. Michael and Vincent both told the court with some confidence that they had gone to the garage and arranged to buy a car at about half past four in the afternoon of the murder. If true, this was a complete alibi.

We have seen in the last chapter how the cousins came to recall their visit to the garage quite late – only when they had heard from Linda about the delivery of the new suite.

Three witnesses came to the trial to support this part of their story.

The garage proprietor, Andrew Zannetos, agreed that he had arranged to sell a car to a man calling himself Galvin who gave Linda Galvin's address. He had a receipt for a £50 deposit – but there was no date on it.

He could not remember the man – or the date. But if the man had wanted finance for the car – as Vincent Hickey did – his application would have to be phoned through to the hire purchase company, General Guarantee Corporation.

Mr Zannetos was asked about how he phoned through these applications for finance. 'Well,' he replied, 'I mean if somebody comes in the morning, for instance, I get in touch with the finance the same day; or if it is late in the afternoon sometimes I leave it to the following day,

178

because I know they close about five o'clock, so I don't normally bother them in the afternoon, late in the afternoon.' (*16.3*)

There were, he said, exceptions. 'Sometimes we get customers who want everything done quick, and, of course, even if it is four o'clock or half past four in the afternoon, and they want to speed things up there is a possibility that I can get in touch with the finance in the afternoon.'

The general rule was, then, that he would telephone the hire purchase company on the same day as the agreed sale, if the sale was in the morning. If it was in the afternoon, or late afternoon, he would leave the phone call till the next day. If a customer was in a hurry, however, he might phone through about the finance in the afternoons as well.

If Vincent and Michael had gone to the Bristol Road garage on the afternoon of 19 September, as they claimed, their application for finance would normally be phoned through the following day.

Michael Hurley gave evidence as manager of the General Guarantee Corporation. He produced the day books for the period. In this, he said, his clerks entered the names of all the people who had applied for finance. There, high on the list for 20 September, was the name J. Galvin. The document strongly supported the cousins' story.

There was more to come. William Mee also gave evidence. He said that he had bought a car from the Bristol Road Garage the previous September. This happened – definitely – in the afternoon, he said. He finished work at 3.30 and could not have gone to the garage before that. He thought the day was a Tuesday, because he was paid on a Tuesday and he needed the car urgently for the following weekend. Mr Mee's name was entered in Mr Hurley's day book for Wednesday and he was accepted as a good credit risk that same day, 20 September.

He could not have gone to the garage on the Wednesday before leaving work at 3.30, and so could never have got to the garage in time on the Wednesday to clear credit control. William Mee must, therefore, have gone to Bristol Road Garage on the Tuesday – the day of the murder. Mee's name appeared *after* Galvin's. The evidence of the three men, taken together with the day book, suggested very strongly that both Galvin and Mee had gone to Bristol Road Garage on the Tuesday afternoon, and that their names had been phoned through, as was Mr Zannetos' habit, on the Wednesday morning, together, in the order in which they went to the garage – Galvin, then Mee.

All this seemed powerful for the defence. Yet the impression given by the alibi witnesses was blurred. What should have been strong evidence to support the cousins' story came over so poorly in court that the prosecution managed to turn it to their advantage.

To start with, Mr Hurley for the hire purchase company admitted he was not the man who dealt with the documents, and was therefore the wrong person to give evidence. Pamela Massey, the clerk, who had handled the applications on the day of the murder, and who had given a helpful statement to the defence, was not called. Mr Hurley was vague, insisting that names could be entered in the book in any order. The fact, he implied, that Galvin was so high on the list did not mean that his application came in early.

The detail of the day book, which, as we have seen, showed entries in different handwriting – first the three by post, then one other entry, then Galvin, then Mee – was not brought home to the jury. Yet the fact that names were entered in different handwriting suggested that they were entered in some sort of order, and that those high on the list were entered earlier than those low down the list. Another point about which Mr Hurley seemed unclear was that Mr Mee's name (and therefore Galvin's) was phoned through early on the Wednesday morning.

There were other problems which blurred the issue. Mr Mee, in reply to Mr Hollis, said he had left work at 3.30, and had gone to Bristol Road Garage 'somewhere between half past three and five' (*16.6*). When he was asked by Mr Judge to estimate how long he had been at the garage, he said: 'Ten, fifteen, twenty minutes' (*16.8*). Then Mr Judge reminded him of his statement to police the previous April, in which he said he and his brother had been 'at the garage for about one hour, leaving at 5 p.m.'. He agreed this was likely to be right (*16.9*).

Vincent and Michael had estimated that they went to the garage between 4.30 and 5.00 p.m. Mee said that he was there an hour, and left at 5.00 p.m. But the Hickeys had not seen the Mees, nor *vice versa*, and Vincent and Billy Mee had been at school together. This enabled the prosecution to suggest that Vincent was clearly making up the afternoon alibi, and had in fact been to the garage the following day – the 20th.

Mr Justice Drake made the point twice. 'There was no suggestion from Vincent that Mee was there at that time and the prosecution say: "Well, there is pretty good evidence, isn't there, that Vincent and Michael were not there on the afternoon of the Tuesday the 19th?"'

And again: 'If Vincent Hickey, alias on this occasion James Galvin, completed his deal as he and Michael say by about 5.30, that might explain their being put in the book against the date of the 20th; but, as I say, it does not seem possible, does it, that both Mee and Vincent were there on the same occasion on the afternoon of the 19th, because the times they referred to certainly overlap.'

The times *did* overlap. But there was, as we have seen, other evidence which the police had at their disposal, and which they had barred from the defence, which suggested otherwise. William Mee mentioned in his evidence that he had been to 'quite a few garages in the area' (*16.8*). If the jury had heard the evidence of the Wytons or of Billy Mee's brother Bob, a picture would have been built up which would have proved it quite impossible for Mr Mee to have been at Bristol

Road Garage at 4.15. To start with, he did not get home from work until four o'clock. Then he had to collect his brother and the Wytons. Then they visited other garages, including one about twenty minutes away in the Stratford Road.

The Wytons and Robert Mee put the visit much later. They all remembered having to move their Mini from the forecourt of the garage so that cars could be put away behind a steel fence. They remembered Gayle being in a hurry in order to catch the shops before they closed at six o'clock. They all recorded how the garage had only been visited as a last resort, on the way home. All this suggested that William Mee's visit to the garage happened later than he thought – well after five o'clock and probably nearer six. If so, of course, it would not have been at all surprising that he missed the Hickeys, who always said they were clear of the garage by half past five, and probably earlier. The order they went to the garage, in other words, was the same as the order their names appeared in the day book: Galvin (4.30 to 5.15 approx.); Mee (5.30 to 6 approx).

There was one problem with this theory, Michael Hickey repeated what he had always said: that he had seen the garage proprietor, assisted by another man, putting cars away behind the steel fence. This suggested, according to prosecution and judge, that Michael was inventing the afternoon visit. For if the Hickeys said, as they did, that they left the garage by half past five, and Zannetos said, as he did, that he never put his cars away before six, the Hickeys must be wrong.

'That may be, you may think,' said Mr Justice Drake to the jury, 'some totally different occasion when Vincent or Michael had passed the garage and had seen someone putting the cars away after six o'clock, and that was being used to embellish the alibi.'

It *was* true that if the cousins went to the garage when they said they did they could not have seen the cars being put away. Was there any other explanation for this contradiction apart from that given by the judge?

Some months after the trial, after much puzzling, Michael recalled that after going home to Linda's for egg and chips, he had been given a lift to the Dog and Partridge by Alan Murray. On their way they had passed the Bristol Road Garage, and Michael had pointed out the car which Vincent had bought that afternoon. It was still on the forecourt, but other cars were being driven behind the steel fence by Zannetos, helped by another Greek. Michael said he had muddled up the incident with his visit to the garage earlier in the afternoon. Of course, this was a shift in his original story, but it was plausible. Certainly, if an alibi had been 'concocted' (the judge's word) for 4.30 to 5.30, it seemed unlikely that the cousins would embellish it with something that regularly happened about an hour later.

181

What about the other man in the office? Mr Zannetos gave evidence before Michael Hickey. He was asked by Mr Hollis, for Vincent, if he had someone working for him in his garage the previous September. Mr Zannetos answered 'No'.

'Is there somebody else who would appear to be a Greek chap?' asked Mr Hollis.

'Well, there's a lot of people calling there from time to time,' replied the garage proprietor, vaguely.

The defence left the matter there. The prosecution leaped to expose the vagueness of the answers. Cross-examining Mr Zannetos, Mr Judge asked again if he had anyone working for him at the garage in September 1978. No, said Mr Zannetos, firmly, he had not.

When Michael went into the witness box later that same day (29 October), he stayed with his story – consistent since he was first arrested – that there were two Greeks in the office. 'There was the man himself who come up this morning and a Greek, a big fat bloke, really big he was,' he said. (*16.25*)

Mr Cox when he came to cross-examine Michael pounced at once on the apparent contradiction.

Q. 'There were not two Greeks. There was one.'

A. 'There was two.'

Q. 'Did you describe the second man this morning – as very big and fat?'

A. 'I'm not quite sure, but I think the man who came up this morning said it was his grandfather, but I'm not sure of that.'

Mr Justice Drake: 'That wasn't the question. The question was how did you describe him this morning?'

A. 'Big and fat.'

Mr Cox: 'You described Mr Zannetos, or one Greek, and someone else there who was very big and fat?'

A. 'That's right.'

Q. 'Moving the cars?'

A. 'The big fat one was. When I got there, he was sitting in the office.'

Q. 'Who was?'

A. 'The big fat bloke. Mr Zannetos was sitting at the desk filling the forms in for Vincent.'

Q. 'Do you recall it being suggested to him that there was a big fat bloke sat in a chair in his office?'

A. 'Nobody put the question to him.' (*16.58*)

Mr Cox changed the subject.

Michael was quite right. Nobody *had* put the question to Mr

Zannetos that there might have been a big fat man sitting in his office. Had they done so, no doubt Mr Zannetos would have disclosed (as he disclosed to me and Ann Whelan in 1984) that his father-in-law, Mr Tsokalides, who was big and fat, was in Birmingham that autumn. He often visited the garage and sat in his son-in-law's office for long periods in the day. Once again, a little piece of evidence which appeared from what was said in court to be part of an invented alibi was a fact which was available, but which no one from defence or prosecution was able to discover.

At least the Hickeys had some witnesses to support their alibi. In the months before the trial, Jimmy Robinson, as we have seen, was putting together his alibi, with the help of witnesses. He and Pat Molloy, he said, had been to the California pub after Carol Bradbury had come out of hospital. They had returned to Carol's for lunch, gone to sleep and woken up in time to see *Star Trek*. There were obviously no documents to support this alibi, but there were witnesses: Carol Bradbury; her daughter Tracey; Vi Collins, the woman who saw Jimmy with the flowers.

In his letters to Carol in the weeks before the trial, Jimmy was confident that 'the truth will come out'. There was never any doubt in his mind or in his letters that Carol's evidence would be valuable to him. He was reinforced in the knowledge that Carol had also given a statement to Pat Molloy's lawyers and would be a witness for Pat's alibi as well.

As the trial continued, Jim's lawyers engaged in fierce discussion as to whether they should call the alibi witnesses. One side (taken for the most part by Mr Fryer) was that Robinson didn't have much to lose, and it was better to call supporting witnesses than to leave him to tell his story on his own. The other (pressed by Mr Draycott) put two serious objections.

The first was that Carol had made contradictory statements to the police. As we have seen, when told by the police that the flowers had not been bought until Wednesday, she had equivocated. However certain she seemed about it later, her detailed statement the previous January would be mercilessly thrown at her by the prosecution. There were obvious problems in calling a thirteen-year-old girl who might not perform at all convincingly in her mother's support. Vi Collins was unlikely to stay firm under cross-examination about the exact day she saw Jimmy from the balcony. The fear that Jimmy would be accused of inventing an alibi might, Mr Draycott suggested, be compounded by the witnesses, rather than diminished by them.

There was a further, more substantial, problem. What was Pat Molloy's position? If Molloy did not stand up for the alibi, might that not finally wreck Jimmy's case? And did not Carol and Tracey say definitely in their statements that Molloy was with Jim that afternoon? If

Molloy said anything different, would not the contradiction be lethal?

The weakness in both these arguments was that the risks were being taken anyway. If Robinson was to give evidence, as he was determined to do, he would be subject also to the charge that he did not say where he was when he was first asked about it; and he too would say Molloy was with him. On both counts, it seemed at least arguable that the dangers were to be run anyway, and that it was better to run them with supporting witnesses than to leave the prisoner on his own.

Caution won the day. On the evening before Jimmy Robinson went into the witness box, he was told of his counsel's advice; that Carol, Tracey and Vi Collins should not be called, and that he was on his own.

Carol had been told by the defence lawyers to stay at home, and not togo near the court until she heard the lawyers' decision. She was outraged. She was prepared to be a witness, and indeed wanted to be one. As she has told me since on several occasions: 'I knew perfectly well where Jimmy was on the day that boy was killed, and I was determined to tell the court.'

Irritated by her ban from even the precincts of the court, and suspecting Robinson of downgrading her role in getting him acquitted, she stopped writing to him. This sent him into a desperate frenzy. He wrote to her each day, passionately begging her to reply. On 31 October, as she tried to follow the trial on television and in the papers, she got a letter from Cartwright and Lewis:

> Dear Madam,
> We write to inform you that upon the advice of counsel, James Edward Robinson has decided against calling you to give evidence at the trial at Stafford Crown Court. This advice has been given him by his barrister in view of the fact that you made two statements to the police which would probably conflict with what you would say in the witness box and therefore Counsel deems it advisable not to put you in that position. There is always such a difficulty with alibi evidence and obviously Counsel advised Mr Robinson in his own best interests.
> We thank you for your continued assistance in this matter.

The letter was a tremendous blow to a courageous woman who was preparing for an ordeal in the interests of the man she loved, and of what she was certain was the truth. She did not start writing again to Jimmy until his letters explaining his own outrage at the decision mollified her.

> Let's get it straight, Cal. I was shocked, sickened and really upset when my counsel said he didn't want to call you. We had a big row,

I cursed and raved at all of them. I wasn't too worried about you being tripped up in the box because I realised that even if you *did* get confused over some details, the basic and fundamental truth would come out and be clear to the jury – but my counsel said, no we can't risk it.

Fortunately for both of them, relations were restored by the end of the trial.

Who can say that the lawyers were wrong? Carol, Tracey and Vi Collins on their own did not make a formidable trio. But they were flesh and blood on the bones of a story which the jury heard only from Robinson. More importantly, however, would the lawyers' decision have gone the same way if they had had the evidence which the prosecution had discovered, and not passed on? What if they had known of Yvonne Hards' statement that there were flowers in the flat when she herself gave Carol flowers on the Wednesday? If this additional piece in the jigsaw had been available to the defence, might they not have decided to support their client's story?

In the event, Jimmy was left entirely on his own to tell his story. He told Mr Draycott:

> I remember talking to a couple of people in the Cali when I came out of the Cali in the afternoon. I says to Pat I was feeling a bit guilty about the way I had served Carol out over the motor and leaving her on her own the day she came out of hospital. I says: 'I'll get her a bunch of flowers' and me and Pat put a quid each towards them and went over the shop opposite the Cali. I remember going down the road with the flowers with Pat, going into the house. I gave Carol – I took the flowers upstairs to her and put them on the bed. . . I think Carol came downstairs and put the flowers in a jug or something. (*17.57-8*)

The only witness called by Robinson's defence was his solicitor, Tony Fryer, who testified on the identification parades.

There *was*, however, some corroboration for the 'flowers' alibi at the trial. It came not from the defence but from a prosecution witness, Susan Bennett, Carol Bradbury's neighbour. Susan Bennett gave evidence mainly about Robinson's gun which had been brought to her house for hiding two days after the murder. This was thought by the prosecution to be highly suspicious. In fact, it was not suspicious at all since Robinson had been arrested for the Tamworth meat robbery on 20 September (the day after the murder) and Carol and Pat were anxious to get rid of his gun quickly in case the police raided her house.

This was the point which Mr Gorman, counsel for Pat Molloy, was

185

anxious to make when he rose in cross examination. But he started with
something else:

> Q. 'You did not actually see Carol Bradbury brought home or
> coming home from the hospital, did you?'
> A. 'No.'
> Q. 'The first that you knew of her being home was when she
> came round at night to see you.'
> A. 'Yes.'
> Q. 'That was the Tuesday. On the Wednesday you had made an
> arrangement with Carol that she would look after Kelly, that is
> your child?'
> A. 'Yes.'
> Q. 'So did you go to Carol's house that morning?'
> A. 'The Wednesday morning, yes.'
> Q. 'What sort of time would that be?'
> A. 'About nine o'clock.'
> Q. 'In the morning?'
> A. 'Yes.'
> Q. 'Did you notice whether there were any flowers in Carol's
> flat at that time?'
> A. 'Yes.'
> Q. 'Was there any talk of them?'
> A. 'When, on the morning?'
> Q. 'On the Wednesday morning.'
> A. 'I just told Carol, like, Carol said: "These are the flowers that
> Jimmy brought me in yesterday" and I said they was nice and that.'
> Q. 'But you saw them did you?'
> A. 'Yes.' (*7.23*)

Susan Bennett's answers to Mr Gorman did not present the whole
picture. She had told the police that in a conversation on the *Tuesday
evening*, the evening of the murder, Carol had told her about a bunch of
flowers which Jimmy had bought her coming back from the pub. When
Mr Gorman asked if there was 'any talk' of the flowers, she'd asked:
'When, on the morning?' When restricted to the morning, the conversation she reported was anodyne.

Her conversation with Carol *on the previous evening* plainly supported an alibi for Jimmy Robinson. It stated clearly that he had brought
flowers back from the pub, and therefore could not have hurtled out to
Yew Tree Farm. Nor did Mr Draycott, for Robinson, carry this matter
any further. His brief included the statement Tony Fryer had taken
from Susan Bennett. When it was his chance to cross-examine Susan
Bennett, he told the judge: 'No Questions.'

Susan Bennett gave evidence on 16 October, Jimmy Robinson on the 30th, a whole fortnight later. Neither Mr Gorman nor Mr Draycott mentioned the connection in their closing speeches, nor did the judge in his summing up. The strength of the 'flowers' alibi was never properly presented to the jury. How strong it would have been if supported not just by Susan Bennett but by Carol Bradbury, her daughter Tracey, Yvonne Hards and Vi Collins can only be left to speculation.

Pat Molloy

Until the last few days of the trial, Jimmy Robinson and the Hickey cousins and their lawyers had good reason to be satisfied with the way things had gone. The three men had acquitted themselves reasonably well in the witness box. Vincent Hickey had made a reasonable show of explaining and contradicting his early confession. Above all, the prosecution evidence against them had been absurdly weak. On the day he gave evidence, Jimmy Robinson wrote to Carol in a cheerful mood. His barrister, he said, was 'delighted'. Most of the 'liars', he felt, had been 'exposed'. He wasn't counting any chickens, he concluded, but the trial was going 'so-so', better than he expected.

This optimism was based on a legal point which was repeated again and again by the judge and the barristers. The point was that the statement of one accomplice is not evidence against another – unless that accomplice goes into the witness box. The jury heard the full story of Pat Molloy's confession of 10 December. They had it in writing in front of them. The statement implicated Jimmy Robinson and the Hickeys in the murder of Carl Bridgewater. Molloy claimed he was upstairs while the others were downstairs, and that he rushed down as soon as Carl was killed to find the other three quarrelling over a smoking gun and a dead boy.

This statement *was not evidence against anyone except Molloy*. So said the law. So said the judge. So said the lawyers. The jury were instructed to put the statement which they had heard, and which they had read, out of their minds except in so far as it implicated Molloy. They had to rule out all consideration that it incriminated Robinson or the Hickeys.

In legal theory this was, no doubt, admirable. In practice the jury had in front of them a statement which said, in effect: 'I was at the scene of the crime, rootling through drawers in upstairs bedrooms, when I heard a shot, rushed down and there were Michael, Jimmy and Vincent standing with a gun over the murdered newspaper boy.' It is almost inconceivable that this did not influence them.

If the judicial authorities were serious about their own rules, if they really meant it when they said Molloy's confession was only evidence against himself, then their best course was to try him separately, and to keep his confession out of the hands and ears of the jury which tried the other three.

As it was, the shadow of Pat Molloy haunted the entire trial. He was kept separate from the other three prisoners, in a row behind them (where he was not safe from constant invective from Jimmy Robinson and Michael Hickey). As the trial went on, the suspense was unbearable. None of the other defendants, their families or their lawyers knew what Molloy would do. Robinson at least knew that Pat's lawyers had talked to Carol Bradbury and her daughter. The others knew that Molloy had put in an alibi notice, saying he was with Robinson at the time of the murder. Would he testify to that? Would he deny his statement and denounce his interrogators? As the case against the three other men stumbled along, the enigma of Pat Molloy grew.

In fact, the matter had been settled well before the trial. It was discussed in the 'brief to counsel' prepared by the Tamworth solicitors Argyle's for Molloy's barristers, John Gorman QC and Malcolm Lee.

After reviewing the evidence, the brief comes to the main point, the confession statement:

> The truth of this statement is of course denied by the accused as are the subsequent admissions, but instructing solicitors feel that its effect must be considered since it would seem to be important to decide whether or not it would be in the accused's interests to give evidence at the trial. Counsel is instructed to advise on this aspect in due course but instructing solicitors feel that the accused's denial of the truth of his statement and admissions is unlikely to impress the jury. It may be such as to convince the jury that he is lying and thereby to increase the chances of conviction. . .
>
> The accused fully appreciates and acknowledges the difficulties of his case, bearing in mind the admissions that have been made, and yet it must be emphasised that the accused's instructions have remained consistent since he was first seen on the 18th December 1978. He has maintained his instructions that he was not involved in the burglary or the murder and does not know who was.

This was supported by Molloy's own statement of evidence which came with the brief, and which said that he had no knowledge at all of Yew Tree Farm and at the time of the murder was snoozing by Carol Bradbury's fire.

The solicitors' brief went on to make some very shrewd observations about the prosecution, and Pat Molloy's own importance to it.

From the prosecution point of view, instructing solicitors feel that they have nowhere near as much evidence as they would like, particularly against the other defendants. With regard to the other defendants, counsel will observe that particularly in relation to the additional evidence, the prosecution are very much 'scraping the barrel'. The position of the accused is an unusual one, in that instructing solicitors feel that any defence would carry more creditability and a greater chance of success if his instructions had confirmed the truth of what he had said to the police. This however is not the case.

The irony of the situation is that of all the defendants the accused is the one perhaps least likely to become involved in such a dreadful crime, and yet he may stand in greatest danger of conviction. . . Instructing solicitors feel that the police who have investigated this case share this view. There has been a suggestion that the accused is a professional burglar who has found himself out of his depth in the company of men of a violent nature.

The advice could be summarised like this. Molloy insists he never went to the farm and doesn't know who did. He says his confession was made under duress, and with the help of information provided by the police. But it will be better for him at the trial if he shuts up about the truth, and allows the false statement to stand. He says he was never there, but he will be better off if he doesn't say so at the trial.

There *was* a perverse logic in this advice. Molloy's statement said he was upstairs at the time of the murder. If he left that alone, and did not come over to the jury as a liar, he would most probably get off the murder charge. There was almost no other evidence against him.

For Molloy to be found guilty of murder, the prosecution had to prove that he knew that a gun was being taken to Yew Tree Farm, and that it might be used there. There was only one flimsy bit of evidence to suggest that. Prison Officer Francis Edwards said he had had a conversation with Molloy in Shrewsbury prison the previous January:

'I said to him: "You don't seem to be the sort of man who would do this sort of thing."
Q. 'What did he reply?'
A. 'He said: "I didn't. I allowed myself to become involved."'
Q. 'What else did he say?'
A. 'He said: "I am not making excuses. I knew he had a gun."'
(*12.14*)

It was not very difficult for Mr Gorman to cast doubt on this evidence.

The officer made no note of his conversation and made no statement about it for two months afterwards. Moreover, even if the account was precise, the words 'I knew he had a gun' could have been a general statement that he knew Robinson owned a gun (as indeed Molloy did know), and need not have referred to the farm at all.

What other evidence was there that Molloy was guilty of murder?

There was the so-called 'confession' heard by Helen Johnston, but that was discredited by her getting the date entirely wrong. All eight identification witnesses at a parade held on 16 January had failed to pick out Molloy from the line. *The only real evidence against him was his statement.* If he denied it, he could be convicted of murder because the jury might think he was a liar. If so convicted, he stood to serve twenty to twenty-five years. If he did not deny it, he had a good chance of being acquitted of murder and convicted of manslaughter or aggravated burglary. In that case, he could be a free man in six to eight years.

The logic seemed inexorable. Mr Gorman and Mr Lee did not take long to agree with the solicitors. By the time the trial started they had all decided that Molloy would give no evidence. He would plead not guilty, but he would not challenge or dispute the statement he had signed which not only put him at the farm, but directly implicated his best friend Robinson and two other men whom he hardly knew in the most terrible murder.

His silence would mean of course that all the contradictions, prevarications and nonsenses which infested his interviews after the confession could not be put to him in cross-examination. He would not deny his confession, so his confession must be true. And if it was true about him, how much more true must it be about his three accomplices.

Molloy knew quite well what he was doing to the other three. But he was out of touch with them, and with Carol Bradbury, perhaps the one person who might have steeled him to face down the lawyers' advice. He had to consider a straight choice between a likely twenty-five years if he challenged the evidence, and more likely ten years if he didn't. He agreed, not without some discomfort, to keep quiet.

The decision was not formally disclosed until the seventeenth day of the trial, at four o'clock in the afternoon when Michael Hickey and his mother had finished giving evidence.

'My Lord,' said Mr Tucker for Michael, 'that is the case for Michael Hickey.'

Mr Gorman got to his feet to deliver the most important sentence in the trial: 'My Lord, we call no evidence on behalf of Molloy.' (*17.33*)

From that moment, the case changed. The defence lawyers who during the prosecution evidence had shown some confidence and gusto, drooped.

In his closing speech, Mr Gorman started by reminding the jury that his client had put in an alibi notice, though he agreed his client had not said anything about where he was on the day of the murder. He continued: 'I shall deal with him on the basis that he was not in the room when that boy was shot and that therefore he had no opportunity whatsoever to stop whoever it was who pulled the trigger.'

Mr Gorman had little difficulty in dispensing with what little evidence there was that his client was guilty of murder. He then went on to suggest intimidation of his client.

'If Molloy had given evidence and said that his statement was false, would you have believed him?' he asked. 'If he'd said it was true, where would that have put him? What would have been the consequences of going into the witness box? With that fear on his shoulders, he cannot afford to tell you the truth, whatever it is.'

Mr Gorman enlarged at length on the 'fear' his client had of the other three accused. He reminded the jury of the statements he'd made to the police that he had been 'threatened by Jimmy and Vinny', and that he was speaking of 'terrible people'. Of Joe Hickey, Michael's father, Molloy had said: 'Anybody who told tales about the family, he would see that they were beaten up.' Mr Gorman used the verbals of police and prisoners to show how Robinson in particular had sworn all kinds of frightful violence to Molloy and hoped he would 'end up dead'. All this, said Mr Gorman, 'shed some light on Molloy's predicament'.

What were the jury to conclude from that? Surely that Molloy had not gone into the witness box because he was frightened of Robinson and the Hickeys.

As Mr Gorman sat down, Ann Whelan, who had sat every day in the public gallery, felt the atmosphere in court harden against her and the rest of the families. 'We felt suddenly that we were being despised and hated all over the courtroom,' she said.

The old fox Jimmy Robinson noticed exactly the same development. He wrote to Carol on 6 November:

Up until Molloy's bloke got up yesterday and persisted in maintaining that load of lies in his statement, I simply know that both judge and jury were sympathetic to the evidence, but that dirty brainless idiot's lies have made them all think again and say: 'Surely no one's mad enough to admit to it if they are not guilty' – but that is precisely what Molloy is doing. It's knocked all our defence for six. . .

Things looked so promising a couple of days ago, and now I'm all dejected and terrified of a miscarriage of justice. . . The atmosphere in court has completely changed round.

A day later, as the judge summed up, Jimmy wrote again to Carol:

As you probably know, the judge finished his summing up and he slagged us unmercifully. I was sick, and surprised as he'd seemed so fair up till then. It was due mainly to dirty stinking evil Molloy sitting in court with a handful of lies that we just couldn't attack or show to be so obviously wrong because he didn't go in the box. What a cowardly worm that man is!

He understood the full significance of Molloy's decision well before the verdict was announced:

I know it's not evidence against me, but what person on a jury would or could ignore it, and *if* they accept it, and jumble me into it, *then* the case comes full circle into a lie. . . Anyway, my love, I'm prepared for the worst but even at this late stage I can't imagine what my reaction will be.

On the final day of the judge's summing up, but before the verdict, Robinson walked into court to see Carol Bradbury and Tracey at last in the gallery. It cheered him enormously. In the last letter he wrote before the verdict, he returned once again to the subject of Molloy:

I just can't grasp the thought that he realises the enormity of the wrong he's doing me. If it was on the Hickeys for putting me in trouble, then it's maybe understandable, but I've never done that man an ounce of harm. On the contrary, I've always been pretty decent to him, and he's deliberately swearing my life away by saying he was involved but knew nothing of a gun in order to be convicted of burglary and leave me facing a murder charge. The bastard knows I'm as innocent as the judge himself. I wanted to jump up and scream 'bastard lies, all lies!' and smash Molloy's filthy pasty lying face in. If he's got a conscience I hope it'll plague and torment him till he dies.

Prison For Life

The jury went out soon after 3 p.m. on 8 November. They were back in their place at almost exactly the same time the following day. Their unanimous verdict was 'Guilty'. James Robinson, Michael Hickey and Vincent Hickey were declared guilty of murder; Patrick Molloy of manslaughter. All were declared guilty of aggravated burglary at Yew Tree Farm. Sentence was held over until the following Monday. Before the court rose, the judge praised the police on a 'thorough' investigation. He praised the jury. The newspapers prepared their headlines –

'CARL'S KILLERS!' – and background stories on the 'petty crooks who killed to cover their tracks'. Few of them found space for two dissident statements. Fred Whelan, Michael Hickey's stepfather, had his own verdict: 'Carl Bridgewater was murdered by a person or persons unknown – not by my stepson.' Mrs Pauline Molloy said: 'Pat told me all along he wasn't there and that none of the others were guilty of it.' (*Express and Star*, 10 November.)

Back in his cell at Winson Green, Jimmy Robinson got out one of his precious letter forms and wrote to Carol.

Hello Cal,

Well, my love, the worst possible has happened as I expected after Molloy didn't deny or defend his lies. I'm in a sort of trance of relief from tension, and I know full well the facts haven't sunk in or the realisation that I've been found guilty. At the moment, darling, I'm not thinking of me but of you and I can visualise how destroyed you feel. Cal, you must be brave whatever happens, hold onto the truth darling. Let both our clear consciences give us some sort of comfort because they are clear, and not in anyway troubled from guilt. However wrongly I've been convicted and however we may try to console our poor troubled minds, give a thought to the terrible injustice Molloy has done not only to you and me but his family and children by saying he was involved. He and he alone has got to live with the knowledge of those lies and what he's done to everyone connected with him. . .

Please be realistic and realise that the judge is going to life me off on Monday. Cal, it's no more than the real murdering bastards deserve. I mean that. Sadly, though, darling and tragically for you and I and all our children, they've got the wrong man in my case.

There had been some method in the delay of sentence over the weekend. Police and prosecution hoped that once the verdict was through, and all hope shut off, the final truth about the murder of Carl Bridgewater would be revealed. After all, *who* had pulled the trigger? Was there, among the three men convicted of the murder, perhaps another man upstairs with Molloy, perhaps a driver or a lookout man who, by suddenly agreeing he was there and filling in the details of the murder, might get himself a much lighter sentence than the man he denounced as the one who fired the shot? More than one man, after all, could not have shot Carl Bridgewater. All sorts of promises and deals were still available that weekend. Vincent Hickey, after all, had started the whole prosecution rolling with his 'revelations' at Bromsgrove. He had made almost an art of informing on his fellow criminals. If one of the four men *had* pulled the trigger, surely Vincent (or Molloy) would say who.

From all three men all through the weekend there was nothing but silence. When they came up for sentence on 12 November, Robinson and Vincent Hickey were sent to prison for life with a recommendation that each serve twenty-five years. Michael Hickey was detained at Her Majesty's Pleasure. He could not be sentenced for life, since he was under seventeen when the crime was committed. Pat Molloy got twelve years.

The judge also passed sentence on the other crimes, to which the defendants pleaded guilty. Robinson and Michael Hickey both got twelve years (to run concurrently) for the Tesco and Chapel Farm robberies. Vincent, who had the nerve to plead not guilty to Chapel Farm, had the file on the case left on the table, without being judged. John Burkett, who pleaded guilty to the Tesco robbery, got twelve years.

Jimmy Robinson had a message for Mr Justice Drake when he wrote to Carol the next day:

He might bow me down, but he'll never break me, because I know that for all his wisdom and for all the power of the legal system behind him, he's wrong, terribly wrong and somewhere, as happens very occasionally, the legal system and procedure has gone wrong, drastically wrong. Not much to hang a hope on you might think, and I don't either, but just knowing I'm innocent and being done for nothing gives me a perverse kind of gloating feeling that for all their high-sounding words and legal jargon and the smug and clever arguments they've trotted out, they're thick as shite and still *wrong*.

As the weeks went on, Jimmy Robinson's letters seemed in a curious way to take on a new spirit and a new confidence. Before the trial he had engaged almost exclusively in chit-chat and love talk. After the trial, he turned again and again to the lessons of his experience which seemed to educate him. Late in November, he wrote:

Darling, the sentiments you expressed about law and order and crime and punishment (before all this happened to change your opinions) weren't at all wicked. They were and are right. Certain crimes do deserve very harsh punishment and I still hold with that view and believe in it, especially where young kiddies are concerned. I understand your meaning, though, Cal, and how out of your love you're so disillusioned as to the way the law seems to be so set and rigid on the one hand and yet can be twisted and manipulated if the 'old boys act' is needed, such as with this spy merchant Anthony Blunt. You see what's sickened me is that the thing you and I and thousands of others have always believed to be the best in the world and above corruption – British Justice – is just a sham. It only applies if the 'establishment' isn't threatened. The two laws apply every time, the *haves* and the *have nots*. You and I were looking for truth and justice, and, knowing it wasn't done, it's knocked all our faith cockeyed.

As I've said before, darling, judged on the evidence, the verdict and the sentence was correct but (and this is what we must try to establish) the fucking evidence was wrong and that false evidence is what we were tried on. We were just scape goats, handy bodies to satisfy the public's demand for justice – revenge call it what you like. We didn't have a chance. Oh well, darling, time will tell, you just keep your chin up and don't despair.

As he wrote in all his letters, Jimmy Robinson and the Hickey cousins who had been stunned by the verdict and the sentence into a stupefied silence, imagined that time would be very long indeed.

So did the courts and the lawyers, who realised that with so definite a jury verdict there would be small chance of an appeal.

So did the Staffordshire detectives who chalked the Carl Bridgewater case up as yet another triumph for law and order.

In fact, it was only four and a half weeks before the Carl Bridgewater murder case rose again to push them from their stools.

CHAPTER FIVE
Murder at the Farm
NEXT DOOR

Almost exactly a month after the Carl Bridgewater trial finished at Stafford, it cropped up in conversation at a social evening at Holloway House, the farm next door to Yew Tree Farm. On 14 December 1979, Farmer Hubert Wilkes, aged seventy, who farmed Yew Tree Farm as well as Holloway House, was host at an early Christmas celebration with his part-time book-keeper and secretary, Janet Spencer, and her husband, Hubert Spencer, the ambulanceman whom the police had at one time suspected as Carl Bridgewater's killer. Also in the house sampling Mr Wilkes' extensive range of liqueurs and spirits was his daughter Jean, aged thirty-four, an air hostess who was home on holiday.

Exactly what was said about the case, and by whom, has never been established. Soon afterwards, Jean Wilkes left the room to relieve herself. She went upstairs. Not long after that, Bert Spencer went out too – ostensibly for the same reason. He went outside.

Spencer was away for quite a long time. His wife started to worry about him. Soon after midnight she got up and walked down the room towards the door by which Spencer had left. To her surprise, she heard a noise from the door behind the settee on which the old man Wilkes was sitting. Her husband Bert put his head round the door.

'Are you all right?' she asked.

'Quite all right,' Spencer replied. 'I'm just feeling a bit sick.' He took his head away and closed the door again. Janet Spencer walked on towards the settee. As she reached it, her husband came in again. He walked straight up to the arm of the settee and raised a shotgun to the temple of the unsuspecting farmer. He fired the gun at point-blank range. The noise was terrific. Janet Spencer stood still, paralysed by terror. She expected that Bert would turn the gun on her and shoot her too. Instead, he came towards her. She closed on him, grappling with the gun. He shouted at her to let go, that the gun was loaded. But she struggled grimly, pulling at the gun, a piece of which seemed to come off in her hands. She screamed for Jean. The air hostess rushed into the room, saw her father and screamed in turn. 'Ring for the police!' shouted Janet. Bert Spencer pushed his wife away, strode towards Jean and punched her a tremendous blow in the face, knocking her to the floor and causing her to bleed profusely. She picked herself up, darted to the far door, ran through into the hall, across the dining room, back into the sitting room and through into the kitchen. She managed to unlock the kitchen door before Spencer could get to her and flung herself desperately into the night. She could hear Spencer coming out of the kitchen door behind her as she ran down the drive and out into the road, hoping desperately for a passing car.

None came. She turned left out of the gate and ran down the road towards the A449. As she ran, she heard another blast of the shotgun, not far behind her. Hysterically, she knocked at the door of a bungalow about a hundred yards up the road. There was no reply. She stumbled off down the bridle path which runs to the back of Prestwood Hospital. The grass was too long for her to run. Scratched and bleeding, she climbed over the hedge and crept along the field following the fence to a group of houses just off the A449. The elderly couple at Crickets Cottage opened the door at about half past twelve to a woman, with blood all over her face and her clothes torn, shouting for a telephone. They had no telephone, but they took her to a house next door, where she finally called police and ambulance.

Janet Spencer meanwhile was having an even more terrifying time. When Bert had first pushed Jean around the house, she had managed to reach the telephone. As she lifted the receiver, however, Spencer returned almost at once to pull it from her hands. He beat her on the head and shoulders with the butt of another gun, larger than the one she had broken in her first fight with him. When Jean made her dash for the kitchen door, Janet fled from the front door. She hid behind a tree in the garden and saw a torch flashing in the farmyard. She crawled through the garden and into a field, losing one of her shoes in the process.

She crawled right across the field and somehow got over the hedge into the A449. As she slithered along the side of the road, she saw an ambulance and flagged it down.

The driver of the ambulance was Arthur O'Nions and his attendant driver was Barrie Thomas. Later that night, Mr Thomas described what happened.

'Mr O'Nions slid his door open as we stopped and I saw it was a woman. She jumped into the ambulance and climbed over him into a gap in the centre of the vehicle between me and Mr O'Nions. Her face and clothes were covered in blood and she was hysterical. We tried to calm her down, and I thought she said: "Somebody has shot my husband." We asked her to lead us to where it happened. She said: "Don't take me back. He'll kill me." She was still hysterical and we went towards the lane.'

As they got to the turning of the lane, Janet became more and more hysterical, screaming at the men that they must not go down to the farm or she would be shot. To mollify her, they turned into the lane and parked. Barrie Thomas courageously offered to walk up to the farm and see what was going on while Janet stayed with Mr O'Nions in the ambulance.

As he got out of the ambulance, however, Mr Thomas saw a white Ford Cortina estate coming slowly up the road from the direction of the Stewponey pub. Mr Thomas remembered that his instructions to go to Holloway House Farm that night included a warning to look out for a white Cortina Estate which the man responsible for the shooting might be driving. He stepped into the road and flagged down the Cortina. It turned into the lane and stopped on the other side. Barrie Thomas walked towards it. As he did so, he heard the woman screaming a warning at him from the ambulance. He tapped on the white car's misted window, and the driver wound it down. To his astonishment, Barrie Thomas recognised at once his colleague, ambulance station officer Bert Spencer.

'Hello,' he said. 'What are you doing here?' When Spencer didn't reply, Mr Thomas added helpfully: 'There's been some trouble at one of the farms down here.'

Spencer replied: 'Yes, it's me; I've had a mental blackout and I've shot a friend of mine.'

Grim proof that this might be true was a shotgun which Mr Thomas then noticed on the passenger seat, within Bert Spencer's easy reach. As Barrie Thomas asked for the gun, a police panda car drew up beside the ambulance. A policeman came up, and Spencer handed his loaded shotgun, butt first, through the window. Ambulanceman Thomas then got into the Cortina, and Spencer drove him back up the lane to Holloway House Farm. The ambulance departed to take Janet Spencer to Corbett Hospital. The police car followed Spencer's Cortina.

As the Cortina drove off, slowly, to allow the police car to catch up, Barrie Thomas asked nervously whether Spencer had any more guns. 'No,' Spencer answered 'but I'll give you this cartridge.' He put his hand in his pocket, wound down the window and threw a cartridge hard over the fence onto the righthand side of the road.

When they got to the farm, Barrie Thomas inspected the body of Farmer Wilkes who was quite dead. He looked up, and saw Spencer gulping from a whisky bottle. He was still clutching the bottle and gulping from it as he and Mr Thomas went back into the road to look for the police officers. PC Griffith and PC Carter from Wombourne police station, who had been on patrol when they were sent to the farm, arrived at once and took Spencer back into the house. He took several more gulps of whisky before PC Carter relieved him of the bottle. Within a few

minutes the sitting room and kitchen were swarming with police officers. When Detective Sergeant Tony Holdway of Staffordshire CID
came in, Hubert Spencer immediately recognised him.

'Hell, Tony, I know you,' he said cheerfully and shook hands with the
astonished officer.

'Yes,' Sergeant Holdway replied, 'I know *you*.' No doubt he remembered interviewing Bert Spencer as a suspect in the Carl Bridgewater murder slightly more than a year previously.

Spencer kept wondering aloud what had come over him. 'Oh no. I've
beat up my wife and killed my best friend,' he said. Aggressively, he
demanded to say goodbye to his 'best friend'. As he moved towards the
dead body, Sergeant Holdway took hold of him.

'You will have to say goodbye to him from there,' he said.

Spencer announced that Holdway was not big enough to stop him,
and made to push through the ring of officers. At once he was handcuf-
fed and quickly on his way to Wombourne police station. Twice on the
way there the police car had to stop to allow their charge to get out and
be sick.

At Wombourne, Bert Spencer was to meet another old acquaintance.
Three almost simultaneous telephone calls had been made shortly after
midnight by duty police at Wombourne to the top officers of Staffordshire CID. Something rather strange had happened, they reported. An
old man had been shot in the farmhouse, and it rather looked as though
it might have something to do with the Carl Bridgewater murder.

Chief Superintendent Robert Stewart and Chief Inspector Weslea
Watson were soon travelling to Wombourne. They arrived together at
about two in the morning, and went in to see Bert Spencer.

As they walked into the charge room. Spencer got up and warmly
shook hands with DCI Watson. 'How are you, Sir?' he asked, recognis-
ing him as the man who had interrogated him about Carl Bridgewater.

'Are you all right?' Watson asked in reply, and promptly cautioned
Spencer.

'I'm told I did it, but I can't remember a thing,' said the ambulanceman.

The two senior officers turned at once and headed for Holloway
House Farm.

The appalling scene which greeted them there must have seemed
awkwardly familiar to both officers. There was the victim, shot through
the head at point-blank range while innocently sitting on a settee. The
weapon was a 12-bore shotgun, sawn-off. When they heard the story of
the cartridge thrown out of the window into the road at Ashwood Lane,
they could hardly help recalling the cartridge case which has been found
in Doctors Lane – the continuation of Ashwood Lane – no more than a
few hundred yards away, on the day after the Bridgewater murder.

199

When they heard that the cartridge case was of Eley manufacture, the coincidence seemed complete.

After all the tests and photographs had been carried out, Hubert Wilkes's body was taken to Wordsley Hospital mortuary, where Dr Benjamin Davis carried out an autopsy. The wound in Mr Wilkes' head was startlingly similar to the one Dr Davis had analysed in the head of the newspaper boy fifteen months earlier. The range at which the shot had been fired was almost exactly the same in both cases – something less than three feet.

Chief Superintendent Stewart also attended the autopsy – with the third of the three top officers who had been disturbed that night – Superintendent Eric Lycett. Chief Inspector Watson, meanwhile, went back to Wombourne, where, in the early hours of the morning, he interviewed Janet Spencer. Mrs Spencer had been brought to the police station from Corbett Hospital where she had been treated for severe injuries to her face and body. Watson took a statement from her, which has never been disclosed.

Did she discuss the Carl Bridgewater case, and the similarities between the two murders? As long as the statement is not disclosed, we shall not know. Certainly, Jean Wilkes, in *her* statement made at Holloway House between three and four o'clock in the morning to Stewart, Watson and WPC Rawlings, nowhere referred to Carl Bridgewater. However, when Watson and Stewart, after what must have been only a very short rest, came back to Wombourne to interview Bert Spencer at 11.35 the next morning, the Carl Bridgewater case was high on their agenda.

At the start of the interview, Chief Superintendent Stewart made it quite clear that they knew Spencer had shot Wilkes. Could it have been the effect of drink? he asked. Spencer doubted it. 'Have you had any turns or fits, loss of memory, etc.?' asked Stewart. 'No,' was the reply. 'No treatment for disorder or depression?' Stewart asked again. 'No,' was the reply.

When pressed about the details of the previous night's horrors – the fight with his wife and Jean Wilkes in particular – Spencer said he could not remember any details, and pointed to his head suggesting there was something wrong in that department. When it came to the guns and ammunition at Holloway House, he was more accurate and specific: there were three shotguns in the house, he said, and cartridges of every kind were kept in the drawer of Mr Wilkes' desk and in the food cupboard. The interview went on:

Stewart: 'You are quite experienced with guns?'
Spencer: 'Yes, I used Mr Wilkes' when I wanted, and that is the single-barrelled 12-bore.'

Stewart: 'Do you use Mr Wilkes' ammunition?'

Spencer: 'He bought a whole carton about two years ago. He gave me some three months ago. I got some that I bought six months ago. They are in a cupboard in a cartridge belt in my home.'

Spencer then began to remember that he had used two guns the previous evening – one which had come apart while fighting with his wife, and another larger one with which he had chased Jean Wilkes, and which ended up in his car when he was flagged down.

Finally, DCS Stewart got round to the broader issue.

Stewart: 'Is there anything else you can bring to mind that you think can help?'

Spencer: 'I just haven't got a reason.'

Stewart: 'You were questioned at one time about Carl Bridgewater?'

Spencer: 'Yes. This officer questioned me' (indicating Mr Watson).

Stewart: 'Did that upset or have any effect on you?'

Spencer: 'Yes it did, it had an effect. The effect has been invisible up to now.'

Stewart: 'It did affect you?'

Spencer: 'It did upset me, it really did, I think that's perfectly natural, don't you?'

Stewart: 'Is there anything else you would like to say about the matter?'

Spencer: 'No, Sir.'

Stewart: 'I am referring of course to the effect that you were questioned.'

Chief Inspector Watson then took up the questioning, and used some of the information he had gleaned from Jean Wilkes and Janet Spencer during the night.

Watson: 'When did you last talk to anyone about the Carl Bridgewater murder?'

Spencer: 'The last person I ever spoke to was Mr Wilkes about the time of the trial.'

Watson: 'When they were convicted?'

Spencer: 'Yes.'

Watson: 'I suggest you talked about it last night.'

Spencer: 'I don't recall talking about it last night.'

Watson: 'If Jean Wilkes says that amongst matters discussed was the Carl Bridgewater murder and that you talked about being inter-

*rogated and answering questions on a pro forma, a questionnaire,
would that be the truth?'*

Spencer: 'No, I didn't talk about that last night. At least I don't
remember talking about it.'

Watson: 'What do you remember talking about?'

Spencer: 'Price of turkey. Turkey trade.'

In all his interviews, Spencer kept repeating that he could think of 'no
reason', 'no reason at all' why he should have murdered a man whom he
continued to call his 'best friend'. This view was confirmed by Jean
Wilkes.

'A man called Bert Spencer helps out on the farm occasionally, usually on a Saturday,' she said. 'He has done odd jobs around the house
too; he's recently decorated the spare bedroom and is working on the
tiling downstairs. Bert's wife, Janet Spencer, does the secretarial work
for my father on the farm books . . . The secretarial work is always done
on a Thursday night. Janet and Bert always come together, they are
more or less friends of the family and the book-keeping night is also a
social occasion.'

Jean Wilkes was consistent about this. Soon after her father's funeral,
she went to stay with an old family friend, Michael Howard, who
farmed at Droitwich.

'She was absolutely stunned, dumbfounded,' Michael Howard told
me in May 1985. 'She would return to the subject almost every hour of
the day. She would hold her head and say: "Why, why, why did it
happen?" She just couldn't come to terms with it or explain it. She
hadn't got a theory. She said she felt very sorry that Spencer had done it.
The relationship between the Spencers and Wilkeses, she said, had
been a very pleasant one.'

Philip Wilkes, the younger of Mr Wilkes' two sons, was equally warm
about the Spencers. 'Mr Bert Spencer has worked part-time for my
father for the last six months,' he said. 'They were very good friends; I
have never known them have an argument. My father thought a lot of
Bert Spencer, and he was at the farm most weekends . . . I can give no
reason at all for what happened at the farm last night.'

Anthony Wilkes, the elder brother, was also interviewed by the
police. For some reason, he wasn't asked about the relationship between his father and the Spencers.

If the awful possibility that the Holloway House murder may have
had some connection with the one at Yew Tree Farm had not occurred
to Chief Superintendent Stewart already, it was conveyed to him in no
uncertain terms in a letter written that very morning – 14 December – by
Ann Whelan, Michael Hickey's mother.

Ann Whelan had got up early to go to see Michael in Liverpool prison. On the radio she heard the report of the shooting at Holloway House. Before she left she sat down and dashed off a letter to Stewart.

Dear Mr Stewart,

I sincerely hope that the man accused of the murder of Mr Wilkes of Holloway House Farm will be questioned very deeply and at some length about the Carl Bridgewater murder, as I think you know as well as I that my son Michael and the other three are innocent of this crime.

Surely the police and yourself want to find the persons who really did commit this awful murder. Because I do, and our fight has just begun.

In Liverpool prison, she told Michael about the curious murder of the farmer who farmed the land at Yew Tree Farm. She wrote to Jimmy Robinson and told him. Robinson wrote to Carol on 9 January 1980:

Mr Fryer had read of that shooting and hadn't put any real significance on it until my letter arrived. He scanned the papers every day and said how quiet it had been kept, you know no big morbid headlines about what a fateful tragic place it was etc. No. The dirty bastards kept it quiet because they knew it would raise eyebrows and people would realise how strange and incredible a coincidence it was.

Press, radio and television in the Midlands and nationally hardly commented on the coincidence of the murders at the two farms. The *Express and Star* on the day after the murder referred to the closeness of the farms in a lowly paragraph. The *Birmingham Evening Mail* on 14 December, in the third paragraph of its front page story, mentioned that Holloway House Farm was 'only 500 yards from the farm where newsboy Carl Bridgewater was killed'.

After these early reports, the media fell silent. Of course, the geography itself was not enough to sustain much interest. And no one in the media knew that Spencer had been a suspect for the Carl Bridgewater murder.

The Staffordshire police *did* know, however, and in the early weeks after Farmer Wilkes' murder the police made some effort to find out if Hubert Spencer had killed Carl Bridgewater. On 19 December, only five days after the farmer was shot, they visited Donald Spencer, Hubert's brother, at his home in Great Arthur Street, Smethwick. What worried them particularly was the piece of card which had been found on the journey to the pub made by the two brothers' families only four weeks after the Bridgewater murder. The card, they reminded Donald, had referred to the Bridgewater murder and had seemed to be a message to Bert directing him to the killer. The card had been picked up in the road as the two families made their way back from the pub. Donald Spencer remembered the incident: 'On the way back from a local public house as we came across Telford Way, my daughter or Bert's daughter, who were walking in front of us, picked up a piece of cardboard lying on the footpath. They showed it us and we read the message on it. It mentioned Bert by name and gave some indication that he could have had something to do with the Bridgewater murder. Bert didn't say much about it, but insisted that we took it almost immediately to our local police station. Since then Bert has not mentioned that murder inquiry to me.'

Donald Spencer could offer no explanation whatever for this episode. He concluded: 'I know of no reason why Bert should have done what he is alleged to have done. I have seen him twice since the incident happened and he maintains that he can't remember anything at all about it. He seems his normal self.'

Spencer's statement was taken by Detective Sergeant Holdway, who was now hot on the trail of the suspect he had hunted in the original murder inquiry. On 3 January 1980, he went to Corbett Hospital and collected the daily record sheets from the ambulance liaison office. He was told that the sheets were kept for the last three years, so he took all of them for 1977, 1978 and 1979.

Many of them were missing. For 1977, the records were missing for seven days; from 1978 the records were missing from 1 January to 12 October – for the whole of the first nine and a half months. For 1979, only thirteen days were missing.

The sheets recorded the movements of ambulances and patients in and out of the hospital. Each movement was filled in at the time by the ambulance officer in his handwriting. The sheets therefore would give a very clear account of who was on duty at the ambulance liaison desk at any given time. But the gap which Sergeant Holdway found in the records made it impossible to say who was on the desk on 19 September 1978, because the sheet for that day was missing.

So were the sheets for the whole of the first nine and a half months of 1978. This huge gap in the records could hardly be explained in terms of carelessness for a day or even a week. Quite unusually, a whole block had disappeared.

Some time that January (1980) DCI Watson and Sergeant Holdway interviewed Spencer's boss, Barry Chambers, who ran ambulance control for the area from the headquarters at Smethwick. Barry Chambers told the officers that a very strict procedure governed the movements of ambulance officers. He explained that it was part of Spencer's job to move between the various hospitals for which he was responsible – not just Corbett, but Wordsley, Ridge Hill and the Limes Hospital at Himley. It was also his job to travel to see patients who might have a special problem with ambulances. He was, therefore, quite often on the move from Corbett. How were his movements recorded?

That was very simple, Mr Chambers replied. Ambulance control had to be informed of every movement made by any of their officers. If an officer wanted to move from his post, he was obliged to telephone ambulance control at Smethwick and report where he was going and when he was leaving. These reports would then be set down in a book. Strict penalties applied to officers who moved without reporting.

Naturally, Chief Inspector Watson asked to see the book. Mr Chambers and his staff went to get it. They came back dumbfounded and embarrassed. The book which covered September 1978 was missing. Indeed, it was the only such book in recent history which was not there.

What period did the book cover? Some years later, in June 1985, Mr Chambers told me: 'The period would vary according to the number of entries, and how long it took to fill up the book. We would just finish one book and then start another. Obviously, when the officers came to see us [in January 1980], the book for September 1978 had been completed, and we were well into a new one. The period covered by one book could be a year, or as much as eighteen months.' The books, he said, were carefully kept, but this one had just gone. No one could provide any explanation for what had happened to it.

Mr Chambers also confirmed to me that Hubert Spencer had easy access to the book. He himself had worked for some years as a control officer at Smethwick. Indeed, one of his duties was to record in the book the movements of other ambulance officers. Anyway, Mr Chambers went on, 'the book is for reference, not just for control but also for the officers in the different hospitals. If they wanted to check their movements for some reason, of course they had easy access to the book. We didn't keep it hidden away, for that reason.'

Neither Mr Chambers nor anyone in ambulance control or at the hospital could provide an explanation as to these missing documents. Bert Spencer, Chief Inspector Watson was assured, was a 'most meticulous man' who kept all his records in perfect order. How he could have 'lost' nine and a half months of sheets in 1978 was a mystery. That the ambulance control book at Smethwick could have gone missing at the same time was an astonishing coincidence.

Sergeant Holdway recorded the missing hospital sheets in a brief statement dated 3 January. On 2 April, DCI Watson took a statement from Barry Chambers. The statement seemed to support the theory that Spencer was at Corbett Hospital all the afternoon of the murder, as he had claimed.

On the possible movement of Spencer to other hospitals, Mr Chambers said: 'The procedure was that Spencer would notify ambulance control at Warley by direct line, informing us that he was out to one of the hospitals and giving details of a telephone number where he could be contacted.'

So much for the procedure. What of the documents? Mr Chambers' statement did not include any reference to the book where these movements were recorded, or to the fact that a bit was missing, or to the fact that Spencer would have had access to it. Indeed, there was no reference in Mr Chambers' statement to *any* documents recording the movement of ambulancemen.

Instead, Mr Chambers' statement went on to say that if Spencer had gone in his own car to another hospital, he would have claimed expenses from the Regional Health Authority. 'I am aware,' he went on, 'that checks have been made and no claim was received from Spencer for September 1978.'

No claim was received for all September. Was that not in itself extraordinary? Would an ambulance officer whose duties included moving between hospitals in his own car, and who could claim for every mile, go for a whole month without claiming expenses? Mr Chambers told me he thought this was 'quite probable'. Other ambulance officers I spoke to at Wordsley ambulance centre were more dubious. They told me that Spencer travelled a lot, and always claimed expenses.

Mr Chambers' statement ended: 'Whilst Spencer's position did permit him to be away from his post I am certain that if he had been absent for a period of something like two hours, he would have been missed and someone would have reported it.'

This conclusion avoided the possibility that Spencer himself may have reported his movements that afternoon.

There were, of course, independent witnesses about Spencer's movements that afternoon. In particular, there was Mrs Riebold, the ambulance secretary, who worked with Spencer at Corbett and had given a clear, unequivocal statement only a week after the murder that Spencer was working in the hospital all afternoon.

On 17 January 1980, the detectives went to 84 Kingsley Road to talk again to Mrs Riebold. She gave them another statement: 'I have always got on well with Bert, he is always full of fun,' she said. 'I have never known him to be bad-tempered although on very rare occasions he has reacted to other people's bad temper . . . I am still positive that I was correct in saying he was at the hospital all that day except for perhaps leaving for lunch round about 1 p.m. Sometimes he had lunch a little earlier or a bit later and he may have done that day but he would only be away about an hour.'

This was the only part of Mrs Riebold's statement which dealt directly with Spencer's alibi. Though Mrs Riebold agreed that it was part of

Bert's duties regularly to visit Ridge Hill Hospital her statement did not say *how* or *why* she could be 'positive' that Spencer was at the hospital all afternoon. It did not say how close she worked with him, or whether she was with him all the time, or whether she had any certain way of checking his movements.

Nor could Mrs Riebold help with the mystery of the missing hospital documents. 'I never knew what happened to the sheets,' she said. 'They had nothing to do with me. I didn't know that they were kept. I have helped to look for some sheets that are apparently missing, but haven't been able to find them. I can think of no other place in the hospital where they might be.'

Mrs Riebold said she regarded herself 'as a friend of Bert and his family. I live in the same road and I visit their home occasionally. They have always seemed a very happy family. I was stunned,' she went on, 'at receiving the news that Bert had been arrested for shooting Mr Wilkes. I can think of no reason why he should do such a thing. I believe it completely out of character. He used to talk a lot about Mr Wilkes and obviously thought a lot of him and said he enjoyed working on the farm. As a matter of fact when this happened, he was going to have the next week off, to help Mr Wilkes with the turkeys for the Christmas period.'

Reassured that Spencer's alibi was intact, the Staffordshire officers relaxed their inquiries on any possible link between the two murders. They interviewed a prison officer called Stephen Jackson, who said he had bought Spencer's blue Vauxhall Viva from him in January 1979, soon after Molloy and Vincent Hickey had been charged. Spencer had then bought a white Ford Cortina estate.

Sergeant Vincent Potts, scene-of-crime officer, also made a statement saying there were 'no fingerprints of Hubert Vincent Spencer found when I carried out my examination of Yew Tree Farm, Lawnswood Road, Wordsley'. Finally, the gun expert Thomas Warlow confirmed that there was no connection between the cartridge case found at Doctors Lane on the day after the murder, and any of the shotguns found on Mr Wilkes' farm.

It was clear that the Staffordshire police officers were quickly satisfied that Hubert Spencer had nothing to do with the Yew Tree Farm murder. But at the offices of the Director of Public Prosecutions, as lawyers studied the papers for the prosecution of Spencer on the Wilkes murder, there was considerable unease. No member of the public knew that Spencer had been a suspect in the Carl Bridgewater murder. Once that fact *was* known, there was an unhappy coincidence between the two murders. The lawyers for the convicted men, especially Tony Fryer, were already asking awkward questions about the two murders. Before long, no doubt, they would hear about the questioning of Spencer soon after Carl's murder. Would they not want to know why he was questioned and what the evidence was which prompted police to question him again a few weeks later? The Staffordshire police had carried out an inquiry and were satisfied that Spencer was innocent of the murder. But would it be right or sensible to withhold from the convicted men's lawyers, who were by now considering an appeal, the evidence which had led to Spencer in the first place?

Spencer was due to be committed for trial by Wombourne magistrates on 27 March. In early March there were a series of conferences between Staffordshire police and the Director of Public Prosecutions and his staff. The DPP finally decided to disclose the information. On 25 March, two days before the committal hearing, Mr Chance from the DPP's office wrote to all four lawyers representing the four convicted men.

> There is material which I propose to disclose to the Court and to your client prior to the consideration by the Court of your client's application for leave to appeal. The material arises from a charge of murder preferred against Hubert Vincent Spencer who is due to be committed for trial by the Wombourne magistrates on 27 March.

The material was not sent until 12 June, a few days before Hubert Spencer stood trial at Stafford Crown Court.

To the lawyers and families of the convicted men, especially to Ann Whelan, the bundle of documents came as manna from heaven. She sent them at once with an exultant letter to Michael. Almost every item in the bundle had new information which seemed to point to Spencer as the murderer of Carl Bridgewater. The most remarkable of these were the first two in the bundle, the statements made by Roger Edwards, the company director, who said that shortly before three o'clock on the afternoon of the murder he had seen a blue Vauxhall Viva driven by a man in uniform turning into the driveway which led to Yew Tree Farm. This statement, first made on the day after the murder and repeated and clarified to senior police officers seven weeks later, had not been disclosed to the defence at the trial. The Vauxhall Viva could not have had in it any of the four defendants in the Carl Bridgewater trial, all of whom were seen in pubs in Birmingham at almost exactly the time Mr Edwards saw the Viva.

Of course, the statement could have been *found* by the defence, if someone on their behalf had been prepared to search the 7,000 statements made. Indeed, if someone for the defence had even bothered to look at the statements made the day after the murder, they would have come across Mr Edwards' sighting. Even then, however, on its own it was just another sighting of a car near the farm, and not specially important. It was only in connection with Hubert Spencer and the prolonged investigations by the police of all other departments which employed men in uniform that the statement took on an electric significance. All the other coincidences – Spencer knew the farm, he knew Carl Bridge-water, he collected antiques, he had a gun licence and shot in the area – piled on top of Mr Edwards' solid foundation.

The Director of Public Prosecutions was quite aware of the signifi-cance of Mr Edwards' statements. In his letter to the defence laywers which came with the bundle, he wrote:

Many inquiries have been made in an endeavour to establish the identity of the driver of the car described by Mr. Roger Macara Edwards, without success. It will be appreciated that uniforms of the kind mentioned by Mr Edwards are worn by persons engaged in numerous differing occupations.

As though to back this up, the DPP included a statement from the retired farmer Fred Jones, who was living at Yew Tree Farm at the time of the murder, but had since left and was living at Bobbington. Mr Jones said:

The mouth of the driveway at Yew Tree Farm was frequently used by motorists as a place to turn around, mainly local residents dropping their children off to catch the school bus and again in the afternoon to collect their children returning from school. These turns being 8.45 a.m. and between 4 and 4.30. I have also seen other motorists use the driveway quite frequently at the turning point.

Fred Jones' statement at the trial had made no mention of all this turning about in the driveway. Instead, the impression was created of an isolated farmhouse, and great significance attached to all the sightings of cars in the area.

One further effort was made to distance the Vauxhall Viva which Mr Edwards saw from the Vauxhall Viva which Spencer drove. On 23 May (long after it was known to police that the prosecution were about to disclose all the documents which incriminated Spencer) DCI Watson and Sergeant Holdway paid another visit to Mrs Riebold, this time at Corbett Hospital.

They had come to ask about Bert Spencer's uniform. Mr Riebold said:

During the time I worked with Bert Spencer he was always of the same rank, and the insignia he wore was always two pips. He very rarely wore his uniform jacket, he felt the heat a lot. It would have to be a cold day for him to wear his uniform jacket. When he did wear it in the cold weather, he would usually take it off in the hospital and leave it on the back of his chair. On days when it was reasonably warm, he didn't wear the jacket at all, not even when he went to other hospitals. I never saw him wear a hat. He might have kept the jacket in his car when he was not wearing it, but I'm not sure of that.

Mrs Riebold could not, of course, be sure what he did in his car. Bert Spencer would not wear a jacket in the office unless it was a cold day. But when he drove home for lunch (as Mrs Riebold said he did) he would take his jacket with him, and might wear it. Still, it had two pips on it, while Mr Edwards, as he drove past, always on the move, said he'd seen only one.

Also enclosed in the bundle of documents was the statement of Alfred Bishop who had also seen what he thought was a blue Vauxhall Viva going down the drive to the farm about an hour earlier than Mr Edwards had.

There were also all the statements from the Staffordshire police officers who interviewed Spencer and made the inquiries about uniformed officers in the area; information about the piece of card found in Telford Way, including a copy of the card; statements from Kenneth Farndon and Robert Thompson, friends of Spencer; three statements from Barbara Riebold, two about the alibi, the other about the pips; the statement of the senior ambulance officer, Barry Chambers; and the statements from the man who bought Spencer's car, from Fred Jones about the turning cars, and from Thomas Warlow about the cartridge case. Also included was an even bigger bundle of all the witness statements which would provide the basis of the prosecution case against Bert Spencer at Stafford Crown Court. The Carl Bridgewater case was referred to only by the three policemen who interviewed Spencer after the Wilkes murder – DCS Stewart, DCI Watson and DC Wheawall. There was, however, a curious omission. A statement from Jean Wilkes, taken from Kidderminster Hospital in January 1980, broke off in mid-sentence after two pages. There was no reference in those two pages or in her earlier statement, taken in the early hours of the morning after her father had been shot, to a conversation between Spencer and Wilkes on the Bridgewater affair. This conversation had been reported by the police officers, who said they had heard it from Jean Wilkes.

There were other documents and statements which must have been relevant to Spencer but which were not supplied by the DPP. The statement made to DCI Watson by Janet Spencer at 5 a.m. on the morning after Hubert Wilkes was shot was not supplied. The evidence about the missing ambulance book at Warley was not supplied. The evidence about the expense claim forms from the West Midlands Regional Health Authority was not supplied.

The final document which *was* supplied was Spencer's criminal record, which showed him convicted of three cases of wilful damage at Smethwick Juvenile Court when he was nine; of larceny when he was ten (for which he spent a month in a remand home) and of office breaking and larceny when he was twenty-five, for which he was fined £25.

The defence lawyers had no time to absorb the documents properly before the trial of Hubert Spencer opened. Ann Whelan collected the bundle from Tony Fryer on 19 June. Spencer's trial opened at Stafford on 23 June, and Ann attended every day of it. The atmosphere was very familiar to her. This was the court where her son had been convicted. The prosecutor of Spencer was the prosecutor of her son, Philip Cox QC. Mr Chance, the representative of the Director of Public Prosecutions in both cases, was in court. Several of the policemen who gave evidence against Spencer had been witnesses in the Bridgewater case.

There were, however, two absent friends. At no time in the proceedings did Ann catch a glimpse of Detective Chief Superintendent Stewart or DCI Weslea Watson. They did not give evidence and they did not attend the court. They had been on the scene of the murder of Hubert Wilkes as quickly as they had attended Yew Tree Farm after the newspaper boy had been shot the previous year. They had conducted many of the most important inquiries on that fatal night. They had interviewed Jean Wilkes at the farm and Janet Spencer at Wombourne. They had interviewed Spencer himself briefly immediately after the murder, and at considerable length the following morning. Their statements about these interviews were in front of the court, and yet they were not called.

One effect of this omission was to cut down to one the references in court to Carl Bridgewater.

Both DCI Watson and DCS Stewart had raised the Carl Bridgewater murder with Spencer in their interviews after the Wilkes murder. Watson had told Spencer that Jean Wilkes had reported a conversation not long before Hubert Wilkes was shot in which Spencer had recounted his experiences in the Carl Bridgewater inquiry. Because Stewart and Watson were not called, the jury never heard about this conversation. Jean Wilkes gave evidence but she was not asked about it, and did not mention it. Thus neither the jury nor any of the many reporters at the trial heard that Carl Bridgewater's murder had been a subject of conversation shortly before Farmer Wilkes met his violent death.

The single reference that was made came from the evidence of Detective Constable Wheawall, who interviewed Spencer at length on the night of the Wilkes murder. Wheawall was told by Spencer that Watson was trying to 'make something out of' the Bridgewater case. 'I don't think Jean brought that up tonight,' he said, 'but it didn't cause me to flip.'

Since the prosecution was obliged to bring DC Wheawall to court, there was no escaping this reference. But prosecutor Cox went to some lengths to make it clear that this reference did not, in his view, provide a credible motive for the murder. Mr Cox concluded: 'We know not, perhaps we will never know, why this man did this terrible thing.' The prosecution insisted, and Mr Justice Glidewell agreed in his summing up, that the evidence supplied no credible motive whatever for the murder of Farmer Wilkes.

In this, the prosecution greatly assisted the defence lawyers, who never denied that their man had shot the farmer. They insisted however that his mind had gone blank, perhaps as a result of alcohol, and that he had not formed the intention to kill which is necessary for a murder verdict. The fact that the prosecution insisted that there was no motive greatly helped these arguments.

Mr Justice Glidewell impressed on the jury that the Yew Tree Farm murder could not possibly have had anything to do with what Spencer had done at Holloway House Farm.

> Members of the jury, you know the material facts about that other murder. It had taken place in the very near vicinity to this farm, and the trial had taken place and the verdicts had been given just over a month before the incident of 13/14 December. Whether in fact that had any relevance, whether it had any effect upon the defendant's mind, is really a matter of pure speculation. It was a matter that the defendant raised. It is accepted that he was interviewed. Nothing is to be deduced from that. Because he was one of 17,000. The police obviously interviewed everybody they possibly could who might have had any information, and, as you know, this man had a gun licence.
>
> There is nothing more than that about the police interviewing him about the Carl Bridgewater murder, and certainly you must not draw any deductions of any sort from that. I am sure that you you will not. Whether it had any effect on his mind is a matter of speculation. As I say, he said that it did not cause him to flip, and by that you may think he meant 'to lose mental stability'.

This had little basis in fact. There were not 17,000 people interviewed in the Bridgewater inquiry, but 7000. Spencer, as the DPP's documents proved quite clearly, was *not* interviewed in a random way because he had a gun licence. Indeed, the first interview of Spencer never mentioned guns or licences. He was interviewed because of an anonymous telephone call immediately after the murder. Six weeks later, he was interviewed again, by a senior officer, when it was found that he drove a car of the type seen going into the farm that afternoon, that he knew Carl Bridgewater, that he collected antiques, that he used guns on Yew Tree farm, and so on.

At any rate, the jury, on such a direction, would inevitably ignore the Bridgewater case as a possible motive for the killing. That possible motive, surely relevant in all ordinary circumstances, was withdrawn from them *by the prosecution*. Indeed, Mr Cox went out of his way to be as fair as he could to Hubert Spencer. When the judge was summing up about the effect of drink on the mind and on intention, Mr Cox intervened to suggest he was being too stringent in the test he was applying, and that Spencer might be acquitted of murder if his mind was merely 'confused by drink'.

The jury, however, were not very impressed by this. Spencer had 185 milligrammes of alcohol per 100 millilitres of blood – about twice the limit allowed for driving. Considering the huge amount of whisky he had gulped from the bottle after the murder, considering the evidence that Mr Wilkes had an alcohol level in the blood of only nine milligrammes, and considering Jean Wilkes' evidence that he had had two large Scotches, perhaps three, before the murder, the notion that Spencer could put the whole thing down to the drink was grotesque.

The jury did not take long to make up their minds. They went out at a quarter to eleven on 26 June and came back at half past two, immediately after lunch. They were unanimous. Hubert Spencer was guilty of murder. He was sentenced to life imprisonment.

The single brief reference to the Bridgewater case in the evidence at Spencer's trial was hardly worth reporting, and hardly reported. The judge's dismissive reference to the matter in his summing up effectively shut up any busybody journalist who had come to the trial hoping for some copy to connect the two murders.

There was no reason at all why the awful murder of Carl Bridgewater should not now gently disappear from public consciousness.

CHAPTER SIX
Campaign

Pat Molloy Tells His Story
If Pat Molloy had been at Yew Tree Farm when Carl Bridgewater was killed, he would have been delighted by the outcome of his trial. By skilful use of his right not to go into the witness box, and through the fortunate fact that there was little or no independent evidence against him, his lawyers had managed to persuade the jury that he had no part whatever in the killing, and did not even know that a gun was being taken to the farm and might be used there. The sentences handed down to Robinson and Vincent Hickey were a terrifying measure of the value of his lawyers' advice.

If Molloy had tried to establish an alibi and failed, he too would have been sent down for twenty-five years. As it was, he had a stiff sentence for manslaughter. If he kept his head down and behaved himself, he could expect to be out in eight years. Considering the help he'd given to the Staffordshire police, there was no reason why he should not be a likely candidate for early parole, and be free even sooner.

He could rely on the prison authorities, of course, to keep him apart from the other three. Even though he and Michael Hickey were both sent to Liverpool, they were kept in different parts of the prison. Michael was abused and attacked by the prisoners. On one occasion he found some razor blades in his cell with some written advice to 'do the decent thing'. Pat Molloy could thank his lucky stars he was not in the same position. He was ignored as the man who *hadn't* murdered the boy.

Like the other three, Molloy was told immediately after the trial that there was not the slightest chance of a successful appeal. The jury verdict had been unanimous, the judge's summing up flawless in law, the sentences absolutely in line with precedent.

This was confirmed in writing by Malcolm Lee, Molloy's junior counsel at the trial, on 28 November, sixteen days after the verdict. 'The task of the accused in attempting to prove an alibi,' wrote Mr Lee, 'would have been hopeless, and might, quite wrongly, have involved him in the risk of being convicted of murder rather than manslaughter.

214

Thus I have no hesitation once again in confirming that it is my opinion that the accused took the only proper course open to him at trial.' There were no grounds for appeal either against conviction or against sentence and the clear advice which flowed from Mr Lee's opinion was for Molloy to shut up and bite the bullet.

He did quite the opposite. From the first day after his conviction, Pat Molloy started to campaign against the verdict which had singled him out for special favour. Immediately, he demanded forms under the Criminal Appeal Act, on which he could seek leave to appeal. He proceeded to fill them in himself.

On 11 December, a month after the trial, he wrote of his confession (Exhibit 54):

> My statement is not a true account, and is a revenge statement against the Hickeys and Robinson. My alibi notice is perfectly sound, but I was unable to use it due to the witnesses failing to appear in court. I wish to call all three witnesses in support of my alibi. Their names are Mrs Carol Bradbury, Miss Tracey Bradbury and Miss Sonia Bradbury . . .
>
> To get the truth out of Vincent I made that statement and put Michael in it as well. At the time in question, I did not know the Hickeys to speak to, but I thought by what Vince was saying to the police he must have had first hand knowledge of what happened at Yew Tree Farm, and was covering up for someone and was trying to involve me, Jim and John Burkett.

To this first letter giving grounds of appeal there was no reply from his own lawyers. But Molloy did send a copy to Tony Fryer, Jimmy Robinson's lawyer, who wrote back on 22 January 1980: 'Unfortunately, as stated here, the matter carries no weight at all. If the position is as stated, you should of course have gone into the witness box.'

Knocked back (with every justification) by Jim's lawyer as well as by his own, Molloy might have thought it better to let things rest. On the contrary, however, a few weeks later, he was at it again, with more forms for the Court of Appeal, and more grounds. 'I ask leave to appeal against conviction on these further grounds – that I was never allowed to contact my fellow-accused at any time.' In this short document he demonstrated how the other three accused had regular access to one another at Winson Green, but he was not even allowed to write to Jimmy Robinson to discuss their joint defence or their joint alibis.

A week later (20 March) yet another form was filled in in Molloy's careful handwriting. 'Sir, I ask permission to submit further grounds for appeal, which are as follows: that I was advised by my Counsel not to go into the witness box. By taking Counsel's advice, I gave up the right to call my alibi witnesses.'

On 26 March, still further 'grounds for appeal' went to the Court of Appeal from Liverpool prison in the name of Pat Molloy – this time about Helen Johnston and James Dundas-Ure. Of Johnston's evidence, Molloy wrote: 'I state here and now I was never in that pub in the evening with Jim Robinson.' On the conversation with Dundas-Ure, Molloy said: 'I am now saying that Jimmy Dundas-Ure is a liar, and I heard nothing spoken relating to 30 years for Carl Bridgewater.'

On 16 April, he wrote about the complete lack of any evidence that the four men met after being at the two pubs.

> We were all supposed to have set off from these points and started up old bangers, collected a shotgun (blind drunk too, remember) and still got to Yew Tree Farm for 3.25 p.m. to be seen by a witness. . .
>
> Is it likely that literally scores of trained experts following what they termed four drunken robbers, couldn't find a hair, a print, a button, a footprint, a shred of cloth either at the farm or on any of our clothing? Where did the stuff they said we nicked get to? Not one shred of evidence to tie either of us to it, and if we talked so freely in the pubs etc about actually shooting the kiddie, surely we'd have dropped it out: 'Wanna buy a clock or a pan etc', regarding the stolen stuff.

On 1 May, he was at it again:

> During all my time on remand I had numerous interviews with my solicitor, and I gave the details to him, chapter and verse, on my statements, how they came to be made, and I said all along that I wanted to give evidence in the witness box. But I was persuaded not to give evidence, and Mr Gorman asked me to sign a form and at the time I could not see any harm in signing that.

The Irishman was like a beaver in his cell, scribbling away in outrage at almost everything that had happened at the trial. Judge, lawyers (including, especially, his own), police, prison officers, all of them came under attack. Nor was he operating entirely on hunch, or on his own observation. He was reading law books to help him. Proof of that comes from the letters he wrote in those early months after conviction to Carol Bradbury, who, in spite of Jimmy Robinson's fury against his former mate, still continued to write back in a friendly and sympathetic way.

He started by trying to blame Carol for the disaster, suggesting that he did not go into the box because she and her daughters had not appeared as witnesses. This was not so: the cause and effect were the other way round. By early January 1980, this rather pathetic attempt at self-justification and his attacks on everyone else had turned into remorse: 'It has escalated from my lies and a case has been built up on the strength of what I said. I have helped to convict innocent men, and I did not mean it to go so far as it went. But I will try to put it right on appeal and I hope I will be believed – there is no reason why I should not be. There is no evidence to connect me or Jim with it, other than my lies.' (18 January 1980)

To this theme he returned again and again, in letters almost every week: 'I regret now not giving evidence, but I hope to put it right at the appeal. I will do my best for all of us given the chance and will' (25 January 1980); 'Tell Jim not to despair as all of us will be proven innocent of this' (3 February 1980).

His last letter to Carol rejoiced that he had been taken off Category A status on 4 February. In his letter there was a new, mysterious tone: 'You see, you do not know what happened at Wombourne. I did write to you eight months ago explaining everything that went on. That letter had to be rewritten; I will tell you about that when I see you again. What I have said on the appeal forms is not enough, and you know that, but it is all I am allowed to say. I can't invent grounds without something solid to back it up.'

Although Pat Molloy enclosed a visiting order with his letter, Carol did not see him. She had cracked under the strain. She had a nervous breakdown and went into hospital. Carol never wrote to Pat again. 'What happened at Wombourne' was not disclosed for another eight months.

In the meantime, Pat was absorbing the news of the documents released by the Director of Public Prosecutions about Hubert Spencer, and writing about it to new correspondents: Fred and Ann Whelan. Ann Whelan had driven Carol to Liverpool to see Pat as early as January. Before long, Ann was writing to Pat, and changing his attitude to the Hickeys. Ever since he heard that Vincent had accused him of Carl Bridgewater's murder, Molloy had been consumed with bitterness against the whole Hickey family. Michael's abusive appeals to him during the trial to 'get up and tell the truth' had not helped. Pat described the Hickeys to Carol in a letter soon after the conviction as 'pure tinkers'. The letters and visits from Ann and Fred completely won him round. He went to see Michael and apologised. He became more and more disturbed by what he had done.

In May, he wrote to Ann: 'There is times I do worry over this terrible affair, not so much for myself but for the others, Michael mostly. The consequences for them are awful, their young lives will be wasted away in these places if we fail to put over our innocence.'

Ann Whelan also engineered what seemed impossible, a reconciliation between Pat Molloy and Jimmy Robinson. Robinson was persuaded to put aside his detestation of Molloy in the common interest of preparing an appeal. All through the summer and autumn of 1980, Molloy kept up an extraordinary correspondence with the Whelans and with Jimmy. He was, as he put it, 'like a cat on a hot tin roof' about new information. He wrote to the National Council of Civil Liberties and to Justice, both of which organisations responded favourably. He wanted to know more and more about the Spencer affair. He prepared his letters with questions and instructions, many of them extremely shrewd (it was he, for instance, who first suggested that the ambulance records might show whether Spencer had made any move on the day of the murder). He changed his lawyer to a London firm which, he was told, specialised in criminal appeals, and then was forced to change back again when legal aid was granted only to the trial lawyers. The cowed, tragic figure who had sat on his own on a back bench in the dock at Stafford was transformed into a fighter determined to free himself and the three men he had helped to convict. Unity between all four of them was the key to success, he insisted. 'We must have one Counsel for all of us,' he wrote repeatedly.

From time to time, he referred in an oblique way to the mystery of 'what happened at Wombourne' which he had mentioned to Carol. He was intrigued by Ann's accounts of Dave Waller's case against the Chief Constable of Staffordshire. Waller, a Dog and Partridge regular, alleged, as we have seen, that he had been beaten up in Wombourne police station while being questioned on the Bridgewater murder and the Hickeys' alibi. Molloy wrote to Ann on 8 June 1980: 'When you see Dave Waller tell him I will fully back him up over what happened at Wombourne as I seen it happening.'

When Ann visited Pat in Liverpool on 9 June 1980, he surprised her by taking out the upper row of his false teeth and showing them to her. There was a crack from top to bottom in the centre, which had plainly snapped the row in two. It had been stuck together again. Pat explained that the teeth had been broken during his interrogation at Wombourne.

It was the first hint of violence. There was no more word of it, except for vague references to the Waller case, until October when Pat Molloy wrote a long statement for his lawyers. The document, dated 8 October 1980, was formally signed by Malcolm Lee, Molloy's barrister, and incorporated in the official documents for Molloy's appeal. It was quite different in tone and content to what had gone before.

To explain: last year of 1979 I had reason to write to a friend about what happened at Wombourne murder HQ. In that letter I described the feelings and mental torture I underwent at the hands of the Regional Crime Squad, and how I came to sign the statement Exhibit 54. I posted this letter in the usual way – it was censored by

218

the prison at Leicester. A week later the prison officer in charge of the segregation unit brought my letter to my friend back to me, and a covering letter from the Home Office Cat A committee which I said I could not write to anybody about the ill-treatment I received at the hands of the police. It also said the only person I could write to about this matter was the Chief Constable of Staffordshire or a solicitor.

When I made the opening ground, last December 1979, I was still under the Cat A restrictions, and I thought at the time I could not accuse the police of brutality in my grounds, and how that Exhibit 54 was obtained.

What happened to me was this. I was taken to Bournville to wait for some men to take me to Tamworth. A blanket was placed over my head and I was taken to Tamworth, as I thought. But in fact I was taken to Wombourne murder headquarters and I was there two days before I really knew where I was. I was taken into the doctor's surgery to be questioned.

Molloy then alleged that he had been assaulted more than once while at Wombourne. His statement went on:

I was told all about Vince Hickey and Jim Robinson. I was shown a statement signed by Vince Hickey saying he was the driver and me and Jim and John Burkett was at Yew Tree Farm with him. I was very upset over this as I knew me and Jim were not at Yew Tree Farm. But neither could I remember where me and Jim was at that time for sure. The police came back later that night after the pubs closed loaded up with bottles of ale. They said I could have a crate of them if I said I was at the farm screwing. I was questioned and insulted and called a thick Irish Mick. I was struck on the face several times which broke my teeth. I was repeatedly asked to sign a statement saying I was at the farm upstairs, robbing it.

The meals I received were liberally dosed with salt, and I was refused a drink. In the end I had to cup my hands in the lav basin and flush the toilet to get a drink of water. During the night, I thought long about how Vince was involving me and Jim in a murder which I knew nothing about. Also what they had told me that Joe Hickey had informed on me, Jim and Burkett. I was told that Jim had put me in for the Tamworth meat offence.

Molloy then said that he decided to make a statement implicating the other three men in the murder; and that the words of the statement had been put in his mouth by the police. He went on:

I signed Exhibit 54 out of revenge on the others and out of fear of more beatings and ill treatment. As soon as I signed it, conditions changed for the better. But I never for one moment thought it would be believed. But it was, and they recruited the lowest of the low out of the prisons to back it up. Also a barmaid and others. I was also threatened with more beatings if I did not come across with more to involve Michael Hickey.

On its own, such a statement must have seemed incredible to Malcolm Lee and the solicitors who asked Molloy to make it a formal ground for appeal. After all, Molloy had not mentioned anything of this in the run-up to the trial, and the police had no chance to comment on any allegations of violence against the Irishman. The excuse that he was a Category A prisoner hardly affected his discussions in privacy with his lawyers. But as the case of Dave Waller progressed, the fact that Molloy, a suspect for the murder, should have been threatened and beaten did not look so strange. When Dave Waller finally accepted his £1,000 from the Staffordshire police in exchange for a pledge not to continue with the action, Pat Molloy wrote testily to the Whelans: 'Like Michael I am a bit disappointed over Dave Waller giving in so early. If he had held out, he would have got seven to ten grand.'

With the allegations which he had been bottling up for so long finally out in the open, Molloy bent himself with greater and greater effort to unite the four men in a powerful appeal. In the first five months of 1981 he wrote almost every day to this or that organisation or to the Whelans or to his family or to Jimmy Robinson with new ideas and new tacks for inquiry. In May, he finally sacked Argyle's and Malcolm Lee, arguing that their behaviour at the trial was crucial to his appeal. When Tony Fryer wrote suggesting a meeting to discuss common ground with Jimmy Robinson, Pat Molloy replied enthusiastically, and fixed up a date: Friday, 12 June. In the same week he agreed to take the truth drug, and was delighted when Ann Whelan offered to pay for it. He was in good spirits. On 10 June he got a letter from his old pal, Jimmy Robinson. It must have comforted him: 'You know how out of order you was, Pat, with your particular brand of insanity, and so do all of us. Still, Pat, I know too your utter remorse, and I accept it, and I do also appreciate your great determination to see the truth finally emerge.'

The same day, Pat Molloy wrote to the Whelans warmly to thank them for a blanket they had taken him the previous weekend. He was full of new points on the case, a new ground of appeal he had just put in, and the argument which Michael had for a separate trial. As with so many other letters of the time, he seemed far more concerned with the convictions of the other three than with his own. 'I am an easy-goin' sort of chap,' he wrote. While the letters from the others all reflected the depression, loneliness and drudgery of prison life, Pat Molloy seldom wrote about such matters. He was delighted, almost honoured, that he had won back the friendship of Robinson, and the trust of Michael Hickey and the Whelans. He was determined to do all in his power to put right the wrongs he had done them. His behaviour in those eighteen months after his conviction is quite impossible to explain in terms of his guilt.

On Friday, 12 June 1981, the very day he was to meet Tony Fryer, Pat Molloy played a game of football in the exercise yard. No one saw exactly what happened. In the middle of the game, he collapsed unconscious and was taken to Leicester Royal Infirmary. He never regained consciousness. His death certificate pronounced death by brain haemorrhage and shock.

Jimmy Robinson wrote to Ann Whelan: 'I'm afraid my gut reaction was one of resentment at his dying more than sympathy or sorrow.' What infuriated Jimmy was 'the lies Pat's taken to the grave with him . . .' He wanted to know whether Molloy had made any official affidavit denying his confession, or any statement which could be presented officially to the Court of Appeal. 'Will the Crown smugly sit back on their laurels well satisfied at the way things have turned out? It's an enormous *get out* for them.'

The following month (July 1981) Jimmy Robinson was moved from Hull prison to Gartree, near Leicester, where Molloy had died. His first letter to Ann from there showed that, once again, his compassion had won the battle over his indignation.

It was a very strange and traumatic experience to arrive in this establishment where poor misguided PM met his tragic and untimely end, and speak to people who were in fact possibly the last persons he spoke to. Let me say now I feel guilty (but still bitter) re certain remarks I made concerning the man, because without doubt the poor fellow was indeed doing his very utmost to make amends.

In Aylesbury prison, Michael Hickey was overcome with grief and despair. He wrote a message for the wreath which the Whelans sent to his funeral at Tamworth. The message was dictated on the phone to Ann Whelan by a prison officer:

Pat,
What can I say that hasn't been said already, following your leaving us? But Pat I know you will still be with us when we finally do get the justice we have all been seeking since our wrongful arrest which has broken the hearts of our family and friends.
I only wish you could be here to hear our wrongful convictions

put right. Because Pat we will continue to fight to clear us all, and when that day comes, then I will know you are finally at peace. I will say goodbye now Pat but I want you to know you are sorely missed.

The disunity between the defendants which had done so much damage to them during the trial had been healed even before Molloy's death, but his death presented immediate problems to the other three. Molloy's insistence in open court that his confession had not been freely given, but had been twisted from him in a mixture of deceit and terror, was vital to the appeal. Without it, the three were saddled with his confession, unchallenged on oath, and with what they could do to pick holes in the prosecution case. Fortunately, in this second effort, Ann Whelan had been very active, with substantial success.

Helen Johnston contradicts herself (Twice)

Ann Whelan's New Year Resolution for 1980 had been to see all the main prosecution witnesses personally, to discover if there was anything they could add to what they had said at the trial. She was told by Michael's lawyers that there were no grounds for appeal as the case stood at the trial, but that if any new evidence appeared, the chances of an appeal might change.

In the period after Michael's arrest, both Ann and Fred had thought it possible that Jimmy Robinson and Pat Molloy were guilty. The trial convinced her that the entire prosecution case against all four men was wrong. She therefore determined not just to bring the four men together (in which, as we have seen, she was singularly successful) but also to approach the witnesses against Robinson and Molloy as well as the witnesses who spoke directly against the Hickeys.

High on her list was Helen Johnston, the Dog and Partridge barmaid who had said she'd overheard two incriminating conversations in the pub – one between Robinson and Molloy, the other between Robinson and Carol Bradbury. Though Mrs Johnston's evidence was highly suspect (the date on which the first conversation occurred was at least three weeks out), Ann had been surprised at the weight given to it both by the prosecuting barristers and by the judge.

On 21 January 1980, therefore, she went to Helen Johnston's home and talked to her. She explained who she was and how much she believed in her son's innocence. She begged the barmaid to think if there was anything she may have misunderstood or overheard wrongly in the conversations. The discussion was hampered by Helen Johnston's huge family. Ann left before long, after writing down her telephone number.

On 7 February, two and a half weeks later, Helen Johnston rang Ann and asked to meet her. She said it would be difficult to talk with all the children around. So Ann collected her and drove her back to the Whelans' home at Hollywood. There Helen Johnston said she thought she *had* been wrong about the conversation about the gun. She thought perhaps that Molloy and Jimmy were discussing another job with a gun. She even had doubts whether a gun had come into the conversation at all. Ann Whelan thanked her, and drove her home.

On 20 February, Helen Johnston phoned again, asking for another meeting. She suggested a pub in Selly Oak – not the Dog and Partridge. Ann went to the pub, with Vincent's mother, Ann Hickey. Once against Mrs Johnston expressed doubts about what she had said at the trial. The two mothers pressed her, if the doubts were genuine, to consider making a formal statement withdrawing the evidence about the conversations. Mrs Johnston promised to think about it.

Exactly a month later, on 20 March, Mrs Johnston again phoned Ann Whelan. She was now prepared, she said, to see Ann's solicitor and make a statement retracting the evidence of the two conversations in the pub which had done so much damage to Jimmy Robinson. Elated, Ann phoned her solicitor, Richard Gilkes, to fix up an interview. Mr Gilkes thought it better than Mrs Johnston should go to Tony Fryer, who was Robinson's solicitor, and a meeting was finally arranged for the afternoon of 28 March. Once again, Ann Whelan was organiser and driver.

The interview was recorded on tape. The barmaid was confused and hesitant. She started by saying: 'I did tell one or two lies which I know was wrong. I'm trying to put it right now, but I know I might even go to prison for this.'

Mr Fryer tried to take her carefully and logically over the two incriminating conversations she told the trial she'd overheard in the Dog and Partridge: the first between Robinson and Molloy in which the newspaper boy was mentioned, and Molloy kept repeating: 'Whatever you say, whatever you do, keep your word, the gun went off accidentally'; the second between Jimmy and Carol in which Carol had allegedly said she would 'shop him for the paper boy'. Both conversations were bitterly contested by the people who were said to have taken part. Neither was heard by anyone else.

Mrs Johnston insisted she *had* heard Molloy and Robinson talking about a gun going off accidentally, but now realised that this was referring to the 'Tesco's job' – the robbery at Castle Vale in which Robinson had been involved, and in which John Burkett had fired his gun. Mr Fryer pressed her again and again to say why she had thought the conversation was about Carl Bridgewater, but she had no adequate reply.

Had the newspaper boy been mentioned in the pub at all, by either Robinson or Molloy? Mr Fryer demanded an answer, but he didn't get one.

Fryer: 'What had Pat said about the boy?'

Mrs Johnston: 'You see, they might have been talking about the newspaper boy themselves I mean.'

Fryer: 'Yes' (puzzled).

Mrs Johnston: 'And I may have got it wrong.'

Fryer: 'Did you know what he said about the boy?'

Mrs Johnston: *Pause (ten seconds). No answer.*

Fryer: '*Did* Pat say anything about the newspaper boy?'

Mrs Johnston: 'This is – I'm only trying to explain like. This is what they were on about. They didn't mean that they had anything to do with it, like.'

Fryer: 'They may have been talking in general about the murder?'

Mrs Johnston: 'Yes, yes, and I got it all wrong. And I think that's all really, what they was on about and I picked it up all wrong.'

On the second incriminating conversation – Carol's threat to 'shop' Jimmy over the newspaper boy – Mrs Johnston was much more specific. She definitely had *not* heard any such conversation. 'I've lied where I shouldn't have lied,' she said, and again, later on, 'I've lied more or less all the way.'

Why had she lied? Mrs Johnston said she had been threatened. She was very unclear about these threats, and indeed more than once in the interview changed the description of the men who threatened her.

Sitting in on the interview, and intervening only rarely, Ann Whelan sensed that Helen Johnston was intimidated by the solicitor, and confused by his constant demands for rational explanations. Helen Johnston had told Ann Whelan in the security of their homes that she had not heard any of the incriminating conversations but had made them up to assist the police with the case against their suspects, who, Mrs Johnston assumed, had committed the murder. The explanations to Mr Fryer about the threats were, Ann Whelan felt, invented to justify the lies.

After Mrs Johnston had gone, Tony Fryer did his best to make some coherent sense out of what Mrs Johnston was saying. He constructed a written statement, which began: 'I don't know what is going to happen to me but I must get things off my conscience because I told a number of lies at the time about the matter.'

The first and most important of these lies, the statement said, involved the conversation between Jimmy and Pat about the gun going off accidentally. Her new statement went on:

Jimmy and Pat were in there talking, but I couldn't really hear

what they were saying because the juke box was on. I did hear
them on about a job and a gun, but I didn't know what they were
talking about and I just took it to mean the Carl Bridgewater murder. In fact, on reflection, I don't think they were on about shooting anyone, but they were on about a job they were going to do in
the future and were discussing whether or not to take a gun. I told
the police as their having said they were on about the newspaper
boy, which was totally untrue. I never heard Pat say to Jimmy
about the gun going off accidentally.

It was also 'totally untrue' that Pat had reported this five or six times,
and, the statement continued, 'I never heard Carol say "I'll shop the
pair of you for this murder", I never said that to the police.'

It was a reasonable shot at a coherent statement from an incoherent
interview. Helen Johnston agreed it, but Tony Fryer was not happy with
it. He arranged to visit Mrs Johnston at her home to go through it with
her again before asking her to sign it.

The Staffordshire police, meanwhile, had heard that Mrs Johnston
was casting doubt on her evidence. They acted swiftly. On 29 March, a
Saturday, the day after the interview in Tony Fryer's office, Helen
Johnston was visited by DCI Wood.

She told him she had been to Tony Fryer's offices and said that the
evidence she'd given at the trial was totally untrue. After some questioning by Chief Inspector Wood, however, she decided that the evidence given at the trial was totally true. Wood left. On Monday (31
March), the day that Tony Fryer was to visit her to finalise the statement, Helen Johnston rang the solicitor with the news that the police
from Wombourne had been to see her. They had told her, she said, that
she must not see Fryer again or have anything to do with signing anything.

Tony Fryer said later (in a formal statement):

I was not made aware by Mrs Johnston's call as to how the police
knew of her visit to these offices, but I did understand from her
that they had warned her, as I had done, that she could at some
stage be charged with perjury or perverting the course of justice if
it transpired that she had lied at Stafford Crown Court.

She informed me that she was extremely worried that the police
would keep calling to see her and would harass her.

Tony Fryer said that she must seek another solicitor, who had nothing
to do with the Bridgewater affair. He had no further contact with her.
The statement he had taken from her stayed unsigned.

The police, as she feared, had not finished with Mrs Johnston. On 10

April, Chief Inspector Weslea Watson visited her at her home. After a long interview, Mrs Johnston decided that she had lied to Tony Fryer and that her evidence in court was true.

There was little more that Ann Whelan could do. The first prosecution witness she had seen had agreed, of her own free will and in order to calm her troubled conscience, to retract her evidence. She had rung Ann to offer this retraction. She had retracted her evidence to a solicitor. Yet now the retraction was null and void.

Nothing more happened for six months. In October 1980 Mrs Whelan got a phone call from a journalist working for Central Television. He told her he had read that the four men were hoping to bring new evidence to the appeal. Apart from the material about Hubert Spencer, which had just been publicised in a powerful article by Aileen Ballantyne of the *Guardian*, was there, he asked, any other new evidence which might be brought to the Court of Appeal? At once, Ann Whelan disclosed that Helen Johnston, a prosecution witness, had retracted her evidence in a statement to a solicitor.

Within hours Central Television were round at Helen Johnston's. To their delight she agreed to give them an interview. On News at Ten that night, the 'lead' story was that a crucial prosecution witness in the Carl Bridgewater murder trial had changed her story. Mrs Johnston appeared for a brief interview. She agreed that she had told lies in court, and that she had not heard the two incriminating conversations. She did not really give an explanation, except to say that she had been threatened. The following morning, the newspapers were full of it. 'CARL WITNESS CHANGES EVIDENCE' was the front page headline, for instance, in the *Daily Mail*.

If Detective Chief Inspectors Wood and Watson were watching the news that night, they must have been the most exasperated policemen in the country. Had they not interviewed Mrs Johnston? Had they not warned her not to make wild statements about her evidence at the trial? Had they not pointed out the dangers of a perjury charge? Yet there she was blurting out a retraction to twenty million viewers. The Staffordshire police called in an outside officer, Superintendent Morgan of the Cheshire police. He interviewed Mrs Johnston on 5 November. She told him that what she had said on the television was the same as what she had told Mr Fryer and that it was all totally untrue. Her evidence at the trial, however, was 'correct'.

That might have been the end of the matter. But the police and the prosecution went to further lengths to shore up their position.

Mr Fryer was approached by the Director of Public Prosecutions and asked to hand over the tape recording he had made of the interview with Helen Johnston. In view of what she had told him about the police behaviour, he refused.

The Director then issued publicly a 'Memorandum Concerning Statements Made by Helen Johnston'. After summarising the events since Helen Johnston was first interviewed by the police, the memorandum moved to a 'summary':

At trial Helen Johnston gave no evidence against Vincent Hickey or Michael Hickey. Her evidence was relevant against Robinson and Molloy. Before the trial she claimed that she had been threatened. She claims to have been threatened since the trial. Since the trial at least three other witnesses for the Crown have complained of harassment or threats or both. There is further material to suggest that efforts have been made to contact a further prosecution witness by persons who have no legitimate reason for doing so. These and other material tends to confirm Helen Johnston's claims of threats.

The Director of Public Prosecutions of course knew his libel law and chose his words carefully. Yet the thrust of this part of his memorandum cannot have been in any doubt. First, Ann Whelan was contacting witnesses who had not given evidence against her son. She therefore had 'no legitimate reason' for contacting them. Secondly, 'at least three' other witnesses had complained of threats or harassment or both. This all 'tends to confirm' that Helen Johnston had been threatened. The likeliest person to be threatening or harassing her was Ann Whelan.

What, however, were the facts? Ann Whelan took the view that the entire case against the four defendants at Stafford was wrong. She had noticed how the division of the defendants into two pairs, and then the separation of Molloy from the others, had done the four great harm. She resolved to fight the case as a whole, and she had a perfect right to do so. The witnesses had all given evidence. They had every right to turn her away from their doors. Mrs Whelan is 5' 7" tall, and she weighs 9 stone 2lbs. Alone, she approached Mrs Johnston. Mrs Johnston then herself contacted Ann Whelan and asked to make a statement to her solicitor. The suggestion that in some way Mrs Whelan had threatened or harassed Mrs Johnston into making a statement was fatuous.

The DPP's memorandum ended with a triumphant final sentence: 'The Crown does not suggest or accept that the evidence given by Helen Johnston at trial should be disregarded or treated as unreliable.'

At trial, Helen Johnston had said she'd heard conversations which gravely implicated Pat Molloy and Jim Robinson in the murder. In February, she'd told Ann Whelan she hadn't heard any such thing. She repeated this on tape to a solicitor, intending to sign a formal statement. Then she told police officers that she *had* heard the conversations after all. Then she went on nationwide television to say that everything she'd said at the trial was lies.Then she told another top policeman it was all perfectly true. The Director of Public Prosecutions concluded that there was no way that she could be treated as unreliable.

The Doubts of Catherine Guy

The second witness whom Ann Whelan visited in January was Catherine Guy. Mrs Guy's short evidence was the only firm link the prosecution could establish between the Hickey cousins and Robinson and Molloy before the murder. From photographs (there was a big debate about how many photographs were shown her) she identified Vincent Hickey as a man who had walked past her window on the walkway to Carol Bradbury's flat. Mrs Guy said she had seen him through the kitchen window as she stood at the sink. Vincent said he had never been to Carol's flat.

When Ann Whelan with Ann Hickey first went to the flat at Wolston Croft, Mrs Guy wasn't there. On 27 March Mrs Whelan went back on her own and talked to Mrs Guy for an hour, openly taping the conversation. She went home and wrote up what Mrs Guy had said. On 12 May she went back to the Guys' house. Mrs Guy read through what had been written, and readily agreed to sign it:

> On my return from shopping one day, I found the police at my home. They were the murder squad on the Carl Bridgewater case. They had just arrested my husband and were taking him to the police station for questioning, but they wouldn't give me a reason why. I then phoned my social worker as I was seven months pregnant at the time, and explained they had just taken my husband away without explanation.
>
> I then went up to the police station with my social worker to find out what was going on. The police then took me into a room for questioning also. They asked me questions about who goes to Jimmy Robinson's flat. I didn't know. They showed me some photographs of Vin Hickey, Michael Hickey, Pat Molloy and Jimmy Robinson just as his hair was growing back. The police asked me did I know Vincent Hickey's face. I said 'no'. They said he's been to Jimmy's a few times. I said: 'If he's been to Jimmy's I must know him'. The police said: 'Well, do you know his face?' I said 'no'. They said: 'Are you sure because he has been to Jimmy's? He's walked up and down the landing with Jimmy and you are always in your kitchen, you must have seen him'. I was confused, but then I thought I had seen his face. But it could have been in a pub.
>
> The police said: 'Well if you think you've seen his face, it must be at Jimmy's'. I have seen a man with a moustache and beard go

to Jimmy's, but I wouldn't honestly say that this man was Vincent Hickey. In fact when I went to Stafford Crown Court to give evidence last year I didn't recognise Vincent Hickey. I had never seen him before in my life.

The only link between the Hickeys and their co-defendants at the time of the Bridgewater murder had been snapped.

The Other Side of Peter Bryant

In January 1981, Michael Hickey became the first convicted prisoner to get Home Office permission to take the 'truth drug'. The supporters of this treatment did not make for it any of the extravagant claims made for the polygraph or 'lie detector.'

The full extent of what it could do was explained by Dr William Canning, consultant psychiatrist at Coleshill Hall Hospital, who administered the drug to Michael and sent in his report in July 1981: 'Briefly the thinking behind abreaction is that a patient becomes disinhibited and less able to censor feelings and thoughts.'

The drug used was Amytal, and Michael reacted well to it. The examination about the murder was thorough and in places tough. Dr Canning concluded: 'Your client stuck to his story throughout the interview and continued to affirm his innocence.'

Dr Canning was specially struck by the set of answers which Michael gave on the subject of Yew Tree Farm itself. 'I questioned him very carefully regarding the geographical location of Yew Tree Farm and I was impressed by the way in which he answered. I am bound to say that I formed the opinion that Mr Hickey did not know the location of the farm, and if this is the case it must cast serious doubts on his being there and being implicated in the murder of Carl Bridgewater.'

The truth drug test, for what it was worth, had been passed with flying colours (and Vincent Hickey passed it in the same way the following month).

The result was of no legal value. It could not be submitted to the Court of Appeal. But it did get a lot of publicity. One young man was so interested in the television report that he telephoned Richard Gilkes, Michael's solicitor, with some more information.

The young man was a petty crook called Robert Gwilliam. He had been in Winson Green prison in 1978 and had tried to escape from there with Peter Bryant. Like Bryant, he had been put on the top security 'E' list, and had exercised with the Category A prisoners, including the three men who were to stand trial for the Bridgewater murder.

Robert Gwilliam remembered that his fellow prisoner and escaper Peter Bryant had given evidence for the prosecution against Robinson and the Hickeys. He telephoned Mr Gilkes (who was also his own solicitor) and offered to talk about Bryant. Mr Gilkes invited Gwilliam down to his office, discussed Bryant's evidence in the case, and took a formal statement, dated 19 February 1981.

Bryant's evidence had been extremely damaging to all three men, particularly to Robinson who was alleged to have confessed directly to the murder and to trying to sell off the antiques from Yew Tree Farm.

Robert Gwilliam said:

I always exercised with Bryant between 15 December 1978 and the end of February 1979. At no time did I hear any of the conversations said by Bryant in his statement of July 9 1979 to have taken place.

I asked Robinson and the two Hickeys if they had done the murder, and they always denied it. They never said anything to me which could have implicated them.

Once when Bryant and I were still on G Wing, he told me that we might get off on appeal if we were to put Robinson and the two Hickeys 'in' for the murder. This was said in the presence of Robert Phillipson.

This statement was submitted by Mr Gilkes as part of Michael Hickey's case for an appeal. As soon as the prosecution saw it, they passed it on to the Staffordshire police, whose officers went at once to Wakefield prison. Serving a life sentence there for a murder in a drunken fight outside a nightclub was Robert Phillipson, who had been mentioned at the end of Bob Gwilliam's statement. The police spent some time with Phillipson.

Robert Phillipson was a cautious man, who would not do as the police suggested. As soon as they had left him he wrote some detailed notes of his visit which he at once made available to the defence lawyers.

The notes provide an interesting insight not just into the truth of Bryant's evidence but also into the way the Staffordshire police conducted their business in the Bridgewater affair:

I was interviewed by two police officers today and shown a statement signed by R. Gwilliam stating that Peter Bryant said to him in my presence, 'If we put in the Bridgewater killers, we might get out sentence reduced on an Appeal'. I was asked by these officers if I recalled him (Peter Bryant) saying this. I replied, 'Answering a question out of the blue like this, without time to think, I don't believe I could recall anything that was said two and a half to three years ago.'

I then went on to say, 'As I remember him [Peter Bryant] this is exactly the type of thing he would have suggested as he was always looking for ways to get out of gaol. He was an inadequate and could not cope in prison. He even tried to escape from the coach travelling to (or from) Court. He was then segregated from other prisoners and when he was allowed back amongst the main flow of inmates, he couldn't face it and asked to be separated again, but the only way he could be separated was to go on Rule 43 (for protection). To do this he had to make up a story that other prisoners were going to attack him, which he went ahead and did.'

It was then that the officer in charge (who was doing all the talking) they told me that he [Peter Bryant] had gone ahead and testified against the Hickeys and Robinson. I told him that whilst I was there and exercising in the same group as one of the Hickeys and Robinson, that though I never spoke to them personally the story I had received was that they had totally denied it [the crime] so how Peter Bryant had come up with anything other than the same story was a mystery to me. The officer told me that it didn't matter though as he was not the only prisoner to testify against them.

He then told me that the thing he found unusual about the case was that Molloy had not contested or disagreed with any part of this statement when it was produced at the trial. He said, 'It is the only case I have seen like it for a long time. There is always *something* the Defendant disputes even if it is only to say that "they are not my exact words but how the officer wrote them down". But Molloy didn't even do that.' I agreed it was unusual and that perhaps Molloy was covering up for someone else and that the Hickeys and Robinson were really innocent. Then he changed the subject. The officer had been writing nearly all the time and he now said to me 'Sign this and you can go'.

The statement he had written contained bits of what I had said, well hardly anything of which I had said really. Only that I had been on remand between certain dates and had exercised with all the above mentioned and had not spoken to Robinson or Hickey and could not recall the conversation between Gwilliam and Bryant. I told him, 'If you put in that [statement] that this is exactly the sort of thing Bryant would have made up, but having only just, after two and a half years, been asked if I could recall him saying it, I would have to say no.'

I told them that having met these people for only a few months, two and a half to three years ago, and never having seen them since, I would need to think about it a bit to try and remember individual conversations (the one in question or one very similar to it I thought I could recall already) as I cannot usually remember conversations a week old without giving them some thought.

He then said, 'Are you going to sign this statement?'

I replied, 'That is not my statement, that is chosen parts of what I have said, parts chosen by you for a purpose only you know.'

I then further said, 'Let me write my statement if it's a statement from me you want.'

To which he replied 'No! This is the only information we require.'

So I then said, 'It is incomplete, you have not written everything I have told you.'

He then asked, 'Are you going to sign this or not?'

I replied, 'No. It is incomplete, it is ambiguous and misleading. It can be construed wrongly because reading Gwilliam's statement and then the one you have written it gives the impression that I have no idea what he is talking about and therefore he is not telling the truth but I do know what he is talking about; it is just that I cannot recall this exact conversation at the moment.'

The officer then said, 'So be it.'

He then wrote at the bottom of the statement 'Refused to sign' and then they both signed it.

I thought for a minute and came to the conclusion that if they produced the statement for some reason and said that I'd made it but refused to sign it it would be just as ambiguous signed or unsigned.

I said to him, 'If you let me add to the statement that he might well have said this but at the present moment in time I cannot recall it, I will sign it for you.'

To this he agreed and after re-writing the second page of the statement he wrote this agreed piece and he started to add a bit more but he left the bit more unfinished and said 'Here you are'.

I crossed out 'the bit more' and initialled it and then signed it. I only agreed to sign it because of the agreed extra piece which was a bit fuller and not so ambiguous but it was still not a complete picture of what I had told him.

All this I have written here is what I recall now straight after the interview, but even this has bits missing. One of the missing pieces is near the beginning of the interview where the officer was telling me how Robinson and Co. deserved everything they got doing what they did, and he asked me my opinion of it. There are other bits I've left out too. He asked me about my case and said I shouldn't do so long as I hadn't meant to do what had happened and how it could have happened to anyone. He said he knew of a similar case to mine where the fellow had got out after five years three months and that I should do about the same, but as I believe this length of imprisonment to be absurd for a lifer (though I know there are such cases) except in special cases, I knew I could not believe what he was saying and that he was just trying to be liked by saying things that I would like to believe.

I do now definitely recall Bryant saying to Gwilliam in my presence, 'if we put Hickey and Robinson in for the murder we might get out sooner if we appeal' or words to this effect.

These notes were passed to Tony Fryer as soon as he arrived on 19 October to take a statement from Robert Phillipson. The prisoner gave Mr Fryer a long and generous statement, repeating that he was now certain Bryant had said what Gwilliam reported. He went on: 'I also recall Bryant saying to Gwilliam on another occasion about telling on a prisoner called Connors who was also in at the time. He was on to Gwilliam about "dropping Connors in it". I gathered that it was half what we knew and half what he would make up in order to make things worse for Connors and to ingratiate himself with the prison officers.'

The evidence of Bryant which had not been challenged by any independent witness at the time, *was* now challenged by two independent people with nothing to gain from what they said. Peter Bryant himself did not benefit for long from the good favour he won for himself by his evidence. Before long he was back in Dartmoor prison, and was not released until December 1985.

The Lord Chief Justice Steps In

Soon after Robert Phillipson's statement was taken, the defence lawyers heard that a date had been set down for their application to the Court of Appeal for leave to make a full appeal: 1 December and, if necessary, 2 December 1981. At last, after two years, the case would be back in open court. The news was greeted with much delight by Jimmy Robinson in Gartree and Michael Hickey in Aylesbury. From Vincent, who had been in Long Lartin prison near Evesham ever since the verdict, there had been a long and brooding silence. Vincent had sacked his trial barrister, choosing Patrick Bennett QC in place of Desmond Hollis. For Michael and Jimmy the lawyers were the same as at the trial.

Presiding, rather unusually for a mere leave to appeal application, was Lord Chief Justice Lane, the country's top judge. He was flanked by Mr Justice Goff and Mr Justice Taylor.

The defendants' lawyers had agreed among themselves that the case should be led by Patrick Bennett for Vincent. Mr Bennett opened on the importance of the evidence of Roger Edwards, the man who had seen the Vauxhall Viva turning into Yew Tree Farm, and its driver in uniform. Could this have been Hubert Spencer? he asked. The Lord Chief Justice intervened: 'He looks nothing like him, does he, Mr Bennett?' Mr Bennett agreed at once, and proceeded to say at great length that the last thing he intended to do was to suggest that Mr Spencer had done the murder.

When the Lord Chief Justice insisted that if Spencer *had* done the murder, he must have been 'part of a team', Mr Bennett suggested that, for all he knew, Spencer may have been the fifth man – he may have taken part with the men he was representing! From that absurd moment, the whole appeal collapsed.

The appellants' lawyers appeared to be drained of all fight and confidence. Though Mrs Guy was brought to court, the defence did not even formally submit the statement she made to Ann Whelan. Though Robert Gwilliam came to court, the defence did not submit his statement about Bryant, nor the support he got for it from Robert Phillipson. All these matters, for some inexplicable reason, were not even raised.

When the defence referred to Helen Johnston, the Lord Chief Justice publicly rebuked Mr Fryer for interviewing her without a representative of the police or Director of Public Prosecutions present.

The entire case against the defendants had rested on admissions made by Vincent Hickey and Pat Molloy when they were held incommunicado in prisons without access to lawyers, friends or family for periods ranging from a week to ten days during which they were rigorously interrogated by a hostile and determined police force. On this the Lord Chief Justice had no comment. For a solicitor who interviewed a woman who had come to his office of her own free will to make a statement, but had not asked a policeman to be present, the Lord Chief Justice reserved the most stinging rebuke.

In the press box the view was unanimous at the first interval (when most of the journalists left). The case was lost. It hardly seemed worth coming back the next day, 2 December 1981, to hear the Lord Chief Justice's judgement.

The following were the main points plucked out by the Lord Chief Justice to summarise the case against the three men.

1. 'Robinson did stand on a parade and was identified by three separate witnesses, two of comparatively small weight. There was a Miss Stagg, a very impressive identification witness . . .' Lord Chief Justice Lane did not point out that none of the witnesses picked out Robinson from the parade itself, and Miss Stagg, the 'very impressive identification witness', was very impressive on the colour and length of Robinson's hair, when he had no hair at all.

2. 'Vincent and Molloy had access to a Bedford van.' There was no evidence that Molloy had access to any Bedford van.

3. 'There was further evidence that Vincent and Michael left the Dog and Partridge and Robinson and Molloy left the California public house shortly before 3.00 p.m. on 19 September, which would give them ample time to be at the scene of the farm at the time when the witnesses say the burglars were to be observed.'

Mario Sabetta, a key witness, was said to have seen two of the murderers in Lawnswood Road at 3.25 to 3.30. The very fastest time that the police could do the journey from one of the pubs to the farm, along routes they had planned and knew well, was twenty-seven minutes. Yet, in the view of the Lord Chief Justice, the four men had 'ample time' to meet up after closing time, set off in what Molloy called their 'old bangers' and get to the farm by 3.25-3.30.

4. 'Zannetos contradicted the evidence of these applicants [that they were at his garage on the afternoon of the murder]. He said he was visited by them on the following day.'

Mr Zannetos said nothing of the kind. He said he could not remember the men or when they came in. His evidence was they must have been there on the Tuesday evening of the murder or the following morning, and the documents tended to support their story that they were there on the evening.

5. On the contradictions of Helen Johnston, the Lord Chief Justice once again waxed indignant. The tape of the interview with Mr Fryer, he suggested, did not match the statement which he had drawn up from the interview. On tape, Mrs Johnston said she had remembered a conversation about a gun going off accidentally while in the statement she said she had not. But then the Lord Chief Justice said this: 'For a time on tape it seems that she was trying to apply the conversation to a robbery called the Tesco robbery and not to the Carl Bridgewater events. But when one relates the time she overheard the conversation, the Tesco robbery had not taken place.'

The Lord Chief Justice plainly forgot that the time of that alleged conversation was the subject of some controversy. It could not have been when Helen Johnston said it was, because Robinson was in prison at the time. It must have been much later – after 23 October, and quite possibly (if any such conversation took place at all) after 23 November, which was the date of the Tesco robbery.

The Lord Chief Justice ended his section on Helen Johnston with this: 'It is clear to us that Mrs Johnston, if she were here, would not say that she had lied on oath. If on the other hand she were here and her evidence was that she did lie on oath, it would not, in the face of what we have already said, be credible evidence; it would not be credible evidence in the light of what occurs on tape.'

Mrs Johnston, in short, was altogether incredible, except when she gave evidence at the trial. From then on she either backed up what she had said there, which was credible, or she denied it, which was incredible.

After backing up the trial judge in not insisting that Linda Galvin should be called to give evidence, the Lord Chief Justice went on to explore the main submission of all three applicants: namely that the Spencer episode constituted new evidence; and that if the Spencer story had been in front of the jury, the four men might not have been convicted.

To counter this, Lord Lane relied on the evidence of Mrs Riebold, whom he described, quite inaccurately, as 'the lady in charge of him at the hospital' (if anything, he was in charge of her). He then insisted that if Spencer had been at Yew Tree Farm 'he must have been one of a team'. Why? 'Because there is no doubt and the evidence shows quite clearly that there were three or four people sighted by witnesses who were plainly taking part in this offence . . . What are the alternatives? That Spencer was on his own? That is flying in the face of all the evidence, because there were two vehicles, to say the least.'

Earlier in his judgement, the Lord Chief Justice had been over this ground most thoroughly. He had said: 'Two vehicles were seen by witnesses at the house at the material times, namely about 3.45 to 4.45. There was a light blue Cortina estate and also a van, either a Transit van or a Bedford van, that type of vehicle.'

Let us recap. There were twelve witnesses called who saw vehicles at or near the farm. Eleven of them saw one vehicle. Only one person – Wendy Stagg – at the very end of Lord Lane's time schedule (4.45) saw two vehicles, and one of those was a plum-coloured saloon car which was never traced anywhere, let alone to the defendants. Everyone else saw one vehicle. Some said it was an estate, some said it was a van, some said it was a car. Only two people saw a van 'at the house'.

One of these, Brian Clarke, was certain he saw an Austin/Morris J4 – neither a Transit nor a Bedford. The other, Mrs Dorothy Southall, who only caught a glimpse of the roof of the vehicle, was sure it was a van but couldn't be sure what make. The other two vans were seen by Stephen Bridgewater. He saw a Ford Transit, parked in the road not far from the farm, but he couldn't remember the day; and John Wakelam who 'seemed to remember' a 'tatty-looking and dirty light blue van, possibly a Bedford' which was 'coming from the direction of Yew Tree Farm' at 4.35.

There was *no direct evidence* that two vehicles were 'at the house'.

What of the other assertion of the Lord Chief Justice that there 'were three or four people sighted by witnesses who were plainly taking part in this offence?'

No witness saw four people. No one who said they saw a van saw anyone at all (even Mr Wakelam who said he saw 'possibly a Bedford' couldn't remember anything about any of the occupants or how many there were.) Of the eight witnesses who saw cars, three saw no one at all. Wendy Stagg saw two people in one car, one from another; Mario Sabetta saw two; Terence Madeley saw two; Terence Phelps (at after five o'clock, *after* the Lord Chief Justice's deadline) saw two or three; Mr Mills saw two in a car driving along the main A449 road. Not one of

these people seen were 'at the house', as the Lord Chief Justice suggested. All were outside the premises, either in the road outside or in a car
some distance down the road. There was, in short, no justification whatever for saying that 'three or four people' were seen who were 'plainly
taking part in this offence'.

The Lord Chief Justice concluded: 'The motiveless, drunken killing
of Wilkes, which was Spencer's undoubted crime, contrasted as sharply
as could be imagined from the highly motivated killing of a potential
witness to the burglary.' All three judges, he said, were satisfied that if
the Spencer episode were introduced to a jury it would be regarded 'as a
red herring'. The applications to appeal were rejected.

As the judges gathered up their papers no one noticed Ann Whelan
getting to her feet. The judges looked up in horror when she began to
speak from the back of the court. 'Justice,' she said, her voice high with
nervousness, 'has not been done and has not been seen to be done. And
you, Mr Stewart,' she went on turning to the Chief Superintendent who
was sitting not far away 'you! I challenge you to take the truth drug as
my son has done and see whose lies have won the day.'

The judges scuttled for cover, and the court was swiftly cleared. Outside, I came across the crumpled figure of Tony Fryer, nerving himself
to go down to the cells to tell his client the result. At least at the trial, he
reflected, they had expected to go down. Here, they had hoped at least
for leave to appeal in a case which was shrouded in controversy. The
scene in the cells that afternoon was best described by Jimmy Robinson,
in a letter to Ann a few days later:

Honestly, Ann, afterwards the three of us sat there so stunned and
miserable, we're human, and even though we realised the cards
were stacked against us, we'd still *hoped* and prayed in our heart of
hearts not for miracles, not for what is termed a 'result' – no, Ann,
all we'd prayed for was that the truth would win, and those dirty
twisted evil bastards made a mockery of it. Poor Michael was dis-
traught. Honestly, Ann, I longed to put my arms around him and
try somehow to comfort him. I *felt* so for him, I've got kiddies
slightly younger myself and it broke me up to see a youngster trying to bear up and be even more of a man that he already is. Sadly,
though, such displays of affection are construed by the zoo keepers
as sexually motivated, as apparently love, compassion, understanding are emotions beyond our capabilities . . . That's all now,
Ann, you *remember* no more talk of letting anyone down, okay?
You've got my complete confidence and gratitude.

The reports in the papers were short and final. There would be no appeal. The Lord Chief Justice had had the last word. That was surely the end of the matter.

The Home Office Investigates

Many convicted prisoners protest their innocence after trial. After a while, however, the tendency is for the prisoners to settle down and conform to prison discipline. Young Michael Hickey, however, reacted in a quite different manner. The longer he was in prison, the more outraged he became. In April 1982, four months after leave to appeal was turned down, he was moved from Aylesbury to Long Lartin where he saw his cousin Vincent. Michael inspired even Vincent to campaign about their innocence. They were enthusiastically supported. By the end of 1982, the cousins were treated by their fellow prisoners as though they were innocent of the murder.

Michael, however, was not satisfied with good will. Apart from a few protests organised by his mother, a whole year had passed without a single major article or television programme highlighting his innocence. It was time, he reckoned, to take things into his own hands. He persuaded an initially reluctant Vincent to join him in a demonstration. On 26 February, with the full support of the other Long Lartin prisoners, they climbed onto the roof of the prison and painted a huge sign over it: 'SPENCER KILLED CARL'. They stayed there in freezing weather for twenty-one days – a very long protest. Almost daily, Ann organised pickets and protests outside the prison, but they were never joined by more than a handful of friends and supporters. On 17 March the cousins climbed down, to be met by furious authorities. Both were sentenced to 112 days in solitary confinement.

There was some good news, however. There had been a substantial movement in the case. In December 1982, a prisoner at Long Lartin, George Wells-Johnson, wrote this letter to Michael Shersby, Conservative MP for Uxbridge.

> I am writing to bring to your attention the case of Michael Hickey who is serving a life sentence for the murder of Carl Bridgewater.
>
> I am in no way writing to you to curry favour or gains with parties concerned in this case. I am writing to you because of my conscience of the matter in question. You are my MP . . .
>
> I have known young Michael Hickey for just over a year. He was put to work along side me in the prison laundry, to be my number two in fact, on the job I do. As you can well imagine I was not very pleased with this because of what he was in prison for, 'the killing of a young boy'. I have children of my own.
>
> In the course of the days weeks and months going by, I have got to know this lad very well. He has always protested his innocence

238

of the murder of CARL BRIDGEWATER. I have got to know him better than his own parents, I spend more time with him than anybody else has ever done. I am an old hand compared with this young man. He is not blessed with a good education or a sensible outlook on life. What boy is at that age? I got sick to death of him keep on protesting his innocence and asked him if I could read his trial papers, so I could point out to him his guilt by the evidence presented and shut him up once and for all.

On reading the papers I saw that there was no real factual evidence presented at his trial. I honestly couldn't believe somebody could be found guilty on the evidence presented. Thinking deeply about what I had read, I made up my mind I would find out if he was guilty. He is not clever enough under constant questions, day in day out for months to not slip up in some way. I asked him things that the police could never have thought to ask him, I did this over many months. *He is not guilty of the murder*. When you get a person in after a time, they usually confess, usually to somebody who has got close to them in prison, such is the relationship of young Hickey and myself. I would know if he lied. He is young enough to be my son and not clever enough to convince me he is not guilty if he is. The boy never deviates in his answers in any major way.

In Wormwood Scurbs prison is a man who has confessed to his solicitor of CARL BRIDGEWATER's murder. Why is this being suppressed? You will have heard of the so called prison grape vine. Believe me it really works, for instance if I wanted to send a message to an inmate in another prison I would give the message to a man going to another prison he in turn would pass it on until it reached its intended party. I have found out via the grape vine that this man in Wormwood Scurbs will not or cannot say anything because of pressure by the police 'concerned in both their cases' not to say anything, it has been said if he keeps quiet he will only serve eight years of his life sentence.

Anybody with a grain of common sense after reading and seeing the evidence that convicted M. Hickey will see that this young man should never have been found guilty. At the very least he should be given a retrial, as a matter of fact and record no real evidence was present at the trial. You will say that the legal minds of the country know much more than me about this, I agree with that. But you know as well as I do that nobody will admit to a mistake of this magnitude, least of all the police or Home Office unless first a scape goat is found to blame for this grave mistake.

. . . I am an out and out TORY, all my family are. We are beginning to wonder though, have we made the right party choice. Willie Whitelaw sits on a fence never going either way, he is not the right man for the job, a lot of people think so. Him and his office must know that M. Hickey is not guilty, yet will never agree it is so. How much better for the party if Whitelaw comes off his fence puts his foot firmly on the ground and opens up the Hickey case. How much the public will think of the man if he is seen to put errors of justice right.

You and your fellow MPs must get together and ask the Home Office to reopen this case, you should all read the trial papers and see what sort of evidence can convict your sons or mine to life imprisonment. Give the lad a retrial it will prove once and for all his guilt or not. If the Home Secretary is so sure of his guilt, then he should have no worry about a retrial. There is such a lot being covered up by certain people because of the scandal it will cause if it came out.

I know I am only a prisoner and only one voice of many, but if a prison inmate can be convinced by facts think of the public's reaction at this injustice.

Do yourself a favour and read the transcripts, you will see I have a point.

This powerful letter was sent on by Mr Shersby to the Home Office. Mr Shersby wrote back to his constituent saying he had recommended that a minister look into the case.

George Wells-Johnson had kept a copy of his letter, and it found its way, as all such documents did in the end, to Ann Whelan. She passed it on to Roy Hattersley, MP for Birmingham, Sparkbrook, whom she approached as Shadow Home Secretary. Roy Hattersley was immediately impressed by the letter, and raised its contents personally with the Home Secretary, William Whitelaw. He also went on local television to demand a public inquiry into the case.

On 14 March, Central Television confirmed that the Home Office were discussing whether or not the case should be re-opened. On 22 March, five days after Michael and Vincent came down from the roof, Ann Whelan was watching the news on television when she heard that the Home Office was holding a special inquiry. She phoned the Home Office the next day, and was delighted to hear the news confirmed. Some weeks later, she heard that the investigation would be conducted by the Assistant Chief Constable of Manchester, Bill Donnan, assisted by one of Manchester's top detectives, Detective Chief Superintendent Frank Ridgway. Ann Whelan protested that the inquiry would not be held in public, and was told in another Home Office reply that its findings would not be published. The 'usual procedure' was being followed. The police would carry out all the inquiries and would make recommendations. No one would ever know what they found out, or even what they recommended. Only the action taken by the Home Office would be announced.

Others, however, were carrying out inquiries which would lead to some more public knowledge about the case. Tom Sargant, veteran investigator for Justice, the British Section of the International Commission of Jurists, got a copy of the Wells-Johnson letter, which impressed him. Tom Sargant had access to the prisons.

He visited Wells-Johnson who told him to go to see another prisoner who had been in Wormwood Scrubs with Spencer – Michael Ishmael. Ishmael was serving a sixteen-year sentence for armed robbery. On 5 April Tom Sargant went to Gartree and took a signed statement from Michael Ishmael:

In 1979/80 I was on a 28 day laydown in Winson Green, where I met Michael Hickey and Jimmy Robinson. They were protesting their innocence.

A year later, I went to Long Lartin Prison, where I met Vincent Hickey and was convinced that all three were innocent. This was through prison talk.

In 1981, after a 56 day laydown, I went to Wormwood Scrubs D. Wing, and a man called Spencer served the food on the hot plate. It was common prison knowledge that he had killed Carl Bridgewater, and I made a point of getting to know him. He used to bring little pieces from the hot plate to my cell for a chat. I said to him . . . 'look here, you've got four kids doing life for you, if you've got any decency, why can't you help them' . . . He said 'Honest it was an accident, but the kid lived along by me, and I was frightened they would think I had done it on purpose.'

I asked him to ease his conscience, and when I saw him, he said he hadn't had a wink of sleep all night. I told him to keep thinking about it.

The next day, I was put in the segregation unit and moved to Parkhurst.

Spencer never went into details but kept saying it was an accident.

Spencer's alleged confession to Michael Ishmael, which was published in the *Daily Mirror* on 21 April, was taken seriously by Chief Superintendent Ridgway. He visited Gartree prison to interview Ishmael. The prisoner, however, had been greatly depressed by the reaction of the prison authorities to his story. As he said in the statement to Tom Sargant, he had immediately been exiled to the segregation unit at Parkhurst. Now, he was worrying about his Category A status. He had long been due to be taken off the strict security associated with 'Cat A', and he feared that any further talk from him about the Spencer affair would jeopardise his chances of getting off Category A. His case was due to come up only a few days before Ridgway arrived at the prison. When he got to the room scheduled for the interview with the chief superintendent, Michael Ishmael was surprised to see a group of prison officers waiting with the policemen. He said he did not want to say anything with the prison officers there, but they insisted. He therefore decided to say nothing, and left the room. DCS Ridgway submitted his findings to the Home Secretary on 26 June.

It was *five months* before the Home Office responded. Ann Whelan heard of their decision through a letter from her MP, Hal Miller. Mr Miller passed on a letter he had had from Home Office junior minister David Mellor. This letter said that prisoners in Wormwood Scrubs and Spencer himself had rejected the notion that Ishmael and Spencer had even met, let alone passed information to one another about the Bridgewater murder; and that police had 'not discovered anything new, significant, and relevant to Spencer which could serve to implicate him more deeply in the case'. Accordingly, the Home Secretary could not find any grounds to justify any further action. The case was closed (again).

Spencer's own denial of any confession to Ishmael got considerable publicity. Letters from prisoners to newspapers are scrupulously controlled, and seldom allowed. Hubert Spencer, however, was permitted to write to his local *Express and Star* in outrage at Michael Ishmael's allegations. He described himself, with many references to his art work in prison, as a 'model prisoner'. The letter was seen by Michael Hickey who promptly wrote personally to the reporter, Tony Bishop, challenging Spencer to take the truth drug about the Carl Bridgewater murder. The challenge was passed on by Bishop. Spencer's reply appeared in the *Express and Star* on 3 November: 'I have no intention or desire to allow that useless and obnoxious concoction to be injected into the system. I would however encourage the Hickeys to take as much as they can get. I understand it is quite poisonous.'

Michael Hits The Roof

Michael Hickey was not in a mood to continue this correspondence. He was pondering the collapse of this latest initiative to open out the case. From experience, he knew that a setback like that could plunge him, his cousin and Jimmy Robinson into another year of silence. Once again, he took action himself, this time alone. He had been moved during the summer away from Long Lartin – and Vincent. He was now at Gartree prison, near Leicester. On 24 November, just a week after he heard of the Home Office decision, he put on five jumpers, two pairs of long johns, three pairs of jeans, and four pairs of socks under a new oversize pair of training shoes. He crammed three balls of string in his pockets, and a pair of scissors. Inside his clothing he wrapped round four bin liners, a blanket and a sheet on which he had written in ink, in huge letters: 'SPENCER KILLED CARL. WE ARE INNOCENT.'

As he was called out for work that morning, he made a dash for the prison roof. He had talked to other prisoners about it, and planned his route with great care. Before any of the warders understood what was happening, he was on the flat roof of the prison in the freezing cold – his only protection against which was his clothing and the bin liners.

Reporters who came to the prison, alerted by Ann, shouted up at him. Fashioning a loud-hailer from some old cardboard, Michael bellowed down to them that he intended to stay on the roof until he was forced down, or until a public inquiry looked into his case. The reporters asked how long that might be, and he replied that he would see them at Christmas (four and a half weeks off). They laughed and went away with their pictures.

Some time later Michael wrote to his mother a long and detailed account of what followed. The problems for him were prodigious. The weather was extremely cold. There was no shelter. One night soon after he went up:

> . . . the wind had turned into a gale, and it got worse as the night went on – it didn't stop until seven in the morning. To start with I just held on to the few bin liners I had around me for as long as I thought I could, but then they started to split, and half of one of my top bin liners blew away. It was then I realised that the wind was not going to stop, and it had started to rain. So I took a blanket I had with me, and hooked it over the brackets of the guttering just to hold the wind off. Even though the blanket got sopping wet, it stopped the wind. That was to me the worst night I had, worse than when it was six below, because I had to hold everything and tuck everything underneath me. Many times I would get cramp and my hands were completely numb. It was times like this that I thought of asking for a ladder, and about a warm bath and bed, but I'd just think to myself: 'it will be a better, milder day tomorrow'.

He could not have survived for more than a few days without the sudden, spontaneous and almost unanimous support of the inmates of Gartree prison. Before long, all sorts of useful things started arriving on the roof. By the end of the second week Michael had amassed 100 new bin liners, and a huge assortment of coat hangers, broom handles, pillows, and blankets. There was also an endless supply of radios – perhaps the most precious of all prisoners' possessions – which kept breaking down in the frost and damp, but were instantly replaced. With his invaluable scissors, and string, Michael managed to make himself a sort of shelter near the entrance to the roof. He built a dam against the wind out of his own excrement.

Food was a constant problem, and one which would soon have defeated him had it not been for the solid support he got from the prisoners beneath him. The authorities did not relish a violent confrontation on the roof which would be dangerous not just to Michael but also to prison officers. They decided therefore to 'starve him down' and went to enormous lengths to cut off the supply of food. To start with, he would put a line of string around his hand and wait for a call from one of the windows beneath him. Then he would dash to the part of the roof over the window, lower his line and pull up a food parcel.

The authorities soon got wind of this. Wardens listened at the doors of cells and in the television rooms for any such calls. 'In the end,' wrote Michael 'I was sent up a plan that some one had come up with.' The plan contained an intricate code with letters and numbers which would be held out of windows to let him know where his food parcel was coming from. After a few weeks, Michael had strings with hooks hanging down to almost every window in the prison. He would then watch out for the code, and, after a dummy run or two to confuse the warders, he would rush to the correct window and haul up his food. Often, the plan would go wrong – or (the worst frustration) a parcel would slip off its hook and crash to the ground below. 'These nights,' he wrote, 'someone would come to the nearest window, and lean out and throw up in a sock some tea or coffee.' They even, one day in the afternoon, started throwing up sandwiches, and packets of peanuts stuck on to pieces of wood.

He got a hot meal almost every night. Once, when the prison was searched for drugs and guns and all prisoners were shut up in their cells, he went without his food supply for seventy-two hours, and had to fall back on his miserable store of tins of fish and fruit. But he was very seldom let down.

Michael's report is full of praise and admiration. 'Honestly, they were – and are – marvellous. I couldn't have had any more support. The limits they stretched to keep me up there! Think of the fines they had to pay! It's beyond me how they managed to pay such large and somewhat excessive fines they were handed out. I was told they started at £3. Then after a week, they rose to £5. People were moved from wing to wing. I was told that people in other wings apart from the one I was protesting on were helping out to pay the fines.' In fact, as prisoners have since testified, it was almost an honour to be fined for helping the young man on the roof, and an unofficial whip-round was constantly in existence to help pay the fines.

Many warders were sympathetic to Michael's protests. There were one or two who always led the charge on the food lines, but many turned a blind eye. When one food parcel was stopped by one warder, Michael heard from another soon afterwards: 'He should have let you have that tonight, son. It's bloody freezing.'

When Michael was taken to Liverpool prison after being convicted of the Bridgewater murder in November 1979, he had been spat on, insulted, beaten up and left in his cell with razor blades. He was, in his fellow prisoners' eyes, a child-killer, to be kept in constant isolation and pain. His own courage and determination had sustained him – and changed the prisoners' minds. The well-informed grapevine which runs from prison to prison and is the stuff of day-to-day conversation amongst prisoners entirely acquitted the Hickey cousins and Jimmy Robinson of the Carl Bridgewater murder. As a result, all three were treated with nothing but sympathy and compassion by their fellows.

It was Christmas 1983, and the reporters came out once again to find the young man they had scoffed at a month earlier. He was still on the roof, chanting his innocence through his loud-hailer. On Christmas Day, Michael got a whole Christmas dinner sent up to him on the lines: 'Christmas Dinner from D-wing,' went the message, 'from your pals below. We wish you luck, and hope that something is done soon.'

Still he persevered – through all of freezing January and most of freezing February. When he finally agreed to come down, on 21 February, he had spent an astonishing eighty-nine days on the roof, far, far longer than any other prisoner ever.

This demonstration, perhaps one of the most remarkable acts of endurance in the whole history of protest, was not an immediate reaction to conviction and sentence. It took place *four years after* the conviction. Everyone who commented on it made the point that most guilty prisoners who protest their innocence soon tire of their protestations. When protests go on and on, and increase in their ferocity, the likelihood is that they are justified.

Michael's roof protest brought a tremendous spate of publicity. For the first time, the big television channels devoted substantial feature programmes to the Bridgewater case. On 1 February 1984, Granada's *Last Week, This Week* gave over half an hour to it. This was followed at once by twenty minutes on Channel Four News on 2 February. Soon after Michael came down, the BBC's *Out of Court* team, Sue Cook and David Jessell, undertook a masterly analysis of the case, including for the first time the information that the ambulance record book recording Spencer's movements in September 1978 had mysteriously gone missing.

For Michael, the price was heavy. The prison authorities sentenced him to another two months in solitary. The ordeal, on top of what he had gone through on the roof, was too much for him. Even before he was moved to Albany prison, Isle of Wight, on 25 July, Ann and Fred noticed his spirit slowly fading. The cockiness, the curiosity and the outrage all disappeared.

In its place was a desperate and silent truculence.

The Home Office Investigates Again

Still the case would not lie down. In the week 11-15 June, TV-am devoted an item every morning to the case. On 30 July, inspired by the programmes, a letter was sent to the headquarters of the Staffordshire police. The letter implicated Hubert Spencer in the murder of Carl Bridgewater. It was passed on to the Director of Public Prosecutions, who decided that another secret inquiry was in order. Assistant Chief Constable Donnan and Detective Chief Superintendent Ridgway, whose report had been so concise just fifteen months previously, were wheeled out once more to carry out another investigation.

DCS Ridgway was extremely thorough in his inquiries. He spent a long time with Mrs Barbara Riebold, who had provided Spencer with his alibi. Mrs Riebold's first statement to the police about Spencer was four lines long. Now, her statement ran to nineteen pages. Almost anyone who was remotely connected with the Spencers was interviewed by Ridgway whose attention to detail was legendary in the Manchester force.

But the result was exactly the same. On 13 November 1984, the same dismal letter from Hal Miller was passed on to Ann. 'The results of the investigation have been very carefully considered . . . but the Home Secretary has been unable to find any grounds to justify taking further action in respect of this case.' Once again, there was no information to back up the decision. All inquiries about the nature of the alibi, the statement of Mrs Riebold, the identity of the woman who had written to Staffordshire police in the first place – all were deflected with the pretext 'inquiries of this kind cannot be carried out unless the informants are guaranteed complete confidentiality'. Thus the authorities achieve the form without the content of a fair and impartial investigation. The authorities can say 'we have inquired with the greatest possible care, and do not have to offer a single word to prove it'. As 1984 came to an end, the silence and indifference which surrounded her on every side threatened for a moment to engulf even the commitment and determination of Ann Whelan.

Once again, however, the case rose from the dead.

Reg Hickey Changes His Story

After making yet another New Year Resolution in January 1985 that she would continue to see all the prosecution witnesses who built up the case against her son, Ann Whelan decided to go to London to see Reg Hickey. When we last left Reg Hickey, he was in prison after giving the vital evidence that his cousins Vincent and Michael had worked with him in the area immediately around Yew Tree Farm. Both the trial judge and Lord Chief Justice Lane referred to this evidence as an important part of the prosecution case.

Encouraged by the report of Dr Canning who had administered the 'truth drug' and been impressed by Michael's continued insistence that he had no idea where Yew Tree Farm was, Ann wanted to urge Reg Hickey to consider once more whether he had been mistaken. She had uncovered a small but important fact which no one but the police had known.

In his statement to police after his drive around the area early in 1979 Reg Hickey had said: 'On Monday 8 January 1979 I accompanied the same two officers to the Sedgely area and I directed them to an address at 34 Queens Road, Sedgely, which I identified as having been to with Vinny and Michael Hickey sometime during the period September 1977 and February 1978.'

As we have seen, this was the only address anywhere near the area which Reg could point to as a place where he and his cousins had worked. In February 1980, however, only a year after the statement, Ann visited 34 Queens Road, to be told by Mrs Phoebe Lloyd, the householder, that her roof *had* been mended by some itinerant workers – but in 1974 – when Michael was only twelve and still at school at Tamworth.

Reg Hickey, who was living with his family in Feltham, south-west London, was in bed on Sunday, 3 February 1985, when Ann Whelan called at 8.30 in the morning.

He was nervous and defensive as she explained how important his evidence had been, and how much help people like him could give to put right an injustice.

Reg started by saying that he *had* worked up that way with Vincent, though not with Michael. As Ann persevered, he agreed that he had told lies in evidence. He was, he said, full of fury against Vincent for denouncing him for the Hertfordshire robbery. He reminded Ann that there had been no evidence at all against him and that his four-year sentence was entirely due to what Vincent had said. He had also been promised parole, and a move to a prison in the Midlands, which he badly wanted. He had felt he had no alternative but to co-operate with police, who, incidentally, had kept all their promises. As the conversation continued, Reg Hickey became apologetic and sympathetic. When Ann asked if he would make a statement to her solicitor, he agreed at once. As she left, he put his arms round her and gave her a kiss, adding, 'Don't worry. I will put it right now.'

He was as good as his word. When Jim Nichol, Ann's new solicitor, arrived two days later (5 February), Reg Hickey gave him a detailed statement. Mr Nichol took the statement away, typed it up and sent it back to him for any amendments. The final signed version read in full as follows:

I am the second cousin to Vincent Hickey and Michael Hickey. They were both found guilty of the murder of Carl Bridgewater at their trial in 1979.

In 1979 I gave a statement to police officers investigating the murder of Carl Bridgewater. I have been shown a copy of the statement by Michael Hickey's solicitor Mr James Nichol and I now wish to make a further statement concerning the statement made to the police and the evidence I gave at the trial.

When the police first came to see me I was in Wandsworth Prison. I think it was late at night about 7.30 p.m. and I think I was interviewed in the Governors Office. There were two policemen present together with a prison officer who may have been an assistant governor.

One of the police officers told me that they were investigating the murder of Carl Bridgewater. The officer said that they had Michael and Vinny for the murder. I already knew that because I think I had read it in a paper. The officer said words to the effect that he believed that we all worked together. The officer said that I did not owe Vinny any favours because he – Vinny – had got me 4 years. They said it was only due to him that I had got those 4 years. They told me details about the job for which I had got 4 years that could only have come from someone who had been on the job with me. Vinny had been on the job with me.

The officers then said that if I helped them out with the Carl Bridgewater murder then I would get parole. The only thing on my mind was getting parole, I wanted to be out of prison as soon as possible.

They said that they would transfer me to a Midlands prison so that they could interview in the future more easily. I wanted to be in a Midlands prison. The officers asked me if I would be willing to make a statement saying that I had worked in the area with Vincent and Michael when the murder took place. I agreed to make a statement to that effect even though I had never been in the Wordsley area before and did not know it. The nearest I had been was Kingswinsford and Sedgely. I agreed to make the statement partially because what they had told me about Vinny and because they told me I would get parole.

I was eventually transferred to Shrewsbury Prison.

I remember the same two officers who had seen me in Wandsworth came to prison and took me out in a car. They told me they were taking me out to have a look around the area of the murder.

During the period we were driving around the officers were pointing out places and telling me that I had been working in these places with Michael and Vincent. I just agreed with them although I had never been to many of the places.

In all I went on two occasions with the same officers to the area where the murder took place. On one occasion I was taken to a place where the officers told me that the murder had taken place. They told me to say that I had been working there. I just agreed.

Before I had gone out with the officers in the car on the first occasion they told me that they had me down for three other jobs which they knew I had done. The officers said that if I did not help them I would be done for these three jobs.

The officers appeared to know a lot of detail about these jobs and in particular about one job which would have been very serious for me if I had been convicted of it. They said if I helped them with the Bridgewater murder they would wipe the slate clean together with any other jobs I cared to tell them about. I'm not too sure whether I signed anything to the effect that I had done the three jobs referred to and others.

The statement I gave to the officers was written down by one of the officers and a lot of it is untrue.

In particular on page 2 there is a reference to a lot of places that I had worked at with Vincent. They end with 'Wordsley'. Before going to Wordsley with the police I had to the best of my recollection never been in Wordsley in my life.

On page 5 of my statement to the police I say that I have been to a public house called the Crooked House. I have never been there.

I think it is right that I directed the police to 34 Queens Road Sedgely as I say on the bottom of my statement to the police.

On page 5 of my statement it states that I have been to Kingswinford looking for work with Vinny and Michael. I wish to make it clear that I have only once in my life been to Kingswinford to look for work and this was at the end of 1977 or the beginning of 1978. I do not think I have ever been in a public house in Kingswinford. The only pub that stands out in my mind is 'The Kingswinford' because Vinny's mum used to work there. I have only ever done one job in Kingswinford – even then I'm not sure and may be mixing up this one job with the Sedgely job.

Concerning page 5 of my statement to the police and the paragraph dealing with Wordsley I wish to say that the police officers did take me to all the places but this was the first time that I had ever been. I do not know a public house called the Lawnswood nor have I ever been in Lawnswood Lane except with the police.

249

At the bottom of page 5 of my statement to the police there is a reference to a place called Wall Heath. I have no idea where this is and I do not think I have ever been there.

After making and signing the statement for the reasons outlined above and giving evidence at the trial police officers came to see me on two or three occasions in prison.

At the time of the trial I knew my case was due to be heard for parole so I just went along with the story and the statement that the police had made up.

I honestly believe that I was given parole in August 1980, 10 months before my existing release date, because I had helped the police.

I agree to this statement written down by Mr Nichol.

When the Reg Hickey statement was published in the *Daily Mirror* of 21 March 1985, there was an immediate response from the media. Reg Hickey appeared on regional and national news on independent television all that day, and the following Monday he was on BBC News.

The authorities were silent. There was no answer to this crucial change of evidence from the Staffordshire police, from the Director of Public Prosecutions or from the Home Office. There were no allegations of 'threats' by Ann Whelan; no denunciation of Jim Nichol for seeing Reg Hickey without a representative of the Director of Public Prosecutions.

Reg Hickey's new evidence was the most powerful blow yet to the prosecution case at Stafford. What he had said at the trial was more vital than the 'verbals', the overheard conversations, of Helen Johnston, or the prison 'confession' detailed by Peter Bryant. Reg Hickey had been a substantial witness who had put members of his own family in the area of the murder, of which they had denied any knowledge. He had implied that they knew where they were going if they went to Yew Tree Farm, and had lied when they said they didn't. Now that evidence was removed there was nothing but the single visit to his mother at the pub at Kingswinford after dark to suggest that Vincent had ever been anywhere near Yew Tree Farm. As for Michael, there was now *nothing at all to connect him with the farm*. His insistence under the truth drug that he had never been in the area in his life, which had so impressed Dr Canning, was now, as far as all the evidence was concerned, perfectly true. Moreover, once the Reg Hickey evidence was removed, the case against Michael depended entirely on the testimony of what Pat Molloy had called 'the lowest of the low' from the prisons. Now that Reg Hickey had withdrawn his evidence, the judge's warning that the unsupported evidence of prisoners must not convict stood out sharp and clear. If Reg Hickey had not given evidence at the trial, and if Michael had been tried separately, it is inconceivable that a jury would have convicted him.

Farmer Howards Theory

The *Mirror* article about Reg Hickey had an unforeseen effect in yet another Midlands farm – Upper Goosehill Farm, at Hanbury, near Droitwich in Worcestershire. Farmers don't normally read the *Daily Mirror*, and the farmer there, a dedicated local Conservative called Michael Howard, was no exception. But his housekeeper read the article and showed it to him. On 28 March 1985 Michael Howard wrote to me:

CARL BRIDGEWATER/MICHAEL HICKEY

Dear Mr. Foot, Re The above case and your article in the Mirror, March 26. Bert Spencer, who is serving life for the murder of my close friend Hubert Wilkes, who was the tenant of Yew Tree Farm where Carl was murdered, has confessed to inmates that he killed Carl. Knowing the layout of the farm and the persons as I do, I have no doubt in my mind that Hubert was killed because he confronted Spencer with the fact that he knew that he was guilty of Carl's murder. I have kept all the newspaper accounts, and see Anthony Wilkes, Hubert's son, every Tuesday at market. Admittedly the evidence is circumstantial, but so logical, especially if you knew Hubert as I did. He was himself an amateur detective . . . If I can be of any help, you may contact me.

Contact him I did, and on 22 May 1985 I visited him in his farmhouse where he entertained me royally. He drove me to the Stewponey pub near Wordsley where we met Anthony Wilkes. Mr Wilkes told me about his contempt for Spencer and his fury at what the ambulanceman had done to his father.

Anthony Wilkes also told me that Spencer was 'always nosing about' Yew Tree Farm and its grounds; that he kept a shotgun in the boot of his car for shooting at rabbits and often went out at night on the farm grounds with a big black torch to attract the rabbits; that he had regular access to the grounds of both Yew Tree Farm and Holloway House, and to all Farmer Wilkes' guns. Anthony also told me that he suspected Spencer of stealing one of his father's shotguns, though he could never prove it.

On the drive back, and at his farmhouse, Michael Howard expanded on his views about his friend's death. He had known Hubert Wilkes extremely well for many years. He got to know him first when he started to sell him seed and turkey food at Station Farm, Hagley, which the Wilkeses farmed for many years before going to Holloway House in the mid-seventies. He and Hubert Wilkes had travelled together to the

Royal Shows and their families had gone in tandem to social occasions in the West Midlands and Worcestershire farming community. 'I knew him as well as anyone did,' said Michael Howard. 'He wasn't a popular man. The only other close friend he had was Alec Blount, the local National Farmers Union representative who was at the house for a social drink early in the evening when Hubert was shot. He kept himself to himself and was reserved and a little cantankerous about the outside world. Not many people trusted him, and he trusted very few people.'

Hubert Wilkes had a hobby. 'He had an interest in detective work,' Michael Howard told me. 'I've stood or sat for as long as three hours at a time listening to him conduct the prosecution and defence on various cases, possibly projecting forward what would be said in a court if he went to court on a certain subject, weighing up the pros and cons as to whether he'd win or whether he wouldn't. He used to fight both sides. He also did it with cases of interest in the local press and radio. He had an inquiring mind; a sort of devious mind where he questioned peoples' every action.

'Knowing Hubert, he would have put two and two together in the Carl Bridgewater case, which had been time and time again in his mind. After all, it had happened on his own farm, and he puzzled about it. In my opinion, he would have accused Spencer that night of having a hand in the murder. He was always doing things like that, coming out suddenly, very quickly, and saying: suppose this, or suppose that. Often he would suggest something quite outrageous just to annoy or shock or upset people around him. He was that sort of chap.

'I don't think Jean would have been in the room when he said it. No, I think he mentioned the murder when Jean was upstairs (she said it was raised earlier in the evening anyway) and accused Spencer directly. Perhaps he *had* got something against him. He would have gone into one of his "prosecution" talks, and that could easily have made Spencer flip. I kept this to myself until I read about all the coincidences which fitted Spencer to the murder, and had talked to Anthony. Then I rang the police and gave them my views. I told all this to the police from Manchester who were looking into this last year.'

This was of course speculation, but it came from a man who knew Hubert Wilkes extremely well. It inspired me to try to find out still more about the ambulance officer and his connection with Yew Tree Farm.

The following month (June 1985) I went to Corbett Hospital, Stourbridge, where I was shown round by the administrator, Richard Rogerson. As Mr Rogerson took me into the large reception hall where patients were discharged from ambulances, I could see at once why those who had made inquiries in the past had been impressed by the alibi evidence provided by Mrs Riebold, the ambulance officer's secretary. On the side of the hall, just inside the doors which opened out onto the road, was a small enclosed cubicle with desks for two people in it. This, said Mr Rogerson, was where the ambulance liaison officer sat with his secretary: side by side.

The cubicle had been enclosed, he told me, since 1979. In 1978 it was surrounded by a counter, with the desks still side by side. Obviously if a person sitting at one of the desks testified about the movements of the person sitting at the other, this was evidence of the strongest kind. If Mrs Riebold had indeed been sitting at her desk on the afternoon of 19 September, then she must have been able to give a very accurate report of Hubert Spencer's movements. I recalled visiting Mrs Riebold at her home in March 1984, and asking her about the alibi. She would not talk to me, insisting this was 'a police matter', but she said she had been with Spencer all that afternoon. When I pressed her, 'In the same room?', she had not answered the question, and again repeated she was not going to talk to me.

While I was reflecting on all this, Mr Rogerson went on talking. It was not for several minutes that I realised he was giving me the answer to the questions which were puzzling me. He explained that Spencer was an employee of the ambulance service but that the two secretaries to the liaison officer were employees of the hospital. One worked in the morning, the other in the afternoon.

There were *two* secretaries to the ambulance officer, one in the morning, one in the afternoon. When did Mrs Riebold work in the cubicle? Usually, Mr Rogerson replied, in the morning. In the afternoon she usually worked as secretary to consultants in the closed rooms off the main reception area, or indeed elsewhere in the hospital altogether. As I became rather excited at his information, Mr Rogerson hastened to point out that he was not at the hospital in 1978; that he had no idea whether these circumstances obtained in 1978; that he would ask the administrator of the time if he would speak to me; and that he had no intention of giving me the name of the other secretary who worked in the afternoons, though he was good enough to tell me that she was employed at the hospital in 1978.

It did not take me very long to find that the same rules did apply in 1978 (though John Hodgson, the assistant administrator at the hospital then, couldn't remember details of the crucial week), and that the name of the second secretary was Mrs Celia Johnson. The next month (July 1985) I was in Stourbridge again, combing the houses at the back of the hospital where I eventually found Mrs Johnson. She met me at the door and did not ask me in. She seemed nervous of my inquiries about Spencer and said several times that the police had told her that on no account was she to speak to anyone from the press. All I could get from her was that she had seen the police quite recently.

It was not until April 1986, as this book was being completed, that I discovered that Celia Johnson had been interviewed by Detective Chief Superintendent Ridgway of the Manchester police. She told him she was not at work at the hospital on the day of the murder, but had the day off, either through holiday or sickness. Mrs Riebold, it seemed, had 'doubled up' for Mrs Johnson that afternoon.

Did this mean Mrs Riebold *had* left Spencer on his own for an hour or two that afternoon? This was not clear, but hospital staff noticed that Chief Superintendent Ridgeway made a great many 'test runs' from the hospital to Yew Tree Farm, carefully timing every one. Most of this I published in my *Mirror* column on 18 July.

More information on this subject was soon at hand from the strangest source: Bert Spencer. For many months Spencer had been writing letters to Keith Littlejohn. Keith and his brother Kenneth were in the headlines in the early 1970s when they alleged that they were hired by senior ministers to carry out undercover intelligence work in the IRA, and to take part in any robberies which were initiated by the IRA. It was this commission, they alleged, which led them to take part in the robbery for which they were caught and tried.

Keith Littlejohn, who knew Ann Whelan through his girlfriend, became fascinated by the Bridgewater case and started to write to Spencer under an alias, seeking to trap him into revealing some clue which might implicate him in the murder. The attempt was unsuccessful, as were others of a similar nature. Keith Littlejohn wrote to Spencer about Mrs Johnson, and received a furious reply:

> There is nothing new or odd in the fact that Mrs. Riebold and Mrs. Johnson job-share. It never was any secret, but Foot in his usual style adds a touch of sensationalism to a simple well-established fact.
>
> The police did in fact speak to Mrs. Johnson in my presence at her rightful place of work.
>
> As for your suggestion that Mrs. Riebold would have needed X-ray eyes to have seen me, she didn't need to be bionic in any way to follow what was a regular pattern – of coming to the desk for afternoon tea with Mrs. Johnson and me, taking phone calls while Mrs. Johnson popped to the loo and chatting to various regular patients with whom she was on first name terms.
>
> And always – every evening at around 4.45 p.m. – we were at the desk with hospital workers, generally finalising the day's workload and preparing for the busy morning's rush.
>
> And of course like all good British workpeople, we were waiting to go home.

Two comments flow from that extraordinary letter. First, there is, as we have seen, no record of any Staffordshire police interview with Mrs Johnson. She certainly was not interviewed during the Carl Bridgewater murder inquiry, since her name is not on the list of statements. If she did make any further statement in Spencer's presence, it must have been during the inquiry after Wilkes' death. In that case, it ought to have been disclosed by the Director of Public Prosecutions, but it was not.

Secondly, Spencer places himself in the hospital at 4.45 p.m. That was not an alibi for the Yew Tree Farm murder. Mrs Gladys Jones, the most impressive of the witnesses who saw anything at the farm on the afternoon of the murder, said that when she came out of her house at about 4.30, the car she had seen at 4.00 backed up against the door of the farm had gone.

On the afternoon I spoke to Mrs Johnson, I asked a taxi driver to take me on a run in light traffic from the farm to Corbett Hospital.

The journey took seven minutes, fifty-two seconds.

CHAPTER SEVEN
Conclusion

What can we conclude about the awful events at Yew Tree Farm on 19 September 1978, and the sequel to them?

The evidence about the cars suggests very strongly that only one car was used in the raid on the farm. So many people saw one blue car – and no more. The only witness who saw two cars together near the farm that afternoon may have seen something different to the murder car. Wendy Stagg said she saw two cars at the top of the track, one a blue estate, another a plum-coloured saloon which no one has ever connected with the murder. She saw this at 4.45. By far the strongest 'sighting' witness, Gladys Jones, said the blue car had gone by 4.30.

It is worth recalling that the police themselves, as Sergeant Lessemun told Vincent Hickey in an early interview, thought that only one car was involved.

If there *was* only one car at the farm, how many people were in it? The police assumed from early on that there were more than one. They referred in their statements to 'the killers' or the 'gang', almost always suggesting that three men were involved. All this was based on the statements of Terence Phelps, Wendy Stagg and Mario Sabetta. But, as we have seen, if Gladys Jones' firm evidence that the blue car had left the farm by 4.30 is believed, the sightings of Miss Stagg (4.45) and Mr Phelps (shortly after 5.00) are too late to be relevant. Mario Sabetta, moreover, saw two men an hour before the murder. They were not at the farm, but in the road a good distance away from it.

The truth is that there was precious little evidence from anyone about the number of people involved. As many witnesses saw one man in suspicious circumstances as saw more than one.

There was, however, one part of the evidence which tended to suggest more than one person and possibly more than one car. This was the stolen property which was found strewn around the farmyard and on either side of the wicket gate which led to the path to the farm's back door. Why should any burglar who had just committed a frightful murder chuck some of the property around the two areas of the farm grounds, and take other pieces with him?

Conclusion

The copper kettle to the right of the wicket gate and the silver teapot in the orchard on the other side of the hedge immediately to the left of the gate suggest that a man carrying the two items was surprised by something at the wicket gate, which made him throw the two items leftwards and rightwards from where he was standing. Perhaps he was surprised by the newspaper boy himself; perhaps he was hurrying out of the house after the murder with the two last items when he saw the boy's bicycle and jettisoned the two antiques so he could throw the bicycle into the pigsty where it would not immediately be seen. Either way, it seems likely that these two items were thrown by one man.

The distribution of the property in the farmyard could be explained by the presence of two cars, one of which got away with a share of the booty while the man (or men) in the other (who had committed the murder) chucked all the goods out of the car in a panic.

This explanation, however, fits the 'one car' theory just as convincingly. All the property which went missing could have fitted in a normal-sized car boot. The (very few) bulky items – a teapot, a basin and a water jug – which were found in the yard would probably *not* have fitted in a boot with the items that *were* taken. They could have been placed on the back seat of the car where, unlike the stuff in the boot, they would be conspicuous to an observer. If the man (or men) in one car, in the moment of panic after the murder, sought to jettison anything which would immediately be seen in the car when it left the farm, he (they) could have run into the farmyard, which was overgrown with scrub and surrounded on all sides by derelict buildings, and got rid of the antiques there. After throwing the boy's bicycle into the pigsty, the murderer(s) could leave without anything suspicious on view in the car or, at first sight, at the farm.

All this effort could have involved two or more men. It could equally, however, have involved one man, at slightly different times. One man *could* have dispensed with the property where it was found in a matter of moments. One man *could* have done the murder from one car, and got away with the stolen property in the boot. The evidence supports this theory every bit as much as it contradicts it. Indeed, there is no real evidence either way.

Whether it was one man or more, the evidence suggested, as the police recognised from the first day, that the murderer(s) had some connection with the farm and even perhaps with Carl Bridgewater. He (they) plainly knew his way around. He (they) knew the dog well enough to prevent it barking. Perhaps he (they) came from the area, and knew the newspaper boy. All these points emerge as strongly from the evidence today as they did when the police made them in press conferences after the murder.

A few weeks after the murder, Hubert Spencer seemed a likely suspect. He fitted the sort of man the police were looking for. The coincidences linking him to the murder grew with their inquiries. He was dropped for reasons which are not clear, but chiefly because police attention was switched to another even more glaring coincidence – between the robberies at the two farmhouses, Yew Tree and Chapel Farm. After all that has happened since, and has been recounted here, the finger of suspicion points even more strongly at Hubert Spencer than it did when the police first interviewed him. The obvious links between the murder of Hubert Wilkes and the murder of Carl Bridgewater put Spencer much more firmly in the frame.

Hubert Spencer has always categorically denied that he killed Carl Bridgewater. He has even agreed to do so on television (unhappily the crew were not allowed in to film him – by order of the Home Secretary). It must be said too that former Chief Superintendent Ridgeway, a highly respected and competent officer by all accounts, has submitted a full report to the Home Secretary which does not support the view that Spencer was the murderer. Mr Ridgeway, of course, had access to information and witnesses which have been denied to me (in one case on his express instructions). I cannot demand interviews and call up computerised information as he can. Perhaps he has found the compelling evidence which absolves Spencer. I have not been able to do so. On the contrary, as my inquiries have continued, the case against Spencer became stronger and stronger. Suspicion of him will continue at least until the authorities publish the information which they must believe entirely exculpates him.

Until that happens, this part of the conclusion – the guilt or innocence of Hubert Spencer – is uncertain.

What seems to me quite certain is that Carl Bridgewater was not shot by Vincent Hickey, Michael Hickey, Jimmy Robinson or Pat Molloy; and that none of these four men were at Yew Tree Farm on 19 September 1978 or at any other time.

The case against them started with an accusation and then a confession from Vincent Hickey. This was *not* offered out of the blue, as appeared in court. A detailed account of the events which followed the Chapel Farm robbery, told here for the first time, makes it clear that Vincent did have a motive, however perverse, in making reckless allegations against anyone he could think of who *might* have been responsible for the murder. He was seeking a way out of a nasty robbery charge. He did not have any information about Yew Tree Farm, but he pretended he did in order to save his skin. He had grassed before, successfully. This time he was not successful. 'I was trying to do what I had done at Rickmansworth,' he wrote in his long report of 6 July 1983. 'This ploy would not work this time.'

At the trial, no one could explain the confession of Pat Molloy. Unexplained, and taken together with Vincent's confession, it seemed irrefutable proof of the guilt of the four men. Now, with the publication of Molloy's letters and papers, the confession *is* explained. It was made partly in fury that Vincent should so recklessly and wrongly have involved him in the murder, partly in distress and disorientation after hours of tough questioning in which he was denied access to lawyers or to friends.

To support these two confessions there was not a scrap of tangible or forensic evidence against the four men. The cars they are meant to have travelled in were never identified or found. The gun they were meant to have used was not proved to be the murder weapon. The cartridge cases found with it were certainly not of the type which killed Carl. Moreover the cartridge case found near the scene of the murder, which could have carried the shot which killed the boy, could not have been fired from Robinson's gun. Not a single fingerprint, not a single tyre print, not a single hair off any of the four men's clothes, not a single piece of stolen property linked any of the four with the murder of Carl Bridgewater.

Most of the flimsy props with which the prosecution shored up their case against the four men have now been kicked away. Four prosecution witnesses – in descending order of importance, Reg Hickey, Helen Johnston, Catherine Guy and David Kane – have changed their evidence. Another, Peter Bryant, has been discredited. There is very little credible prosecution evidence left. Indeed, Michael Hickey, now that the evidence of his cousin Reg has been removed, stands convicted of murder solely on what he is alleged to have said about his involvement to a couple of crooks on the make in prison, and to a police informer.

It is no use protesting that these men would have been in prison anyway, for other offences. Poor Pat Molloy would probably have not gone to prison at all if he had not been embroiled in the Bridgewater inquiry. The meat robbery at Tamworth, his only other offence, would have landed him a suspended sentence. No one can say what effect the harsh routine of prison life had on his already frail constitution, and whether, if he had not been imprisoned, he might still be alive.

Vincent Hickey, too, was not convicted of any other crime. No doubt he would have been found guilty of the Chapel Farm robbery, as he clearly was. He might have got eight years for that, and served between five and six. As this book goes to press he has served seven and a half years. He is desparately ill, mentally and physically, and is under the constant care of a Home Office psychiatrist and surgeons at Worcester Hospital, who tend a series of abscesses all over his body.

Michael confessed not just to the Chapel Farm robbery but also to the fiasco at Tesco. He got a total of twelve years for both. With full remission, he would have served eight, and would be due for release in the autumn of 1986. John Burkett, who was convicted with Michael and

Jimmy of the Tesco armed robbery (in which Burkett carried the gun), got twelve years too. He was freed in June 1986, three months before this book was published. Michael's outrage and defiance, which rose in an upward curve during his first five years in prison, subsided into truculent despair when he came down from the roof. Gradually, he seemed to lose interest, telling Ann and Fred that he had done all he could. It was 'up to others', he said, to prove his innocence.

He sank lower and lower until he seemed to lose control altogether. In March 1986 he was transferred to Park Lane, near Liverpool, a secure institution for the mentally ill. Ann Whelan visits him there every week. She is certain that he would quickly recover if he were free. 'He *is* ill,' she says. 'But *why* is he ill? Because he was convicted of something he never did.'

These three men should not be in prison. They were wrongly convicted of murder. A monstrous injustice has been done. It is high time to put it right.

CHRONOLOGY

1978

7 FEBRUARY

Reg Hickey, Tommy Forbes and Ginger Thomas raid house at Rickmansworth, Hertfordshire.

20 MARCH (APPROXIMATELY)

Vincent Hickey's dark blue Cortina estate sold to Mr Christopher Baron, and scrapped. Body of Cortina dumped in Birmingham canal.

27 MARCH (APPROXIMATELY)

Cortina body fished from canal by Waterways Board.

25 AUGUST

Jimmy Robinson has his hair shaved off.

30 AUGUST

Vincent Hickey moves into Linda Galvin's flat.

18/19 SEPTEMBER (NIGHT)

Jimmy Robinson and John Burkett rob a Birmingham butcher.

19 SEPTEMBER

9.30 a.m.
Carol Bradbury comes out of hospital and is taken home by Jimmy Robinson and Pat Molloy.
2.30 p.m.
New three-piece furniture suite delivered to Linda Galvin's flat.

4.20 p.m. (approximatley)
 Carl Bridgewater shot at Yew Tree Farm
5.00 p.m. (approximately)
 Dave Waller's baby born.

20 SEPTEMBER

9.00 a.m.
 Susan Bennett sees two sets of flowers in Carol's house.
11.00 a.m.
 Yvonne Hards sees two sets of flowers in Carol's house.

20/21 SEPTEMBER (NIGHT)

Jimmy Robinson and Pat Molloy rob an abattoir in Tamworth.

21 SEPTEMBER (EARLY MORNING)

Jimmy Robinson arrested and locked up for Tamworth meat robbery.

24 SEPTEMBER

Hubert Spencer interviewed at his house.

30 SEPTEMBER

Vincent and Linda trick old people at Chapel Farm, Romsley.

14/15 OCTOBER

Vincent Hickey taken to Cannock police station for questioning about murder.

23 OCTOBER

Jimmy Robinson released.
 Hubert Spencer finds piece of cardboard about Yew Tree Farm murder, and takes it to Smethwick police station.

16 NOVEMBER

Spencer interviewed a second time by senior officers.

24 NOVEMBER

Jimmy Robinson, John Burkett and Michael Hickey carry out armed robbery on Tescos, Castle Vale, Birmingham.

Reg Hickey, Vincent Hickey, Ginger Thomas and Tommy Forbes convicted of Rickmansworth robbery and deception at St Albans Crown Court.

30 NOVEMBER

Vincent Hickey, Michael Hickey and Jimmy Robinson carry out armed robbery at Chapel Farm, Romsley.

1 DECEMBER

Birmingham Evening Mail front-page headline reads: CARL LINK IN FARMHOUSE RAID.

4 DECEMBER

Vincent Hickey goes to Bromsgrove police station with solicitor's clerk.

5 DECEMBER

Vincent Hickey names Robinson and Molloy as Yew Tree Farm murderers.

6 DECEMBER

Jimmy Robinson arrested.

7 DECEMBER

Jimmy Robinson takes police to his shotgun.

8 DECEMBER

Pat Molloy, John Burkett arrested.

10 DECEMBER

Pat Molloy signs written confession to Yew Tree Farm murder.

14 DECEMBER

Police take Pat Molloy to Yew Tree Farm.

21 DECEMBER

Michael Hickey arrested.

28 DECEMBER

Pat Molloy charged with murder.

1979

12 JANUARY

Vincent Hickey charged with murder.

16 JANUARY

Identification parade for Pat Molloy.

5 FEBRUARY

Jimmy Robinson and Michael Hickey charged with murder.

23 FEBRUARY

Identification parade for Jimmy Robinson.

15 MAY

Jimmy Robinson, Pat Molloy, Vincent and Michael Hickey committed by Wombourne magistrates for trial.

8 OCTOBER

Trial opens at Stafford Crown Court.

9 NOVEMBER

Four men convicted.

12 NOVEMBER

Four men sentenced.

13/14 DECEMBER

Hubert Spencer shoots Hubert Wilkes at Holloway House Farm.

1980

28 MARCH

Helen Johnston sees Tony Fryer, Robinson's solicitor.

12 JUNE

Director of Public Prosecutions sends bundle of documents to lawyers of four convicted men.

23-26 JUNE

Hubert Spencer tried, convicted of murder and sentenced at Stafford Crown Court.

7 OCTOBER

Helen Johnston goes on television.

1981

17 JANUARY

Michael Hickey takes truth drug.

13 FEBRUARY

Vincent Hickey takes truth drug.

12 JUNE

Pat Molloy dies.

1/2 DECEMBER

Leave to appeal for three remaining defendants refused.

1983

26 FEBRUARY-20 MARCH

Michael and Vincent Hickey demonstrate on roof of Long Lartin prison.

5 APRIL

Michael Ishmael makes statement about Spencer to Tom Sargant of Justice.

13 NOVEMBER

Home Office announce result of inquiry into Ishmael statement. No action.

24 NOVEMBER

Michael Hickey starts roof protest at Gartree prison.

1984

21 FEBRUARY

Michael Hickey ends roof protest after eighty-nine days.

30 JULY

Home Office announces new inquiry into case.

13 NOVEMBER

Home Office announces 'no action' as a result of inquiry.

1985

5 FEBRUARY

Reg Hickey makes statement to Michael's solicitor.

21 MARCH

Reg Hickey's statement made public.

INDEX

A SECRET IS A SECRET FOR ONLY AS LONG
AS IT IS KEPT A SECRET. ?